DANNY
WILSON

I GET KNOCKED DOWN
But I get up again

First Edition.
First published 2022

Published by:
Morgan Lawrence Publishing Services Limited
Ridge House Annexe
16 Main Ridge West
Boston
Lincolnshire
PE21 6QQ
www.morganlawrence.co.uk
email: info@morganlawrence.co.uk
Company number: 12910264

ISBN: 9781838232962

Photographs are courtesy of:
Sheffield Wednesday Football Club, Steve Ellis, Barsnley Football Club, Blades Sports Photography, Hatters Heritage, Brighton and Hove Albion Football Club, Alan Roe, Tina Jenner, Chesterfield Football Club, Chesterfield Football Club Supporters Trust Heritage Group, PA Images/ Alamy Stock Photo, Getty Images Sport, REUTERS/Alamy Stock.

Cover design by LCGraphix
Proofreading by Amy Memory

Printed and bound in Bulgaria
by Pulsio Print.

Contents

Foreword by Viv Anderson MBE

The year was 1983 and I was playing for First Division Nottingham Forest. The lads and I were warming up on the training pitch when this tiny, young lad appeared wearing a kit and pair of boots. I remember thinking, *Who's he? There is no way we've bought him. He must be a trialist.*

But he wasn't a trialist, he was Danny Wilson, a midfielder Brian Clough had just signed from Third Division Chesterfield. We had been double European Cup winners two season earlier, and it was a big step up for Danny, so he must have really stood out at that level. Cloughie was very good at picking players, so I knew he must be a useful footballer.

Danny had great attributes; he always wanted the ball, was constantly looking to get involved, and could be aggressive when he needed to be.

For whatever reason, Danny's time at the City Ground was short lived and he soon moved on to Brighton. We formed a friendship and kept in touch, trying to meet up over the years when we could.

In 1991, I had the opportunity to sign for Sheffield Wednesday. Danny was already playing for them, as were a few other lads I knew, so it was quite an easy decision for me to leave Manchester United and join Wednesday.

Danny and I roomed together which developed a bond, and formed a lifelong friendship that has led to us going on holiday together several times. We've also enjoyed quite a few laughs together.

I remember the night before the 1993 FA Cup final when we were sharing a room. I was captaining the side the following day, while Danny was injured and unable to play. I was trying to sleep when I heard a scraping noise. I opened my eyes and saw Danny, fully dressed, climbing out of the window. "Where are you going?" I asked.

"Don't you worry about it," he replied.

A few hours later, I heard the window open again and it was Danny returning from the pub, having enjoyed a few beers with the other lads who weren't playing in the final. Fortunately, our room was on the ground floor, or he'd have never been able to climb the wall and get back in!

Another time we were in America on an end-of-season tour when Danny and I decided to break curfew to go to a club. I asked the hotel receptionist for a recommendation, and she directed us to a club a few blocks away. When we arrived, we were greeted by a huge bouncer who must have been the size of fifteen David Hirsts. He let us English lads in and when we walked through the entrance, I realised I'd taken him to the blackest club in Philadelphia! "Where have you brought me?" Danny asked. It was some place, I tell you.

In June 1993, I was approached by Barnsley chairman John Dennis and asked to become the player-manager at Barnsley Football Club. It was my first management role, and I knew that I'd need someone around me who I could trust one hundred per cent. I immediately thought of Danny and offered him the role of player-assistant manager. It's unheard of now, but we both combined our management roles with playing, so as well as a trusted assistant, I also gained a top-quality midfielder.

Danny was the ideal candidate; he was vocal in the dressing room where he acted as my eyes and ears, he was good on the training ground, helping me run the sessions, and he was great with the press.

Sometimes with an assistant, you are looking over your shoulder, wondering if they are going to try and take your job, but I never felt like that with Danny. He wanted what was best for me and what was best for the football club, not what was best for him as a person.

I left Barnsley after one season in charge, but not before convincing John Dennis that he should appoint Danny as my replacement. He had first-hand experience of all the ins and outs at the football club and I thought he would be the ideal manager. I was delighted to be proven right when he guided Barnsley to the Premier League three years later.

Away from football, Danny is a bit of a bandit on the golf course. He says he plays off a single digit handicap, but he's a lot better than that when he needs to be.

I've known Danny for over forty years and if I had to sum him up as a person, I'd say one hundred per cent loyal in every aspect of his life. A good player, a top manager, a great friend, and a very, very, good family man.

Viv Anderson MBE

CHAPTER 1
Punched on the nose

I, Daniel Joseph Wilson, came into the world on New Year's Day, 1960. I was born in Billinge Hospital, near St Helens, a town more notable for rugby league than it is for football. In fact, my first foray into sport was with the oval ball, rather than the round one.

Wigan, where I grew up, is a big rugby town and I played both forms – League and Union – for my Primary School team, St Mary's. I wasn't particularly big though, unlike some of the giants I played against, so rugby was a no-no for me. Although I was quick, and my pace often got me out of trouble, I knew that one or two hits off some of those boys and it would be game over! I was much better at football, and I'm sure I inherited my skillset from my dad James Wilson.

Dad was born and raised in Orrell, Lancashire, before joining the Navy where he was stationed in Northern Ireland. A talented full back, he joined Derry City who played in the First Division of the Northern Ireland football league. His tough, uncompromising style of play, combined with his naval background, earned him the nickname Tug. Dad's performances for Derry were rewarded with a call-up to the Northern Ireland senior squad, but unfortunately, he was ineligible to play as he wasn't actually Irish. The national team manager assumed he was eligible as there weren't too many English players playing in Northern Ireland at the time.

It was while serving in Derry that he met my mother, Annie Kennedy. The couple's relationship soon blossomed and after marrying in 1945, they had the first of three children; Margaret born in 1948, followed by Mary in 1953.

A few years later, when my Dad's Navy career had finished, they decided to move to Wigan, Lancashire, and then I came along. My sisters really looked after me, and spoiled me rotten, although it probably didn't seem like it to me at the time! Sadly, Margaret has passed away, but Mary still lives in Orrell and we remain close.

Margaret's children, Michelle and Helen, as well as Mary's children, Ann Marie, Nicola, David, and Christopher – who passed away much too early – were a big part of my life growing up. I've always enjoyed being surrounded by family, and I'd like to think I'm still very family-orientated.

My parents had absolutely nothing, but they tried to do everything they could for us, particularly when I started to play football. When I needed a pair of football boots it was a major thing, but they always made sure I got them, even though they had to save up a lot of money. Money they didn't really have. That's where I think I inherited my strong work ethic – from my parents.

Dad worked as an engineer and always rose at four a.m. to cycle the hour-long journey to work. Mum was a cleaner at Billinge Hospital, where I was born. That must have been strange for her to give birth at her place of work. They both worked so hard and didn't have a lot of time to do much else. They certainly never had any money. That was why it was so important for me to try and help them, and share the little bit of success that I enjoyed later on in my career. My wife Karen and I were lucky enough to invite them to come along with us on many holidays. Not only were they lovely people but they were great babysitters too! My dad had travelled all over the world with the Navy, so all he wanted was to be somewhere he could see the sea and be with his family. Mum was absolutely wonderful with our children, and she had the patience of a Saint. I hope I inherited her patience, although I'm sure some may disagree!

Mum never got upset and I never saw her chastise anyone, she just wanted to help people. I can only recall her telling me off once. My parents both smoked, but because money was tight, they'd smoke halfway down the cigarette, nip it, and save it for later so they had something to look forward to. One afternoon while Mum was ironing in the kitchen, I tried one of her fags, having a crafty smoke in the bathroom. When I came downstairs, she smelt it on my breath and slapped me across my head! That was the only time my mother was anything other than lovely. Dad was a bit tougher and very strict as you can imagine, but deep down he was a big softy. Mum and Dad were both very supportive and gave me constant encouragement, especially about my football.

By the time I was thirteen, although I was still playing rugby for the school team, I had realised that football was the sport I was more accustomed to. I knew from an early age that I wanted to try and make a career out of it, be that non-league or as a professional.

Part of my self-belief was instilled in me from my PE teacher Dave Brown, who was also a professional rugby league player with St Helens, and his assistant Jim Yeo. I absolutely adored them. Dave was an icon to me, and I was full of admiration for him. He encouraged me to reach my potential by pushing me and giving me the determination to not settle for mediocrity. I have so much to thank him for. "You've got to make something with all these attributes you have. I don't want to see your talent go to waste," he told me on more than one occasion.

No matter what sport we played at school – athletics, gymnastics, rugby, or football – I gave my all and more often than not I ended up on the winning team. It was a different matter with the academic side of school, though. I could do English, Geography, and Maths, but I just wasn't interested in those subjects. I lost concentration quite easily as my mind wandered towards the next sports day or games lesson. I should have done much better at school, but I just couldn't focus.

St Mary's Primary School was affiliated with a church. My parents were both devout Catholics, so it was a pre requisite for me to attend the church service every Sunday. I found it quite boring in all honesty, but when I got a bit older, I was allowed to go with my friends instead of my parents which was much better. We'd stand upstairs, right at the back and have a bit of a laugh, although I remember one of the parishioners giving me a clip round the ear once for giggling which put me off a bit. My parents always checked to see if I'd attended the service by asking me which priest had delivered mass, so I used to put my head around the door at the start to see who it was – generally Father Flynn – and then I'd go out into the playground and play on the monkey bars with my friends until the service had finished!

When I was fourteen, I took a little job at the social club that was part of the church. I started off collecting glasses before I was later allowed to serve the drinks. Mass finished bang on twelve noon, and at one minute past, Father Flynn would be standing at the bar with a pint and a fag on. I still don't know how he did it. He got changed quicker than Superman!

I was a Liverpool fan as a child. I suppose everyone was in those days. Liverpool was only half an hour from my house and although Manchester was slightly closer, I chose to support Liverpool because they won everything, yet remained so humble. And they did win everything back then too. They were a good team, who played exciting football and had such a great attitude. They'd beat teams by four or five goals, but never rammed it down their opponents' throats. Ian Callaghan was my favourite player. He was a magnificent midfielder with a similar build to me, and I remember thinking, *If he can do it, so can I*. My brother-in-law took me to watch Liverpool play live, even though he was an Everton fan. Anfield was such a special place, especially on European nights. I couldn't watch them too much though because of affordability and I had started to play regularly myself.

My big break in football came when I joined a team called the Double Seven Club which was based in Ince, Wigan. They were a youth club that fielded rugby and football teams, and they had a very good reputation. In the year above me, playing for the rugby side, was a young lad called Andy Gregory who went on to play Rugby League for Great Britain.

I spent my formative years at the Double Seven Club, making friends, having fun, and playing football. A few other local clubs, some of who were very successful, tried to entice me, but I rejected them as I loved the club so much. The only challenge was that the Double Seven Club was located over six miles away from my home, so it wasn't an easy place for me to get to. There were regular buses, but we didn't have any money for a ticket, and my parents didn't have a car, so I had to try and cadge a lift from some of the other lads.

At the age of fourteen, I played men's football in the open league under the tutelage of Brian Hughes and Jack Roden. It was tough but hugely beneficial as it toughened me up. Even at that tender age, I didn't have any fear in me, like most lads at that age I suppose. I don't think I ever shirked my responsibilities, and I held my own against some of the big lads who played at that level. I was a tenacious centre midfielder, and I loved a tackle. It was a very physical league, but my biggest asset was pace. When you're playing men's football as a young lad, you've got to get out of the way quick rather than going toe to toe – I wasn't big enough for that! I soon learnt how to spot the challenges coming my way so I could avoid them. Playing against men and knowing that I wasn't getting kicked from pillar to post was a huge confidence boost, and I developed very quickly. I think that's when I started to think that I might actually have a chance of becoming a footballer.

In those days, Sunderland had a nursery team based in the North West, and I was spotted by Tommy Pendlebury and Burt Edwards, two Manchester-based scouts, who invited me for a trial. I went along, did well, and signed schoolboy forms for Sunderland. I was still able to play for the Double Seven Club, and I travelled up to the North East in the school holidays.

It was a fantastic time to be associated with Sunderland. Bob Stokoe was the manager and they had shocked everyone by winning the FA Cup in 1973. I went to Roker Park to watch the first team players including Billy Hughes, Bobby Kerr, Micky Horswill, and Dave Watson. They were club legends, and for me to see them play in front of forty thousand people was amazing. I didn't ever feel that I would become part of that team, it was just a dream really.

My time at Sunderland was a real eye opener for me and it was my first interaction with the professional side of the game. The man tasked with looking after the schoolboys was the great Peter Doherty, a former Northern Ireland international, who had won the First Division and FA Cup with Manchester City and Derby County during his illustrious playing career. My dad was suitably impressed as he knew a great deal about him.

Peter was full of positivity, and he used to write me a letter once a week giving me little pieces of advice and encouragement.

There was always a paragraph about my parents; asking how they were and reminding me to listen to them and show them respect. Those letters were brilliant, and I've kept every single one of them to this day.

I was let go by Sunderland at the age of fifteen, although I'm not sure why as no one ever gave me a reason. It was disappointing, but it didn't bother me too much because it was a long way from home, and it used to take an eternity to get there. I've always had a positive approach to life, and I rarely let myself get too down and that's due to my upbringing. I always believed there would be another opportunity for me later on down the line.

Not having to travel up to the North East during the school holidays meant that I was able to enjoy the vibrant nightlife of the town. Wigan Casino was in its pomp and that's where my mates and I would sometimes go for an evening out. My mates were Alan and Brian Barton, Stephen Martland, Phil Bulpit, Rod Marsh, and Lesley Matthews who was known as Winker. That's Winker with an I! Great mates. These were the lads who lived in my area, and we did everything together, even though I was a lot younger than them.

Brian used to import northern soul records from America. No one had ever heard of the artists, but his musical taste was very highly thought of by the DJs of the casino. He'd take the records to the casino to present to the DJ who played them and introduced us to the latest hits from the other side of the Atlantic Ocean. Brian was a few years older than me, and I loved him. Sadly, he and his brother Alan both died in their forties.

The must-have fashion item during the early seventies was a barathea, a little blazer people wore with braiding around the sides and the back. It was the thing to wear at the casino ,accompanied by a pair of baggy trousers. They weren't cheap, but Mum somehow managed to get me a second-hand one and Brian's mum sowed the braiding on for me. I loved that barathea and wore it as often as possible.

One evening I'd been to the casino and didn't get home until three a.m. which was later than normal. I didn't have a house key, but that didn't matter as I knew how to get in through the bathroom window. At the back of our house was an outhouse split into two; one side was for coal and the other stored my dad's bike. I ran through the garden, jumped against the wall, and climbed onto the flat roof of the outhouse. I walked a few feet towards our tiny bathroom window that was always left open. I'd always got in through there without any problems and assumed this time would be no different. However, when I lifted the latch and put my head through the window, I saw my dad, who was sitting on the toilet doing his daily duty. He punched me in the nose, thinking I was an intruder, which scared the life out of me! He gave me a house key after that!

When I turned sixteen, I watched my mates take employment at either Pilkington's, a glass manufacturer based in St Helens, or British Leyland, an automotive factory near Preston. They were all grafters, and I respected the boys – that's what they did, and they worked hard for their families –but I never wanted that life for me. I didn't want a nine-to-five job. I'd had a taste of football and that was all I wanted to do.

After my release from Sunderland, I continued playing for the Double Seven Club. We had a terrific striker called Gary Dickens and scouts were flocking to take a look at him. There was one particular game when Bury scouts came to watch us. I had one of those games when you play really well, and they began to take an interest in me, although nothing happened just then.

As it turned out, in the summer of 1976, I was invited to a trial with Wigan Athletic, who were playing in the Northern Premier, the fifth tier of English football. Wigan had actually finished champions a year earlier but were denied promotion to the Football League because in those days there was no automatic promotion. Instead, the team who had finished bottom of the Fourth Division had to be voted out and that didn't happen too often. There was usually a friendly vote where the Football League chairmen stuck together to keep their clubs in the league.

After impressing during my trial, I joined Wigan on a non-contract basis. I was only paid expenses, so I needed a trade to fall back. Even if I signed a pro contract somewhere, in those days football didn't pay much and you needed to make sure you had a backup plan. So, I enrolled to become an apprentice engineer at Ravenhead brickworks in Upholland which was where my dad worked. He'd set it up for me, but after a few days, I knew that it wasn't what I wanted to do for the rest of my life: getting up at six in the morning and coming home at six at night, covered in brick dust. I'd have a shower, some tea, and fall into bed, before rising again the next morning ready to do it all again. That wasn't for me.

That experience gave me the drive to try and succeed in football and to give it a really good go. I decided to make sure that I had no regrets. I'm so grateful to my dad for giving me that experience and opening my eyes to the 'real world'. I think he realised exactly what my attitude would be like after working in the brickworks and that was typical of the support I received from my parents. They were so supportive of my career and if it wasn't for them, I don't think I would have pushed myself as much as I did.

Fred Eyre was the reserve team coach at Wigan and one of football's big characters. In the early sixties, Fred had the distinction of becoming Manchester City's first apprentice, which involved him cleaning the boots of Dennis Law and Bert Trautmann. He left Maine Road without making a first team appearance and dropped down into the non-league scene where he combined his football career with running an office supply company. He became a very successful businessman.

We still didn't have a car, which meant it was difficult for me to get to and from training, so Fred agreed to pick me up and drop me off each training day – in his Rolls Royce! I lived in a council house and all of a sudden, a Rolls Royce was pulling up outside. All the curtains were twitching, and I'd walk out of my house with a pair of boots in my hand and a big grin on my face. Fred was great to me in that respect.

The biggest adjustment for me was the transition from training two or three times a week and then playing at the Double Seven Club, to training every evening. I found it very demanding, especially as I was often exhausted from my job at the brickworks. It was a big change, but I soon got used to it and reaped the rewards. I enjoyed stepping up to a better level of football, but the professional game seemed a million miles away, so the focus was on enjoying each match.

I made a few appearances for the reserves before breaking into the first team who were managed by Ian McNeill, who was in his second spell at the club. Ian was assisted by Kenny Banks, a former Wigan player and an absolute gent.

I remember one day walking into training and spotting a little brown envelope on my peg. I opened it and couldn't believe it when I discovered it contained a single one-pound note, It was heaven, and I couldn't believe how rich I was. That was the first time I'd ever received payment for playing football.

The Northern Premier League was a fantastic standard, it was like a throwback to the Football League. Boston United, managed by Howard Wilkinson, who went on to win the First Division title with Leeds United, were the standout team. They paid a lot of money which attracted several ex-pros. They had Gordon Bolland, previously of Chelsea, Bobby Brown, who was a former Sheffield Wednesday striker, and a young Lawrie Madden who later became my teammate at Wednesday.

It was great to have the opportunity to test myself against players with Football League experience, but it never bothered me who I was coming up against. Maybe it was naivety on my part, but a lot of the time I didn't even know who my opponents were. After a game, someone might tell me that so and so had played for a big club, but I didn't take any notice before a match which helped me. If I knew someone by reputation and was in awe of them, maybe it would have put me off my own game.

The experienced pros I came up against were fantastic for my development. They didn't like a young whipper snapper like me going past them, and every now and then I'd be taught a lesson. They knew every trick in the book, but I was resilient and often had the pace to get away from them. On the occasions when they did catch me, I always got straight back up and when we came face to face, I didn't back down. I certainly never let anyone intimidate me, that's for sure. Maybe that earnt me some respect from my opponents.

We had some terrific lads at Wigan, many of whom had been knocking about the non-league scene for quite a while.

Ian Gillibrand was our captain, a Wigan legend who spent his entire career at Springfield Park, racking up over four hundred appearances. Everyone looked up to him and he was an inspirational leader who knew the league inside out. He was a brilliant servant to the club. I was incredibly saddened when

I heard that he passed away in 1989 while playing in a charity match. He was only forty years old.

Joey Hinnigan was a fantastic attacking full back who'd be great playing in the modern game. He was a terrific guy and a great help to me.

My partner in the middle of the park was Tommy Gore, a good little midfielder who'd been on the books of Liverpool and Tranmere Rovers. He helped me massively, giving me lots of advice, and we had many chats where he'd tell me what to look out for and how to do certain things.

Those three players in particular were good for me, but everyone in the squad made me feel involved and part of the team, even though I was a young lad.

After the games, there was a good social scene where the lads would go into the club house for a pint or two. I was too young to drink, so I'd occasionally have half a shandy. But more often than not, I'd say my goodbyes and head straight home. I couldn't really afford a drink as I had already spent my one pound.

I was enjoying my football and my performances were starting to garner media attention. The *Post and Chronicle* and the *Wigan Observer* used to report on our matches, and they were full of praise which drew in scouts from other clubs to come to have a look. I'm not sure of all the clubs that were watching me because in those days you didn't find out. There were no agents at that level, no mobile phones or internet either, so all the communication was between the clubs. You only found out about any interest if your manager decided to tell you or pass on messages to other players.

I was already on the radar of Bury from my days at the Double Seven Club, and they'd kept a keen eye on me when I joined Wigan to see how I handled the step up. I must have convinced them that I could play at a higher level because in the summer of 1977 they decided to make an offer for me. It wasn't much of a gamble, because I was playing for Wigan on a non-contract basis, so there was no transfer fee involved and I was still only seventeen with plenty of development ahead of me.

So after just one season with my hometown club, I was on my way to Bury to hopefully achieve my dream of becoming a professional footballer.

CHAPTER 2
Four managers and a pig farmer

Before I signed on the dotted line, Bobby Smith, Bury's manager, visited my house to ask for my parent's permission to sign me. My dad wasn't in when Bobby called, but I knew where he would be. He'd be in the same place he always spent his afternoons.

My dad was a grafter. I've already mentioned that he pedalled his bike to work for a six a.m. start each morning, and when his shift was over, he'd cycle to the Robin Hood pub in Orrell for one pint and a game of dominoes. So Bobby Smith and I tootled down to the Robin Hood and sure enough, there he was, sat down supping his pint with his mates.

Bobby went over to them and introduced himself, before explaining that he wanted me to sign for Bury. Dad listened very carefully, like he always did, and when Bobby finished talking, he got up and said, "You have my permission to sign him, and if he steps out of line, you're allowed to clip him 'round the ear!"

That was Dad. Although he never gave too much away, I knew that it was a very proud moment for him.

The only thing left for me to do was negotiate my contract. Well, that's not quite true. In those days you didn't have the option of negotiating, you were given a contract and told to take it or leave it. I'd been earning £60 a week from my job and signed my first professional contract for a King's ransom of . . . £40! Yes, it was a pay cut, but I'd never have forgiven myself if I hadn't taken the opportunity. Although I was only seventeen, I wasn't going to Bury to play in the youth team or the reserves – I was hoping and praying to be part of the first team.

Even though Bury was only about forty-five minutes from my parents' house, I'd never heard of the place and certainly had no idea where it was. With the exception of my school holiday trips up to Sunderland, and a trip to Derry to see Mum's side of the family, I hadn't ventured out of Wigan very often, so I was full of nerves as I prepared to leave home for the first time.

The club put me into digs with Elsie and Brian Bancroft, a brilliant couple who were like second parents to me. I felt a bit lonely and homesick at times, but they were fantastic and couldn't have done more for me. I have enormous respect for the Bancrofts and the way they helped me start my journey in professional football. They were so positive, but they were also very disciplined. They were huge Bury supporters, so they knew what days I was supposed to be in, and when I shouldn't be in a pub or on the golf course. If they thought I was getting too close to the line, they'd remind me of my responsibilities in a nice and positive tone that still left me knowing what was expected of me. To be honest, I never got above my station anyway and didn't feel I had anything to boast about. Although I had become a professional footballer, I knew I still had a long way to go.

There wasn't a lot of attention from fans away from the game in those days, and there wasn't a lot to do after training which was good as it meant there were no distractions. I could just focus on my football and that was all that mattered to me.

I lived a few doors down from some of my teammates, Alan Woolfall and Steve Johnson, and we became good friends. Steve was a young centre forward who stood six feet tall and weighed twelve and a half stone – he was massive.

Occasionally, Steve, Alan, and I would go to a café called Hames for a coffee or to the local cinema to watch a flick. We were given complimentary cinema passes that allowed us access whenever we wanted to go which was great and helped us relax. The first film we saw, which had been out for a while by then, was *Carry On Camping* with Barbara Windsor and the famous bikini scene – we'd never seen anything like that – or should I say *those* – before!

Bury played their football in the old Third Division (known as League One today), so it was another big step up in quality for me and another huge learning curve. The team was packed full of experienced players who'd been there and done it, and I learnt a lot from my new teammates.

We had Keith Kennedy, brother of Alan, who played for Liverpool, at left back. Tony Bailey was a strong, no-nonsense centre half, and we later signed Pat Howard, who'd been at Newcastle United and Arsenal. He was another centre back, but he played like a modern-day defender. He read the game so well and was capable of stepping out of defence into midfield.

Peter Farrell was a fantastic ball playing midfielder and he played alongside Alan Suddick, who was a legend at Blackpool. Alan was an absolute genius with his left foot, as good as anyone in a dead ball situation.

One lad I'll never forget is John Ritson, a right back who played over three hundred games for Bolton. John was coming to the end of his career, while mine was hopefully just beginning. He always told it how it was. One day, he got me in the corner of the dressing room and said, "Listen, son. I've got a mortgage to pay, so you don't fuck about on that pitch. You make sure you do your job properly because I need the money." Whether that was true or just a kick up the backside for me, I don't know, but that was the biggest lesson I learnt in football. For me, at that age, the game was exciting, a bit of fun and something to enjoy, but for others, it was their livelihood and their families relied on them and their income. John was a great pro and I thought he was brilliant, but I never forgot those words.

A lot of my teammates had second jobs. John Forrest – whose nickname was Jungle – was our goalkeeper. He was only five foot ten which is small for a keeper, but he was agile, a very good shot stopper, and played over four hundred times for Bury. He had a pig farm, so he'd get up at five a.m. to sort his pigs out before arriving for training. And you knew he had a pig farm when you met him because he'd try and get you to smell his hands, jokingly telling you he'd just had it up a pig's arse! He was a great character who later moved into scouting, and I've seen him many times since on the circuit. You don't get many pig farmers in football these days, do you?

Tony Bailey, our centre back, a really funny guy who had played for Derby County, had a waste paper business that he did very well with. Dave Hatton ran a hotel. That was what football was like in those days and it was very demanding for the players to combine a football career with a normal job.

I need to thank Bobby Smith for believing in me and not being bothered by my age. He always said, "If you're good enough, you're old enough." He knew that I'd make mistakes because of my lack of experience, but I would like to think I made up for that with my enthusiasm, and I was determined to repay his faith in me. That was another lesson that stuck with me, and when I later moved into management, I never looked at the player's birth certificate.

I was young and hadn't cost the club a penny, so there wasn't a lot of pressure on my shoulders which helped me adapt to life in the Third Division. Bury's aims were to finish in mid table. We weren't a big club nor an affluent one, that's for sure, so we had little aspiration of challenging for promotion. Along with the players around me, that gave me the freedom to develop.

I made my professional debut on 8th November 1977, coming off the bench in an away game against Cambridge United, who were managed by Ron Atkinson at the time, someone who later had a huge impact on my career.

Nowadays it's all luxury coaches and hotels for away games, but it wasn't like that at Bury in those days. If only! The only time we travelled by coach was if it was cheaper for the club to hire one than pay us petrol money. Overnight stays in a hotel were never an option for us because of the cost. If it was a really long journey, we'd have a sandwich on the coach or a pre-match meal in a hotel, but that was a rare treat.

I came on as a second half substitute and felt I did OK. I noticed the pace of the game immediately; speed of thought required, and the speed of the players was much quicker than I was used to, although having grown up in the Northern League, which was very physical, I found I had more protection from referees in Division Three.

I soon learnt how ruthless football could be when Bobby Smith was sacked, not long after handing me my debut. It was the first time I had known a manager to be sacked, although it certainly wasn't the last. Results hadn't been great, but I felt saddened by Bobby's departure.

I didn't really think about the consequences of a new man coming in and I couldn't worry. I had to be single minded, knowing that if I played well and did my job properly no one could point the finger at me. In hindsight, one or two players were feeling a little insecure, but I certainly wasn't, maybe because of my age.

Bob Stokoe, who had begun his management career at Bury in the sixties, became our new manager. He was the manager of Sunderland when I was on schoolboy forms with them, although he wouldn't have remembered me.

I got my first taste of First Division opponents when we were drawn against West Brom in the fourth round of the League Cup. The match was played on a Tuesday night, at the end of November 1977, and it was absolutely freezing. In the days leading up the game the weather worsened, and it was obvious that the pitch would be frozen solid come match day. My landlady, Elsie, had started working in the wage department of a small company based in Bolton called Reebok. They were continually coming up with new ideas for sports shoes and because of the frost, the club had approached Reebok earlier in the season and asked them if they could design some boots that we could wear on an icy pitch. They quickly came back to us with some ribbed-soled shoes that were a bit softer than the studded boots we usually wore. We tried them during training two days before the game and they were fantastic.

So when West Brom arrived with England internationals Cyrille Regis, Bryan Robson, and Laurie Cunningham wearing their usual football boots, they kept slipping over on the marble-like pitch. We were fine because of our specially designed boots, and we ended up beating them 1-0 in front of almost fourteen-thousand jubilant Bury fans.

Our reward was a home tie against Nottingham Forest in the next round. Forest, who were on their way to the First Division title, were managed by the magician himself, Brian Clough. It was the first time I got to witness Mr Clough's mind games.

Forest's left winger was John Robertson, an absolutely magnificent player, and he was coming up against Gerry Kennan, our young right back. All I could hear was Mr Clough yelling instructions to Gerry.

"Gerry, get tight on him, son. If you get tight on Robertson, he can't play."

So Gerry got tight, but Robbo twisted him inside out.

I GET KNOCKED DOWN

"Gerry, you're too tight, son," Mr Clough shouted. "I wouldn't get that tight if I was you."

Mr Clough talked poor Gerry out of the game. It wasn't Gerry's fault, but we lost 3-0 with John Robertson grabbing Forest's third goal. I was mesmerised by Robbo who was an absolute wizard on the ball.

Still learning my trade in the league, these two cup games gave me a real desire to reach that level. I'd had a glimpse and I wanted more. But first and foremost, I had to play consistently for Bury. I already knew that I wanted to be a big game player, someone who rose to the occasion, but I also realised that one or two good games in the cup wouldn't make my career.

Playing in front of large crowds was something else I had to get used to. At Wigan, we only had one stand, but Gigg Lane was a proper ground, very compact and atmospheric. I was bit nervy at first, but the supporters never put me off my game. Hearing the cheers, as well as the moans and groans, was a whole new experience for me, one I learnt to enjoy. The more games I played, the more accustomed I became to the noise from the spectators, and I found that playing in front of a crowd boosted my confidence. When I received a bit of adulation, I craved more and knowing that my every move was being scrutinised gave me greater focus. The fans were paying their hard-earned money to come and watch us play, so the least we could do was give our all and that's what I tried to do in every game I played.

The pitch at Gigg Lane was one of the best around, it was immaculate. We had our groundsmen, Tommy Marshall and Rodney Lester, to thank for that. Every team who visited us loved playing on our pitch, even the bigger clubs. It was the groundsmen's baby, and no one was allowed on the pitch except on match days. We weren't even allowed to train on it because the turf had to be kept pristine.

Another brilliant character at the club was Les Hart. Now there are legends and then there is Les. After turning down a move to Liverpool in 1936, he joined Bury where he spent the rest of his playing days, even captaining the club for twelve seasons. After retiring, he became first team trainer, coach, and physio, before enjoying a one-season spell as manager where he led Bury to a club record 8-0 victory. He then rejected the Head

Coach position at Leeds United to revert to his previous role as Bury's physio. In total, he served the club for almost fifty years and the South Stand at Gigg Lane has since been renamed 'The Les Hart Stand'.

I was a naïve boy, very gullible, and Les used to exploit that. "Danny, we've got a home game on Saturday," he'd say. "You haven't got any spare complimentary tickets, have you?"

"I might have, Les. Why?" I replied.

"I've got my grandma coming over and she'd like to come to the game. Trouble is, I've already given my mum and dad my tickets," he told me.

"No problem," I replied and gave him my tickets without thinking. Les was getting on a bit, so if I'd done the maths, I'd have realised his grandma must have been one hundred and forty!

Another time he told me, "Back when I was playing, my wife used to go into Bury town centre on a Saturday to do a bit of shopping. She always sat in the same seat, on the top deck of the bus that passed Gigg Lane at twenty-past three, so I knew where she'd be. As soon as I saw the bus drive by, I'd trap the ball and give her a little wave before carrying on with the game."

Fucking hell, that's brilliant, Les, I thought. I believed anything in those days.

If you got a knock, Les would run on with his bucket, sponge, and his secret weapon. I've no idea what it was, but he had this thing that he'd warm up in his hands before putting it on your back, leg, whatever hurt, for a few seconds saying, "This is good stuff, get it on you." It could have been banana peel for all I know, but I believed him, and amazingly the pain always vanished. What a character.

By the time March 1978 came around, I had managed to become a first team regular. I played either in the middle of the park or on the right-hand side of midfield. I always preferred to be in the centre because although I was quick, I wasn't a tricky winger. If I played on the right, I'd be tucked in slightly, rather than running with my feet on the chalk. I liked to get involved in the game and was quite an aggressive player who enjoyed a tackle, and I got more of the ball in the middle.

As a team we were struggling – in fact, we didn't win a single league game that I was involved in during my first season – but it was all about learning and gaining experience for me. Training was tough and you had to put the work in. The work ethic required was the same then as it is today, but we didn't have the modern techniques or facilities. Our training ground was a field that was muddy in the autumn, rock hard in the summer, and in the winter, when the ground was frozen solid, we'd have to train in the car park. We even played five-a-side matches on the snowy gravel, and the lads would be sliding into challenges. We never complained, though, you just got on with it. In fact, the more it snowed the funnier it was.

There is a perception that lower league football in those days was everyone going hell for leather, but that's far from the truth. The Third Division was packed full of very good senior pros who knew the game inside out, so there was always a lot of good football played.

Every day was a school day for me, and I learnt so much during that first season. The experienced players demanded I played in a certain way, and they dictated what I did with the ball. Peter Farrell always wanted the ball played in to his feet, and if I played it in front or behind him, he'd give me a bollocking. Andy Rowlands was a great striker with excellent work ethic. He didn't have blistering pace, so he needed the ball played to his chest or feet. It didn't take long for me to understand how each individual played and I learnt that I had to play to their strengths, as well as my own. That was the biggest learning curve for me.

Every training session, every game, was an education. I received individual coaching from Billy Rudd, who did a lot of work with the younger players. He was a tough cookie and was brilliant for me. I always tried to impress my coaches and wanted to make them proud. Everything was set up to help me develop, and I am very fortunate to have started my professional career at a club like Bury.

I found it hard living away from my parents, but I tried to get back on a Saturday night or a Sunday when I could. Mum was always fantastic to me when I returned home. She'd wash my clothes and then put them in front of the fire to dry, making sure everything was clean for when I returned to Bury on the Monday morning.

I kept in touch with my mates and went out for a pint with them when I came back to Wigan at the weekends. They tried to come and watch me play when they could, but it wasn't easy as they were working long hours. I'm still in contact with many of my childhood friends, although we don't see each other as often as we'd like.

My friends often spent their Sunday afternoons at the pub over the road from my parents' house. When they finished their drinks, they'd knock on our front door, asking if I was in, and even if I wasn't home Mum would always invite them in and ask if they wanted some food. That was typical of Mum. She didn't have a lot, but what she did have she'd quite happily share with others.

Dad was very low-key. His role was to keep the house and the family going, and to keep my feet on the ground. He never once criticised me, he just asked how I'd got on. Dad came to a few games, but work had to come first. I know that he always listened to the game on the radio and watched me on the television. He kept it very cool, but I know for a fact that he was very proud of me.

In contrast, Mum came to watch me at every opportunity she could and that was down to my good friend John Howard. John was a mad sports fan, and if it wasn't for him and his wife Linda driving me up and down the country, I wouldn't have achieved anything in the game. I couldn't afford a car and there were certain places you couldn't get to by bus, so without John, I'd have really struggled. John was eventually best man at my wedding and he and his family remain very loyal friends.

Without John, Mum wouldn't have been able to watch me play and I'm eternally grateful to him for driving her to and from games. Mum used to bring a flask with her that everyone assumed contained coffee. It did, but she also added quite a bit of whisky too! It was a bit of surprise for John one day when he accepted her offer of a sip of coffee from her flask while he was driving along the motorway!

Another time, John and Mum were travelling to Chesterfield to watch me play and they didn't know the route. "Just follow that wagon there, John," Mum said, pointing to a lorry with a Chesterfield address written on the back. "It's going to Chesterfield."

"How do you know that?" asked John.

"Because it says Chesterfield on it," she replied.

No matter where we were playing, if she could, she'd be there. She was a football fan before I started playing, and she liked most sports. She enjoyed a a ten-pence bet on the gee gees now and then.

We finished the 1977/78 season in fifteenth position and Bob Stokoe left to become Blackpool's manager. He was replaced by Dave Hatton, a teammate who was given the job of player-manager. Dave reminded me of Colin Todd in the way that he played. He wasn't the biggest, but he was very quick, strong, and clever, and read the game very well.

One of Dave's first signings was Gordon Taylor who joined us from Blackburn Rovers. Gordon was a terrific winger, who was coming to the end of his career, and he had a massive influence on me because he was also the chairman of the Professional Footballer's Association (PFA).

Virtually every day after training, we'd go to Hames, a little café in the town centre, with the team's centre forward Ken Beamish, another new signing, for a coffee and a sandwich. Gordan would arrive with his copy of the *Telegraph* and complete the crossword in two seconds flat!

While we discussed football, Gordon often spoke about contracts, not in any great detail, just little remarks that I took on board. I learnt so much from Gordon that I never felt the need to employ an agent throughout my career. You don't see that nowadays, players have agents from a very young age, but in those days, I felt that I could stand up for myself to managers and chairman and tell them what I wanted and what I thought I deserved. They never thought it was the same amount as I did, of course, but I learnt to stand my corner.

After he retired from playing, Gordan became the Chief Executive of the PFA, a post he held for forty years. In my opinion, he has done a fantastic job and has given the PFA a strength that they've never had before. He's been criticised for the money he earnt, but the standard of care that players receive today is down to the work Gordon and his team have done. He wasn't the one who put the wheels in motion, people like Jimmy Hill and Derek Dougan did a lot at the beginning, but Gordon took the PFA to another level and you have to applaud him for that. The modern-day players should be grateful to Gordon for the lifestyle they are able to lead. We all paid into the PFA, it wasn't expensive then and it isn't now. It's a drop in the ocean compared to the benefits you get. The fact that you have the power of the union behind you if you find yourself in a difficult situation makes it well worth it.

I firmly established myself as a first team regular during my second year at Bury. One of the most memorable matches for me was returning to Wigan in November 1978 in the first round of the FA Cup. We drew the game 2-2 before beating them 4-1 in the replay a few days later, where I scored the opening goal of the game from the penalty spot. The first of many goals I was fortunate to score against my former clubs.

In all honesty, there were very few highlights that year, and it was a long hard slog of a season. We finished the 1978/79 season in nineteenth place, just six points away from relegation. That meant Dave Hatton was sacked and replaced by Dave Connor, a former title winner with Manchester City, who was taking his first managerial role.

Dave's assistant was George Heslop, a Manchester City legend, and a man with the best hairpiece I have ever seen. I believe George had started losing his hair ten years earlier and then one day he turned up with a full head of blonde hair. The lads teased him in training, throwing muddy balls up in the air for him to head, which he did. It didn't bother him, and his hair never moved. After training he would even wash and shampoo it! What a guy he was.

George was a tough man, a great fella, and was very supportive of me, as was Dave. But sadly, they couldn't keep us up and we were relegated at the end of the 1979/80 season. Dave Connor was sacked and as money was tight, we were told that players would be leaving soon, myself included. Although we'd gone down, I had been playing quite well and had over one hundred games under my belt which was not bad considering I was only twenty years old.

Dave Connor likened me to his former Manchester City teammate, the great Colin Bell, (I think he'd mixed me up with someone else!) and he had arranged for me to have a trial with City, with a view to a permanent move for a fee of around £200,000. But then Malcolm Allison, Manchester City's manager, got the sack and the deal fell through.

I'd had a particularly good game against Chesterfield earlier in the year, and they decided to make an offer of £150,000 for me which was a lot of money at the time. There was no way that Bury could afford to turn it down, so the chairman called me into his office and told me to go and speak to Chesterfield. If the selling club wanted you to go, you didn't really have a choice.

I didn't know much about Chesterfield to be honest. I'd played there a couple of times and remembered seeing the crooked spire, but that was it.

The move turned out to be one of the best things that ever happened to me.

CHAPTER 3
The first trophy

I signed for Chesterfield on 1ˢᵗ July 1980 and knew straight away that I was joining an ambitious club that had aspirations of winning promotion to the Second Division.

Under Arthur Cox's leadership, Chesterfield had finished fourth the previous year and the board backed the manager in the transfer market, boosting what was already a very good team. As well as signing me, they also bought midfielder Phil Bonnyman from Carlisle, goalkeeper John Turner from Torquay, and John Stirk, a right back, from Watford. All told, Chesterfield spent close to £500,000 which was a huge sum for a Division Three side.

The new additions slotted straight in with the existing players, like centre forwards Ernie Moss, Alan Birch, and midfielder Geoff Salmon who was a Sheffield United legend – and a legend in the pub trade!

Arthur Cox was like a sergeant major, very disciplined, and very strict. I didn't mind that though. I liked knowing what my role was and the parameters that I had to work in. He wasn't so regimented that we didn't have the freedom to play, it was more about making sure that his teams were well organised.

He was also very tough. In the middle of winter, he took us running in Curbar Edge, a very picturesque spot in the Peak District. We'd run across the peak, which was covered in snow, but he wouldn't let us wear tracksuit tops or bottoms, even though it was literally freezing. He made us run around in shorts and t-shirts. He was very demanding but that was because he was trying to toughen us up. Arthur was hard that way, but well respected and I learnt a great deal from him.

We had a great coach in Frank Barlow, who is still a very good friend of mine. He was the perfect foil for Arthur's bad cop and was well loved by the players who would go the extra mile for him. In later years, Frank became my assistant and is one of the most loyal, honest, and intelligent colleagues I've ever had. I'd trust him with my life. He was absolutely brilliant, not just for me, but for many players over the years.

Billy Dearden was the reserve team coach, another guy who was brilliant at what he did, and another who is still a dear friend to this day.

I went into digs with a lovely couple called Mr and Mrs Benison and enjoyed socialising with my new teammates, although I remained fully focused on my football.

Once a week we went to a restaurant on Loundsley Green Road called the Olde House which was quite popular as a meet-up place for youngsters. I went in there for a drink not long after joining Chesterfield and met a girl named Karen. We chatted all night and I asked her if she would like to go out again. Thankfully, she said yes, but I was trying to settle at the club, so everything else took a back seat and we didn't see each other again for two weeks when I invited her to John Stirk's birthday party. The rest is history. We married in 1983 and Karen has been by my side ever since. She has been an absolute rock and without her in my life, there is no way that I'd be writing this book now. Karen has kept me focused and has been a wonderful mother to Laurie and Carrie, and grandmother to Arlon and Aoife. I'm very, very blessed.

Even though I had arrived for a sizeable transfer fee, I didn't feel any pressure whatsoever. A few of us had big price tags, so I wasn't alone in that respect, but I also had a lot of confidence in my ability.

For one of my early games, we travelled by coach and had a pre-match meal in a hotel. I didn't have a clue what to order, but I noticed the other lads were eating steak, so I decided to try that. I'd never eaten a steak before then. It's not a meal you'd have before a game now, but it was the done thing back then. I remember Arthur Cox passing me some horseradish to put on my steak which I did. It was awful, and I was almost sick! I still hate horseradish to this day! Sorry, Arthur.

We got off to a fantastic start and by the end of August, we'd only lost two out of our first ten matches and were on track for promotion. But then we were hit with a bombshell – Arthur Cox left us to join Second Division Newcastle United. He came round to say goodbye to us all before he departed and when he got to me, he whispered, "Practice your Geordie, son." The move didn't transpire, but it was nice that he thought I was capable of playing at a higher level.

Arthur signed Kevin Keegan a few years later. I saw them on television standing on a beach in the North East, Arthur with his arm around Kevin who was wearing a full tracksuit with his hood up looking nice and warm. *You've changed,* I thought. I'm sure it was only Kevin who could get away with that! That for me was man management in progress.

Frank Barlow was promoted to become our new manager, although I don't think it's a role he truly relished. He preferred to coach as that's where his strengths lay.

Under Frank, we continued our strong form in the league, but it was in the Anglo-Scottish Cup where we really excelled.

The Anglo-Scottish Cup was a competition formed in 1975 and consisted of twenty-four teams. Sixteen English clubs competed in groups of four with the winners of each group going through to the two-legged quarter finals where they would face Scottish opposition. Manchester City, Leicester City, Chelsea, Newcastle United, Celtic, Aberdeen, and Rangers are some of the teams who entered the competition, and while it wasn't as prestigious as the FA Cup or League Cup, Brian Clough said that winning the trophy in 1977 was the springboard for the subsequent success he enjoyed at Forest.

Chesterfield entered the competition for the first time during the 1980/81 season and we won our group, finishing ahead of Grimsby Town, Hull City, and Sheffield United to draw Scottish giants Rangers in the quarter final.

We battled to a deserved 1-1 draw at Ibrox in front of twelve-thousand fans, before shocking the Scottish Cup holders with a 3-0 victory at Saltergate in the second leg. Rangers were a team full of internationals and we well and truly beat them which showed the potential of our team. At the time, the Rangers fans had a bad reputation, so the pubs in Chesterfield decided not to open as they didn't want any trouble. They needn't have worried though, as the Rangers supporters were as good as gold, drinking in the pubs on the outskirts of Chesterfield instead.

That victory put Chesterfield firmly on the map as not many people had heard of us before then. Rangers certainly hadn't. We were full of confidence going into the two-legged semi final against my old club Bury.

Scoring the opening goal of the first leg at Gigg Lane was a very strange feeling. As soon as the ball hit the back of the net, I ran to the fans to celebrate, jumping around like a mad man. Players don't celebrate against their former clubs these days, saying that it is out of respect. I don't get that at all. What are you supposed to do? Apologise? Every goal is special, and of course you should celebrate. You have a duty to your own fans, too. The best feeling in football is scoring a goal and I made sure I enjoyed every single one, don't worry about that.

Funnily enough, I also scored against Wigan in the FA Cup for the second successive season. I always seemed to do well against my former clubs. I celebrated that one too.

Scoring a goal is a personal thing, but ultimately it means nothing if your team don't win the game. If you want to be successful, you have to put the team first. Yes, individuals can sometimes win a game for you, but you won't achieve anything if you don't perform as a team.

We won the first leg 2-1 and followed that up with a 1-1 draw in the second to set up a mouth-watering final against high-flying Notts County, who were on their way to promotion to Division One.

I started in the first leg of the final which we won 1-0 thanks to a goal by Ernie Moss. Unfortunately, I ruptured my thigh muscle which meant I missed the second leg played a week later.

It wasn't just me who was injured either. Our regular goalkeeper John Turner was out, as was our reserve keeper Phil Tingay, so Paul Gregory, a nineteen-year-old, made his first ever appearance. What a way to make your debut!

County took the lead in the seventy-third minute and with the aggregate score tied at 1-1, the game went into extra time. In the final minute of extra time, Alan Crawford smashed the ball home from six yards to give us a 2-1 victory and our first major trophy. For a Division Three side to overcome Rangers and Notts County was astonishing. It was a very special moment for me to win my first winner's medal. Mind you, I didn't actually get a medal at the time because someone else had pocketed mine by accident and it took the secretary six months to get it back!

The tournament was scrapped at the end of the season which meant that Chesterfield got to keep the cup.

Unfortunately, we missed out on promotion despite finishing in fifth place in the league table, just three points behind Barnsley and Charlton who went up.

The club had spent a lot of money in the hope of winning promotion. The gamble hadn't paid off and there was no more money available for Frank to strengthen the squad. The following season we finished in a disappointing fifteenth and during the 1982/83 season, the team started to be disbanded as Chesterfield began to develop financial problems.

Little Alan Birch, our top scorer, was snapped up by Wolverhampton Wanderers for £200,000 after an impressive display in a behind-closed-doors friendly against Wolves, who had René van de Kerkhof on trial at the time as a potential target.

Alan's strike partner, Phil Bonnyman, also left, joining Grimsby Town. It was a real shame to see that side split up.

I became aware that other teams were showing an interest in me by reading the newspapers, but you never really know which clubs are serious until an offer has been made. Years later, I was speaking to Ron Saunders, who was Liverpool's chief scout, and he told me he'd been to watch me while I was at Chesterfield. "Why didn't you sign me then?" I asked, wondering why I'd missed out on a move to the team I had supported as a boy.

"Because you were shit!" he joked. "We had to come and watch you because you'd been recommended to us, but we already had someone in your position," he told me. He must have meant the groundsman!

My old manager Arthur Cox was rumoured to have made an offer to take me to Newcastle United, but that didn't materialise.

Manchester City were another club that showed some interest, but in the end, it was Nottingham Forest, and Brian Clough, who came in first. They may have known that other clubs were sniffing around, but they came in quickly to try and avoid a bidding war.

Chesterfield were in a real mess financially so when Frank travelled down to the City Ground to meet Mr Clough, he was asked how much the club wanted for me. "We need £90,000, Brian, and we need it yesterday," Frank said.

"Will any of that money go to you for transfers?" Mr Clough asked Frank.

"No, that's just to clear that debt," he replied.

"Well, in that case, I'll give you £90,000 and two players so you don't lose out." That is an example of Brian Clough's understanding and generosity. He didn't particularly see eye to eye with directors at clubs which is why he wanted to help Frank out.

So Steve Kendall and Calvin Plummer went to Chesterfield and stayed there for a couple of seasons.

It was an ideal move for me really; Forest had won the European Cup just two and half years earlier, so for me to go into that arena with players like Viv Anderson, John Robertson, and Colin Todd was an absolute dream.

But before my move was finalised, I first had to travel to Nottingham to meet the legend himself, Mr Clough.

CHAPTER 4
The genius of Clough

When the clubs had agreed on a transfer fee, all that was left was for me to discuss personal terms. So, in January 1983, I travelled down to Nottingham to meet Brian Clough, a man I already had a great amount of respect for.

Mr Clough became manager of Nottingham Forest in January 1975 when they were a struggling team in the Second Division. Eight years later, he had totally transformed the club, leading Forest to the First Division title, two European Cups, one European Super Cup, two League Cups, one Anglo-Scottish Cup, and a Charity Shield.

I was excited to potentially join such a fantastic club, with a manager who was widely regarded as a football genius.

There was a rumour going around that I was going to Forest to replace Mark Proctor. That was a little awkward for me, as I didn't know who I was replacing, and that was nothing to do with me. Anyway, as I was sat in Mr Clough's office with his assistant, Ron Fenton, there was a knock on the door. When it opened, I saw Mark Proctor's head pop through the open doorway.

"Gaffer, can I have a word?" Mark asked.

"Yes, come on in, son," Mr Clough replied.

Mark walked in, saw me, and said, "I'm thinking of going on the transfer list."

"OK, thank you. Off you go," replied Mr Clough. It was quite embarrassing from my point of view as that should have been a private conversation.

When the door closed, the manager asked me what sort of money I was looking for and to be honest, I didn't have a clue. I was very nervous, and in complete awe of the man. I was earning £300 a week at Chesterfield, so I decided to ask for £400.

"Alright, young man," he said. "I was thinking of £350 a week, but you go and have a walk around the ground and then come back and tell me if you still want that £400."

So I had a self-guided tour of the City Ground, taking it all in and imagining myself playing First Division football on the lush green turf. When I returned to his office, the manager asked what I thought of the ground.

"It's fantastic, Mr Clough. Absolutely magnificent," I replied.

"So what about that £400 you wanted?" he asked.

"It's alright. I'll leave the £50 and accept your offer of £350 a week," I replied.

"It's a good fucking job too, son, otherwise you'd be going back to that shithole you've just come from," he said before adding, "And, by the way, you can have the extra £50."

So he gave me £400 a week anyway! That was my first experience of negotiating with the great Brian Clough. It was brilliant. More than educational.

Going into a talented dressing room, full of characters, was a daunting prospect and I admit that I felt a bit nervy. I was going to be playing with big hitters like Viv Anderson, Garry Birtles, Colin Todd, and Ian Bowyer, to name just a few. Many of whom were internationals and superstars. But they were also great people who made me feel very welcome.

Training was much more intense than what I'd been used to, but that was fine by me. I knew the increased intensity would only help me to improve as a player. Ronnie Fenton and Liam O'Kane ran the training sessions, but when the boss walked onto the training pitch, the level ramped up as we all tried to impress him. Mr Clough's presence was enough to make you find that little bit extra because we were all desperate to get into the squad on a Saturday.

I'd played every week at Chesterfield and Bury, and my goal was to play every week for Forest. In my mind, I hadn't come to sit on the bench, that's for sure.

I made my debut on 5th February 1983, in a home game against the reigning European Champions Aston Villa. Talk about being thrown in at the deep end! I didn't play particularly well, but I managed to grab a goal in the first half. Peter Withe had given

Villa the lead just after the half-hour mark. Two minutes later Garry Birtles made a great run down the left-hand side, crossed itin to the box, and I slid the ball home. A goal against the best team in Europe, and a well done from Mr Clough – you can't get much better than that!

When the gaffer spoke to you, he could make you feel ten feet tall, but he could also be quite cutting. We played away at Arsenal in my fourth game for the club. Arsenal were a good side with Pat Jennings in goal, Kenny Sansom at the back, and Tony Woodcock up front. I had a couple of good chances, one that I screwed wide when I should have done better and another where Pat pulled off a great save. We ended up drawing the game 0-0, so we were quite happy coming off the pitch as Highbury was a tough place to go. I thought the gaffer would be happy too. I was wrong.

After the game, we boarded the coach and travelled back up the M1 to Nottingham. We used to park our cars at a hotel in Sandiacre and the coach dropped us off there. I had bought myself a new car when I signed for Forest, a red Ford Escort 1.2L which was a nice little sporty model. As I disembarked the coach, Mr Clough asked me which car was mine.

"That red one over there," I said pointing in the direction of my new motor.

"Is it, young man?" he said before walking over and kicking the back of my car with his slip-on shoes. He then turned to me and said, "You fucking cost me a result today. I've never won at Arsenal, and you cost me a win."

I didn't know what to do. I looked at my pride and joy and saw that although it wasn't dented, it did have a few scuff marks from his shoes. I was just grateful that he wasn't wearing a pair of pit boots!

A couple of days later, Karen received a massive bouquet of flowers at the house. There was no note, but we knew they were from the gaffer. It was his way of smoothing things over, I guess.

Mr Clough would always ask the young lads if they were married, engaged, or had a girlfriend. He felt that those who were in a relationship had more responsibilities, so wouldn't be going out on the town, doing what other young lads were doing. When he discovered that Karen and I were getting married, he was delighted. We invited him to the wedding, along with my teammates at Forest.

He politely declined, which I expected, but he sent a huge bouquet to our house with a card, wishing us all the best for the future.

Towards the end of the season, we played Watford away and I was named as a substitute for only the second time since I'd joined Forest. I knew that Mr Clough didn't like to have to tell the subs to warm up. He expected you to take responsibility yourself and ensure you were ready if he needed to bring you on. During the first half, I was all excitable, running up and down the touchline, trying to impress him. I jogged back to the dugout, and was just to the right of it, touching my toes, swinging my left leg over my shoulder, looking to make a good impression. *Look gaffer I'm warmed up and ready to go on.*

But just as I reached the dugout, vigorously and nervously, I slipped and fell on my arse right in front of the gaffer!

He stared at me for a moment before saying, "You might as well sit down, young man, because you've got no fucking chance of going on after that." So I sat down on the bench and sure enough, I didn't get on.

At the end of the season, in which we finished fifth in the First Division, we travelled to Canada for an end-of-season tour. We played some friendlies in some great stadiums against terrific teams, but we were also given a lot of time for sightseeing. The highlight for me was our trip to Niagara Falls. It was absolutely stunning, and I was glad that I'd taken my camera along with me. In those days, unless you had a polaroid, cameras had a film inside that you had to take to somewhere like Boots to develop, so you couldn't see what photos you'd taken until you got home.

I'd taken quite a few photographs, but still had plenty of space left on the film when I nipped to the toilet. When I returned, I realised that I didn't have as many photos left to take as I had thought which was strange. *I must have taken more than I thought.*

Anyway, when we got home, I asked Karen if she could take the film to be developed for me which she did. A few days later, she went into Nottingham to collect the photos. When she walked through the front door, she flung the photos at me and calmly said, "Don't you ever send me to Boots with your camera again!"

I couldn't believe it when I looked at the photos. It turned out that when I had gone to the toilet, the lads had borrowed my camera and taken pictures of their bollocks, their arses, everything. No wonder Karen was so embarrassed when she collected the photos from Boots!

*****

As well as the trip to Canada with the lads, I also took a short break with Karen, our first as a married couple. Then it was time to return for pre-season training. At Bury and Chesterfield, pre-season consisted of lots of running around the local areas, but at Forest, we went to Cala Major in Spain which was one of the gaffer's favourite places. I think he had a place out there because he loved the area so much.

On the first day, Mr Clough told us that we could have a night out which was brilliant from our point of view. We went into the main strip where the bars were, found a nice place, and one of the lads got the first round in. The order was something daft like sixteen pints of lager and a glass of orange juice for Peter Davenport, who didn't drink. We sat down with our drinks and the next minute, the door opened and in walked the gaffer, wearing a blazer, scarf, and chinos, looking really smart.

The bar went silent, like an old wild west movie, as we waited to see what he had to say. "Right, lads, you lot out," he told us.

We all looked at him confused because he'd told us we could have a night out, and we'd only had a few sips of our first drink. I picked up my glass, but before it reached my lips he shouted, "Oi, I've told you. Out!"

So we all put down our pints and followed him out of the bar towards the hotel. But before we reached it, he turned off left and took us into a piano bar where he'd been drinking with the coaches. There were only a handful of people in the bar, and there was no atmosphere, so he'd decided to get us in there to liven things up.

As we approached the bar, an old guy looked up at Viv Anderson and said, "Can you sing?"

"What?" replied a confused Viv.

"Can you sing?" the old man asked again. This time Viv didn't respond. He knew what the man was intimating. As one of the first black players to play for England, he had learned to ignore it.

The gaffer walked up to the man and said, "Who do you think you are, speaking to my players like that? We know what you're trying to say."

The old fella looked around, saw everyone was staring at him, supped up and left. When the door closed, Mr Clough turned to Viv and said, "Well, Viv. Can you sing or not?"

It completely took the tension out of the situation, and we went on to have a great night. We had a right skinful, and as we walked – staggered more like – back to the hotel, we were told to report at ten o'clock the next morning where we'd be running along the beach. *Crickey,* I thought. *If I'd known that, I wouldn't have drunk as much.*

When we arrived at the beach the following day, nursing a little hangover, Ronnie Fenton told us that we'd be running to the end of the beach and back again. A proper run because it was a very long beach. We all set off together and had run about two-hundred yards when we heard a shout from the side. "What are you lot doing? Get yourself in here." It was the gaffer, sitting in a beachside bar. So we all ran straight into the bar, in full training kit, and had a couple of pints.

He was so unpredictable; you never knew what you were going to get. Sometimes we'd be pleading inside our heads for him to let us train! That was all part of his genius.

A few days later, we played Real Mallorca in an evening game. I have to be careful how I say this – the referee was bent. It was only a friendly, but there was a big crowd, and the ref was completely biased towards the Spanish team. It got so frustrating for the gaffer that at one stage he rose from the bench, walked onto the pitch, and picked the ball up from Colin Walsh, before jogging over to the referee. He lifted the ball towards his face, and said, "We're playing with this mister. It's called football."

The ref looked at Mr Clough, unsure how to handle the situation. Then he exploded and sent the gaffer off. The crowd were going crazy, baying for blood. Mr Clough walked up the tunnel and the game resumed. The next minute, we heard the crowd going mad again. I turned towards the tunnel and saw the gaffer, wearing a hat and scarf, walking along the side of the pitch where he plonked himself down in the opponent's dugout. The referee walked over and had to call security to escort him away.

The animosity in the stadium was so bad that we had to stay inside the ground for two hours after the final whistle. The crowd were stood outside and we were told that it wasn't safe for us to leave the stadium. It was only a friendly and the result didn't matter, but that wasn't the point. The gaffer was so strong-willed and always wanted to play the game the right way, and with fairness. He stood up for us because he didn't like how we were treated by the referee that day.

A few years later, when I was playing for Luton Town, a journalist asked me to give him an example of how Mr Clough looked after his players, so I thought that was a positive story to tell. The article was printed the day before the League Cup final between Luton and Forest. Before the match, Mr Clough came into the warm-up area at Wembley and shouted, "Hey, young man. Come and give us a kiss."

"I can't, gaffer," I replied. "I'm warming up."

"Come and give us a kiss," he repeated.

"Sorry, gaffer," I said. I was getting focused for the match and didn't want any distractions. I couldn't have the opposition manager kissing me in the Wembley tunnel.

A little later, as we were lining up in the tunnel about to walk out onto the pitch, he came over to me, rabbit punched me in the stomach and said, "Don't you ever tell anyone about my holidays again!"

There are so many things that you can say about Mr Clough – and there are many players more worthy to reminisce than me on that subject – but one thing that is definitely true is that he was a genius. He had such a huge impact on me as a player and as a person. There is a reason he was the best manager in the world for a number of years, and the players learnt so much from him.

When he spoke, it meant something, and everyone hung on his every word, whether you were the tea lady or a full international. He was a very genuine man, and very generous, although a lot of people wouldn't know about that side of him.

Mr Clough encouraged his teams to entertain the fans by playing football the right way. "You play on the green stuff, not the blue stuff in the sky," he would demand. Some of the football they played was breathtaking. He made you want to play for him, and he didn't like players who shirked their responsibilities. If you turned away from an opportunity and passed backwards, he'd give you a bollocking because he wanted you to be positive, take chances, and manipulate the ball. "If you're tired, give it to John Robertson and he'll keep it for ten minutes," he'd tell us. He loved exciting football and wanted us to play the game in the way he liked to watch it.

Everyone enjoyed their football at Forest. They beat teams they shouldn't have, and players won medals they weren't expecting to win. One of his biggest strengths was transforming people that others didn't rate or had written off into top players. He polished so many diamonds during his successful managerial career.

They certainly threw away the mould when they made Mr Clough, that's for sure. I'd have loved to have managed against him to see how he handled opposition managers, but he'd retired by the time I became a manager.

It was a real shame, the way he left the game, and the scenes when he said goodbye to the fans were heartbreaking to watch. How he achieved what he did at Nottingham Forest is nothing short of a miracle. As a man manager, he was second to none. If you did well, he'd praise you and if you stepped out of line, he'd let you know about it. Although, you never knew whether you'd get a pat on the back or a punch in the stomach. That was all part of his genius.

I found myself on the bench a lot at the start of the 1983/84 campaign, and didn't make my first appearance of the season until 28th September when I came on as a substitute in a UEFA Cup tie away at German club Frankfurt. It was nice to get my first taste of European football, but I didn't want to spend the season sitting on the bench, I wanted to play. The problem I had was that we had the fantastic Ian Bowyer in the centre midfield spot, so I had to move out to the right which wasn't my strongest position. I'd have played anywhere in that side, but I always preferred to play in the middle.

We also had Steve Hodge, another young lad, coming through the ranks. Although he played more on the left, he was a real attack-minded player. I liked to get forward too, but Hodgey was the better player so it was an easy decision for the gaffer.

I would have loved to stay at Forest for longer, but Mr Clough was very astute at spotting things. He knew that I wanted to play, and that reserve team football wasn't going to cut it. I'd built up a little bit of a reputation as a decent player, so one or two clubs enquired about me. In October 1983, I went to Scunthorpe for a month's loan. Although they were in Division Three, Frank Barlow was Scunthorpe's coach, which was good for me. Their manager, Allan Clarke, had fancied me when he'd been in charge of Leeds United, so I knew I'd play. I had a good time there, scoring three goals in six games, which rekindled my enthusiasm to play first team football.

Other clubs were watching the situation, and when I returned to the City Ground, I wondered if I was going to be sold or would be able to get back into the Nottingham Forest first team. I got my answer ahead of a crucial UEFA Cup tie against Celtic. I'd sat on the subs' bench for the last two matches and expected to be involved in some capacity for the Celtic match. But after training a couple of days before the game, Mr Clough pulled me to one side and said, "Listen, son. We've got a big reserve game coming up. I want you to captain the reserves and show these lads what it's like to be the proud leader of a team."

"Yes, gaffer. I'll do that," I replied, feeling like a million dollars. It was the best way I've ever been dropped!

I had a chance to go to Southampton as a swap deal for a striker called David Puckett. I had all my bags packed, and was ready to go, when the gaffer rang me and told me he'd rather me stay. I'm not sure what happened, but the move broke down.

On 1ˢᵗ November 1983, Brighton and Hove Albion made an offer for me which Mr Clough accepted. Brighton had just been relegated to the Second Division, but I didn't look at it as a backward step at all. When I looked at the players in the squad, and the fact that Brighton was a big, ambitious club with a fantastic fan base that could offer me first team football, I felt it was a step up for me.

I later heard from Brian Moore, the football commentator, who was also on the board at Gillingham, that Mr Clough had told him that he'd maybe made a mistake letting me go. Even all those years later, that one comment made me feel special. That was the effect that the gaffer had on people. It was sad to leave Forest, but it was the right move for everyone.

So just ten months after our move to Nottingham Forest, Karen and I travelled down to the South Coast to begin a new adventure.

CHAPTER 5
Storms, supporters, and a giant spider

Moving from our home in Mansfield down to Brighton on the South Coast was a big upheaval, not necessarily for me, but for my wife Karen who had just completed her NHS exams. As a player, joining a new club can be tough, but the chances are that you already know someone there, and even if you don't, every day you are surrounded by teammates who very quickly become good friends. It's much harder for the wives, girlfriends, and children.

But credit to Karen, she never once complained, and her support and encouragement made the transition so easy for me. She willingly followed me around the country throughout my career.

From a footballing perspective, I had no concerns at all about joining Brighton. We had some phenomenal players. The season before, the Seagulls had been beaten finalists in the FA Cup, and the aspiration was to get straight back to the top flight at the first attempt.

Our manager was Chris Cattlin, a full back who'd played over two hundred games for Coventry City before finishing his playing career at Brighton. I liked Cat a lot. He was energetic and enthusiastic in what he did, and that rubbed off on a lot of players, including me. He liked to join in with the training, telling us how brilliant he was, but we wound him up by telling him he was crap! He was a great character, and also a very astute businessman, who owns a chain of rock shops on the seafront, amongst other things.

Just after I joined, Chris told me that when he went up to the City Ground to sign me, Brian Clough had kept him waiting in an office for ten hours. Mr Clough knew he was there, but he went home for a bit before returning to the ground to complete the deal. That was typical Clough! The gaffer at his best.

Chris wanted to make me club captain eventually, which was a huge privilege, especially considering some of the players already at Brighton. I was fortunate to wear the captain's armband at most clubs I played at, with the exception of Forest. It was very humbling, and a terrific title to hold.

I was still only twenty-two years old, but people started to tell me that I'd become a manager. At that stage, I harboured no ambitions of becoming the gaffer, I was purely focused on my playing career, but maybe I was giving off some signals or signs.

I loved the responsibility that came with being the club captain and I took the role very seriously. I was a talker on the pitch, and I'd like to think that I led by example. I wasn't a ranter and raver. I was only small, so I couldn't yell at a big centre half, or they might give me a clip round the ear! The feedback I gave was mainly encouragement, but I did push players around where I felt it appropriate and thankfully, they responded well to me.

The captain's job isn't just about what happens on the pitch, it's about leading the boys off it too, and Karen played her role in that. She organised social occasions for the wives and girlfriends, making everyone feel welcome. One thing the football fraternity does very well is open their arms to people who are new to the area. Whenever a new player joined, Karen would welcome them and their families and do everything she could to help them settle in the area. She was fantastic.

We had a great set of lads at Brighton and the dressing room ran itself. I'm not saying we didn't need a manager, of course we did, but we made his job easier because no one was afraid to point a finger or be forceful with their teammates when it was needed. The fact that we could be so honest with each other created a great camaraderie and we enjoyed some fantastic nights where we went out en bloc. It was one out, all out at Brighton.

Our team was full of experienced, quality players, like Alan Young, Joe Corrigan, Gerry Ryan, Neil Smiley, Jimmy Case, and Tony Grealish. When I was at Forest, Brian Clough had told me to "Go and learn your trade, and when you think you've got it, go and learn it again." I took that piece of feedback with me throughout my whole career and never got too far ahead of myself. I was always keen to learn, so training and playing with those lads was a dream come true.

I was particularly excited about playing alongside Jimmy Case, who was an absolute legend. During his eight years at Liverpool, Jimmy won four league titles, three European Cups, and a whole host of other trophies, yet he never lost that desire to win.

He was a funny guy too. Jimmy was profoundly deaf, and even though he wore hearing aids, sometimes he couldn't hear you, so you'd be talking to him, and he wouldn't respond. If you didn't know that he was deaf, you'd think he was just being ignorant.

One night, we were in a wine bar/restaurant in the town centre, and before Jimmy went to the toilet, he took out his hearing aid and plonked it on the bar. When he returned, he said, "Right you bastards. I heard you talking about me!" He was a right card, but what a player.

Our England international centre back Steve Foster is one of the funniest men I've ever come across. He was hilarious, an absolute nutter at times – in the nicest way – and great company. Fozzie used to organise the nights out for the lads, and we nicknamed him 'The Bully' because once he said we were going out, you couldn't say no.

In those days, a lot of the pubs closed at two p.m., which meant that we struggled to find anywhere to go if we fancied a pint after training. There were some private sporting clubs situated throughout Brighton, very selective little hideouts, and you had to know where they were. Fozzie knew them all. After training, he'd say, "Come on lads, let's go and have a game of pool and a couple of pints." He loved those clubs so much that he ended up buying one of his own in the Lanes called 'Fozzie's.' His club opened at irregular hours – between the pubs closing and reopening again – and we went there when we could.

Occasionally we'd have a night out wearing fancy dress. I remember Joe Corrigan dressing up as a policeman, standing in the road, stopping cars, and directing them to take alternative routes.

Tony Grealish went as Wee Willie Winkie. We had a meal in a restaurant and were sat near the window that displayed the menu. As passers-by considered what they might like to order, Tony lifted his nightdress up and pushed his bare backside against the window at the side of the menu!

Jimmy Case was dressed as a deep-sea diver, but we lost him later on that night when we went into a nightclub. We later discovered that he'd spent the entire evening sitting in a pond inside the club, with people bringing him his drinks.

On the same night, I ran home at three a.m. wearing a giant spider costume that Karen had made for me. It must have been strange for supporters to see the Brighton and Hove Albion captain running through the streets in the early hours dressed as an arachnid!

We had a group of funny lads, and we had a great time off the pitch. Everything was a piss take until match days when we all became serious. It's absolute heaven if you can have that kind of team spirit, and have players who know when to have fun and when to be serious.

I made my Brighton debut on 3rd December 1983 and made a fantastic start scoring two goals in a 3-1 win over Cardiff City at the Goldstone Ground.

Despite spending a month in Forest's reserves, it wasn't difficult to get back into the swing of playing regular first team football again. In fact, I didn't find the transition from any level of football particularly hard. I always expected it to be tough, especially the higher up you go, but it never really bothered me, and I was always able to adapt fairly quickly. That must have been a dream from a manager's point of view because you don't want to buy someone and have to wait twelve months for them to find their feet. A lot of that was down to my teammates being so welcoming, but it was mainly due to Karen and her selfless attitude.

One of the undoubted highlights of my time at Brighton was beating Liverpool in the fourth round of the FA Cup on 29th January 1984. The build up to the game was extraordinary, with all the talk about Jimmy Case and Graeme Souness going head-to-head. Two hard men. Who would come out on top?

I'd played against Liverpool in my final season at Bury when we were beaten 2-0. We were very much the underdogs then, but at Brighton, we knew were capable of beating anyone. That was our biggest problem because we tended to win the harder games and lose the ones that looked easier on paper.

The pitch on the day was very muddy and slippy, which perhaps suited us more than Liverpool. As the game progressed,

I was as intrigued as anyone as to how the confrontation between Case and Souness would go. I couldn't see either of them backing down. But it turned out to be an anti-climax because Graeme went off with a hamstring injury after just ten minutes. A blow to Liverpool, but it gave us a big lift and we went on to win the match 2-0, with goals from Gerry Ryan and Terry Connor.

It was a huge achievement. I always wanted to test myself against the best and they don't come much bigger than Liverpool, who went on to win the European Cup that season. That was the biggest and best result that I'd had at that stage of my career. To go up against my heroes and get a victory like that was magnificent. We were on cloud nine after that and I don't think our feet touched the floor for a few weeks.

We lost to Charlton and drew to Swansea in our next two games, before Watford knocked us out of the FA Cup. That was our problem – we lacked consistency. That's why we missed out on promotion that year. We were as good as anyone else in the league – better than most in fact – but we just didn't perform to the best of our ability often enough. We finished the 1983/84 season in ninth place. If I'm honest, we should have done much better with the players we had.

On a personal level, I was delighted to score fourteen goals in a season which was the first time in my career that I'd reached double figures. It helped me massively that I played alongside Jimmy Case and Tony Grealish, who were both happy to sit back, because that gave me the freedom to go forward. I had a decent engine and was able to get up and down the park for the entire ninety minutes, and I wasn't a bad finisher either.

Towards the end of that season, I witnessed a shocking incident, when Gerry Ryan broke his leg in a collision with Henry Hughton, Chris's brother. It happened not far from where I was standing, and I felt sickened when I saw Gerry's shin bone poking out of his sock. It was a horrific injury and sadly, Gerry never made it back to the same level he'd been at before. It was a sober reminder that the career of a professional footballer is short, sometimes very short.

I was always quite lucky with injuries throughout my career, but I did suffer with a hamstring problem that wouldn't go away during my spell at Brighton. In those days, the pitches were either rock hard or mud baths, and because I was so quick, I often picked up niggly little injuries. Cortisone injections were popular back then – they helped mask the pain which allowed you to play – but the cortisone would calcify on your ligaments, and that's what had happened to me.

The club had been recommended a guy in Holland, called Dr Smith, by Manchester United's medical team. Bryan Robson had been treated by him and Remi Moses was out there with an ankle injury at the time.

So I travelled over to Amsterdam to begin treatment. The only way that they could remove the calcification and get the blood flowing again was through friction massage. It was horrendously painful. They used their thumbs, the balls of their hands and when they got tired, their elbows.

Remi, I believe, was paying for his own accommodation, and had to take a flat above a brothel because of the rental prices in the Dutch capital. In contrast, Brighton were paying for everything, bar expenses, and had even put me up in a five-star hotel. It was so palatial; my room was almost as big as a football pitch. *I could get used to this,* I thought. Unfortunately, when Brighton got the bill for the first week and realised how expensive it was, they moved me into a little bed and breakfast.

I spent three weeks in Holland, receiving treatment for up to eight hours a day. It was so tiring, sitting and there letting people get into my leg. It was the most painful and distressing treatment I have ever had. I had to try and relax the muscles, but I instinctively tensed which made it even more painful. When they finished prodding me, I'd have half an hour of ultrasound, and by the time I got back to my B&B, my leg felt ten times the size it actually was. It was so painful that I couldn't touch my leg.

Although the club were paying for my treatment and accommodation, I had to pay my own expenses. At the time, interest rates on mortgages were around the twenty per cent mark, so we weren't flush with money, which meant I lived on chips and mayonnaise. The wonderful, glamourous life of a professional footballer!

Karen was great, as usual. It can't have been easy for her to be in a town on her own with no family around her, although maybe she was happy to get rid of me for a while!

When I returned to England and did a bit of running, I felt no pain at all and have never had any problems with my ligaments since. So despite the pain and boredom, the treatment did the trick.

Ahead of the 1984/85 season, we signed Frank Worthington – another absolute legend. Frank was fantastic; his technique and ability shone through. The fans loved him. He was a ladies' man too; their jaws would drop as he walked past. He had everything, the jammy twat!

Frank's first touch was sublime, and if you gave him the ball, you knew you weren't going to get it back for a while. You had no chance of getting a one-two off him, that's for sure. He was so confident and just a brilliant footballer. He had this ability to drift into space using his intelligence and experience, and my job was to find him. If Frank didn't get the ball, he'd go bananas. He was great to play with. I always knew he was a good player, but it was only when I played with him that I realised just how tough he was too. Defenders used to kick lumps out of him, but he always gave as good as he got.

In those days, referees weren't as protective of players as they are now, and the game was much more physical. I always enjoyed a good rapport with refs – I'd tell them they were shit, and they'd say the same to me! We'd grown up with them, come up through the leagues at the same time, so you could always have a bit of fun with referees. There wasn't really a 'them and us' situation like there is now. I think money has caused that divide.

We were also much closer to the supporters back then, and clubs were very much seen as a part of the community. Most of us players had come from a working-class background, so we had that little bit of understanding with the supporters. We weren't a group of big-headed footballers looking to cause trouble, we were just a group of young lads going for a night out. I often spent an evening enjoying a pint with the fans or the supporters' clubs. I was polite enough to listen to their views, even if I didn't always agree with them. You have to respect their opinions because supporters are a big part of the football club,

I never got fed up with the attention from fans and was always more than happy to sign an autograph or pose for a photograph. I accepted that interaction with the public was part of my job as a footballer and I met some wonderful people.

Early in the season, I dislocated my shoulder during a game. It was so painful. Before I left the ground, the physio strapped me up and then sent me home to rest. Later that evening Chris Cattlin decided to drive round to my house to see how I was doing. He knocked on the door and Karen answered.

"I've just come round to see how Danny is," he said.

"I'm sorry, Chris, but he's not in," Karen told him.

"Oh no. What's wrong? Is he in the infirmary?" said a very concerned Chris.

"No, he's fine. He's gone for a pint with the lads!"

When I got home an hour later, Chris was sat in the lounge having a cup of tea. That was how we dealt with things in those days. Alcohol was a good painkiller!

We played some fantastic football during the 1984/85 campaign and finished in sixth place, just two points behind Manchester City who were promoted in third place. Unfortunately, there were no play-offs at that time. We had some memorable results, and I managed to score some important goals.

Moving can be stressful, Karen and I should know, but travelling to Brighton was to hold the most fantastic news, not once but twice.

In mid-April 1984, Karen and I decided to pop out for a bit of lunch at a hostelry called The Ship in Shoreham. On the way there, she joyfully told me that was pregnant, six weeks gone. I could have crashed the car with the tears of joy streaming down my face. What utterly brilliant news.

On the 5th of December, we had the first sight of our wonderful son Laurie James Wilson.

We then, in October 1987, learned that we were soon to have another fantastic surprise. Carrie Ann Wilson was born on the 11th of June 1988. The most beautiful little thing I could ever have wished for. And still is. Family complete.

Both were born at the Royal Sussex hospital in Brighton. Karen gave me the most generous gifts one could ask for. Two of the best moments in my life, bar none. They still have us wrapped round their little fingers, but I wouldn't have it any other way.

It was hard for Karen, who was often on her own with two young kids, but she is a remarkable woman. Away games for Brighton could be four or five hours away, so I'd often walk in at one a.m., and she'd have to be up a few hours later to feed the children. We bounced off each other well, and I tried to do my part and help out as often as I could.

We didn't have any family down south, but Karen's mum, Margot, and my mum used to come and help us out, which was a huge blessing, and a big help to Karen.

Sadly, Margot was taken ill prior to her visiting us in Brighton. Alan Biley, our centre forward and a Rod Stewart lookalike, had a real thing about cars. He used to get a new one every few months, and when he heard that Margo wasn't very well and had never been in a Mercedes before, he took her for a ride in his convertible Merc, all around the town with the roof down. It was a brilliant touch from Alan, and Margot was made up.

Margot passed away not long after Laurie was born, which was absolutely devastating. It was one of the hardest things to know that she was never to meet Carrie, her granddaughter, and vice versa. So sad. She was such a lovely woman, and we still miss her to this day.

Having narrowly missed out on promotion, Chris brought in Dean Saunders, a young Welsh striker from Cardiff, and we also signed Dennis Mortimer, the man who had captained Aston Villa to their European Cup win in 1982. Dennis had an unbelievable CV, and even though he was thirty-three years old when he joined us, he was still a great professional. He did everything the right way: he trained well, ate healthily, and was very athletic. Everything about him oozed class, and I tried to copy him. When the young lads see the older pros who have looked after themselves, it is a real lesson. You can either be a good pro or a bad pro. The good ones have longevity, and the bad ones don't. It was a pleasure to play alongside him in midfield.

Unfortunately, we struggled for consistency and finished the 1985/86 season in a disappointing eleventh in the league table. On a personal level, I'd played some of the best football of my career, scoring six goals in all competitions, which won me the Football League Player of the Year award.

Karen and I travelled down to London for the swanky awards ceremony where Frank Cotton, the Rugby Union prop, and Paddy Crerand, the former Manchester United midfielder, presented me with a beautiful glass decanter and glasses set. It was a huge honour to win the award, but unfortunately, I ended up dropping the set later that evening while I was getting into a taxi. That was another situation that left Karen tutting at me!

In the summer of 1986, the club decided to relieve Chris of his duties, and they brought in Alan Mullary to replace him. I got on really well with Mullars, he had been a magnificent midfield player, one of the top ones in his day. He'd put his arm around me, and teach me midfield things that he specialised in, and I certainly improved as a player under him.

Sadly, the team began to break up, and players were leaving left, right and centre. The lads we'd had were getting older and the manager was looking for younger players. The problem was that it was harder to attract the better players because we didn't look like we were going to win promotion any time soon. We'd been so close, but not quite close enough, and the top players usually want to go to the top clubs.

Results over the course of the 1986/87 season were not good enough and we finished bottom of the league which resulted in relegation to the Third Division. It was a huge disappointment for the club. The town of Brighton was also struggling off the pitch.

Anyone who lived in the South East in 1987 will remember the horrendous storms. The whole of Brighton and Hove, where we lived, was virtually devastated. Everywhere you looked, you could see fallen trees, streets blocked, fences down – it was awful.

A week before the storm, my dad had come down to help me erect a fence between our house and our next-door neighbours'. We'd screwed in these huge fence panels, and they were absolutely solid. . . until the gales began.

One night, Karen and I were woken in the early hours of the morning by a loud crashing noise. We looked out the window and saw that our new fence panels were being thrown everywhere, so we went outside – we probably shouldn't have, but we did – and I was holding the fence panels to try and stop them from going into next door's conservatory. The neighbours were standing there, behind their window, watching us, and even gave us a little wave at one stage. *Come and give us a hand,* I thought.

We were fortunate enough to have a swimming pool in our garden, so in the end, when we realised that we couldn't stop the panels from blowing about and it was too windy to fix them, we chucked them into the pool and went back to bed!

As soon as relegation had been confirmed, Alan Mullary told me that I could be leaving because the club desperately needed money. He asked me if I would sign a new contract to help Brighton command a bigger transfer for me which I was happy to do.

In the meantime, Ron Saunders, who was the manager of West Brom at the time, phoned to ask if I fancied going up to the Midlands to play. As my contract didn't have long left to run, he was hoping to get me on the cheap. I explained that I'd been asked to sign another contract, and I'd need to have a think about it.

"Well we want you to come here, but if you want to sign a new contract with Brighton you do that," he said.

So two days later, I signed my contract. That evening I had another call from Ron. "Why did you sign the contract?" he asked.

"Because you told me to," I replied.

"Oh. I didn't think you'd actually do it!" he said. I think he thought I was using it as a lever to get more money out of him, and he thought he was calling my bluff!

I never asked for a transfer at Brighton, nor did I at any of the clubs that I played for. That's something that I'm incredibly proud of. I didn't have an agent, so there was no one touting me around either. If someone wanted to sign me, they'd have to ask the club, and I had to hope that the manager or chairman would then come to me to see if I fancied the move. I'm not sure that I did find out about every offer, but that was the prerogative of the club. Loyalty was, and still is, a big thing for me. Most of my transfers came about because the teams I was playing for had no money and they needed to sell me to feed the coffers.

It was hard to leave Brighton, and I have so many great memories of my time there. When I joined them, I had honestly believed that we would get back into the First Division, but it didn't work out that way, it was very disappointing.

Not long after the season ended, I was up a ladder doing some painting at home, when Alan Mullary called and told me that Luton Town and Oxford United, both First Division clubs at the time, had made offers for me. The club were happy to accept either offer, and the choice was mine.

So, after three and half enjoyable years living on the South Coast, I was going back to the top flight. The question was – which club should I choose?

CHAPTER 6
A very proud man

Playing international football was something I never really thought would happen. Earlier in my career, I'd received a couple of phone calls from the Northern Irish FA to see if I was eligible to represent them, but I wasn't. Although my mum was Irish, at that time, the rules were that you only qualified if your father had been born in Northern Ireland.

However, in late 1986, the rules were changed, and I believe I became the first player to represent Northern Ireland through my mother's side. It's a shame they didn't change the rules a year earlier as Northern Ireland had competed in the Mexico World Cup in 1986, and it would have been incredible for me to have been part of that squad.

I remember the moment I discovered I'd been called up. Alan Mullary pulled me to one side before the start of training to tell me and then announced it in front of the whole squad. The lads all gave me a little round of applause which was nice.

I felt so emotional, and I couldn't wait to tell my parents that I was going to represent my country. They were both so proud of me when they found out. Mum called her family back home in Northern Ireland to tell them – I think she told everyone she knew!

The only disappointing aspect for me was that my parents couldn't come and watch me play in the famous green shirt because of the troubles going on at the time. Mum's family were from Derry, a Catholic area, and they wouldn't venture into Belfast because it wasn't safe. Windsor Park – where we played our home games – is located in the Protestant area, so it was quite a dangerous place for Catholic people to go.

I'm sure us players were shielded from the worst of things, and

I didn't really appreciate how difficult it was for the people who lived there. I'd been over to Northern Ireland to see family many times before, and it was always a very eye-opening experience. When you can see bullet marks on the walls, spent ammunition lying on the pavement, and the devastation caused by the bombs, it's very humbling. I remember being a child and finding a four-inch brass bullet on the floor that I put into my pocket and brought home with me. Those memories are still imprinted on my mind.

Billy Bingham, who has now sadly passed away, was the national team manager, and he was bringing through a new group of players as a lot of the senior members of the squad had retired after the World Cup. Players like Pat Jennings, Jimmy Nicholl, and Sammy McIlroy would be hard to replace, but we still had some very good players, including Mal Donaghy and Norman Whiteside. Let's be honest, we were never going to win the World Cup, but we had a terrific team, even though we were going through a transitional period.

I felt part of the team straight away, with absolutely no problems at all. My Brighton teammate Steve Penney had also been called up, so I travelled over with him which was nice. When you know players in the squad it helps to break the ice. Everyone was very welcoming.

Billy was a fantastic manager. How he took such a small country like Northern Ireland to two World Cups is nothing short of a miracle. It was dreamland for everyone. He did it through a combination of skill, obviously, but mainly togetherness and team spirit. That was why he was so successful. I could sense the strong camaraderie as soon as I joined up with the lads, and I loved every minute of my time with Northern Ireland. We needed that light-heartedness and banter with everything that was going on with the troubles.

Norman Whiteside was probably at the peak of his powers in 1986. He was a phenomenal talent. Sadly, injuries ended his career prematurely which was a real shame as he was such a class act. Norman was brilliant off the pitch too. He'd come to every game. Even when he wasn't fit, he'd still travel over to cheer us on. He was a great teammate, but unfortunately, I didn't play with him enough times to see how good he really was.

I made my debut on 12th November 1986 in a 0-0 draw away

at Turkey which was a very good result. My second match was another away fixture, and another draw. This time 1-1 against Israel in Tel Aviv.

My home debut was a huge match – a European Championship qualifier against England. They had a very strong side with Viv Anderson, Bryan Robson, Peter Shilton, and Chris Waddle, so we knew it would be a tough game.

The country was always on high alert, but even more so when England came to Belfast. I remember walking out onto the pitch before the game to have a look around. We were all there, the England lads too, when all of a sudden, some sort of explosion went off in a street behind one of the goals. Black smoke rose above the stand, and I heard the sirens from the fire engine as they raced to put the blaze out. It frightened the life out of me. The English players looked terrified too, but the Irish boys just carried on like nothing had happened because they were so used to it.

Inside the stadium, there were some very, very loyal supporters who wanted nothing more than to beat the English, and the atmosphere was quite hostile. The whole occasion was completely new to me, but I saw the people around me remain calm. The lads in the dressing room weren't worried about anything, they were just focused on the game, and that helped me a great deal.

We lost the match 2-0 which was disappointing, although we gave them a good game.

I kept the shirt I wore during my international debut, but after that, I swapped whenever I could. I've got a great collection of shirts from my international days. We didn't swap shirts after the England game, though. We couldn't have done it on the pitch anyway because the fans wouldn't have liked that, but there was even a reluctance to swap in the dressing room afterwards, so I kept my shirt from that match.

After the game, I met Jimmy Nicholl in the players' bar. He was one of the funniest men I've ever met. He always had a story to tell or a joke to play. We'd only just collected our drinks and sat down when the Chief of Police, with his flat cap and cane under his arm, came over and ordered everyone out of the ground because they'd received a phone call to say that some mortars were aimed at the stadium. *Bloody hell,* I thought.

Having delivered his message, the Chief left. I still had half a pint of lager left, so I stood and said, "I'll get rid of this and then get out."

"You'll be alright," Jimmy said, so I sat back down, and he continued his story.

Five minutes later, the policeman came back, yelling, "I'm warning you all, you need to get out right now. If you don't, you will all be under arrest. I want this place clearing now!"

I turned away and was just about to take a final sip of my pint when Jimmy crept up behind me and shouted, "Bang!" It scared the life out of me, and the lager went all over my clothes. Jimmy was pissing himself laughing!

After that, we all left the ground and returned to the hotel. I wasn't used to those kinds of situations, so it was very scary. But Jimmy and the boys had experienced moments like that many times before and had become used to it. Whether it was a crank call or not, I don't know, but thankfully nothing happened.

My next cap came against Yugoslavia in October 1987. At club level, trips abroad were to places like Marbella and Cala Major, but with Northern Ireland, we were travelling to war zones! I remember Sarajevo very well. We trained at the bottom of a ski jump slope, although there was no snow at that time of year, just grass. When I looked up and saw how high the top was it gave me a great appreciation for Olympic ski jumpers – there was no way you'd get me up there!

Yugoslavia beat us 3-0. They battered us if I'm honest, and the score line actually flattered us. That was my first understanding of just how difficult international football was. We got turned over big style by a very skilful team.

At club level, I was used to playing for open and attacking teams, but with Northern Ireland, we were much more disciplined. There were certain parts of the pitch where I wasn't allowed to go, and it was important that we kept our shape, with and without the ball. Billy was very clear about that. We had to be hard to break down and we set up to avoid defeat, rather than to win. We were always in games and very rarely got turned over. We knew that if there was only a goal in it, we still had a chance. If we went in gung-ho, we'd get punished. Billy made us so well organised by ensuring we were all clear on our roles. When I played for Ireland, I was a holding midfielder, with instructions to keep things tight, win the ball back when we were out of possession, and keep hold of it when we had the ball. Going forward wasn't part of my remit. I didn't mind, though, I was just happy to represent my country, I'd have played at right back if it meant I could pull on that famous green jersey. It was always about the team for me. If Billy asked me to run and run until I collapsed, I'd have done it. Playing for Northern Ireland was like that – we did whatever we had to for the good of the team.

International football suits the bigger nations who have huge squads to call upon. We didn't have that, and sometimes we were playing two or three games in a week which wasn't ideal for us. We only had one sub in those days too.

You hear of club versus country rows nowadays, often when a player is carrying a knock and his team don't want him to join up with his national squad. That never happened to me, but that's probably because my clubs couldn't wait for me to go! Seriously, every manager I played under was always very good and never prevented me from playing for my country. We didn't have international breaks back then, but clubs who had three or more players called up were allowed to request a postponement, so there were a lot of matches postponed as you can imagine.

In March 1988, in a game against Poland at Windsor Park, I scored my first, and only, goal for Northern Ireland. Although I played in centre midfield, as I've mentioned, I was employed in a more defensive role for my country, so I didn't get forward too often, unlike at club level where the attacking side was a big part of my game.

With just two minutes on the clock, I found myself standing outside Poland's penalty area. The ball fell to me, so I hit it first time and the ball flew into the top corner. It was an absolute screamer. If you're going to score for your country, you might as well make it a cracker. I'm sure I've added an extra ten yards to that goal in my memory, but I do know that I was outside the box when I hit it. I don't think I stopped smiling for a week after that match, it was another very proud moment.

We drew the game 1-1, and that was the start of a four-match unbeaten run.

In April 1984, France came to Windsor Park, and we held them to a 0-0 draw which was a fantastic result. When you play

France, you know you're going to be coming up against quality players, but we held our own. That was credit to Billy Bingham and his tactics. It wasn't a win, I know that, but it felt like a victory because France were a top team.

Kingsley Black made his debut in that match. He was a very classy player and I helped him settle in by introducing him to the lads off the pitch. But he didn't need any introductions on it – he came in aged nineteen years old and looked like he'd been playing international football all his life. He was fantastic.

A month later, we beat Malta 3-0, and followed that up with a 0-0 draw with the Republic of Ireland. They were managed by Jack Charlton and were a very physical team. The atmosphere at Windsor Park was incredible, and there was so much security around the ground, even at our hotel. Even if we went for a pint, the Special Forces guys would come and sit down with us while we had a drink. I always felt very safe in that respect.

We knew there was a lot of animosity between the two nations, and we were determined to win the match, but unfortunately, we didn't get the victory because it was such a tight game. They had a very strong team with Paul McGrath, Chris Hughton, and Ronnie Whelan, and a draw was still a good result.

We had a lot of leaders in our squad, three of whom went on to manage Northern Ireland – Lawrie Sanchez, Nigel Worthington, and Michael O'Neill. At that time we were all concentrating on our playing careers, so I never looked upon anyone as a future manager. But what you get from playing for your country is an understanding of the differences between club and international football. It must be so hard to only have players together once every few months and expect them to gel. You can't sign replacements if your key players get injured, you have to make do with what you've got. I imagine that is very difficult. That's why I was so impressed when Michael took Northern Ireland to the Euros in 2012. What a job he did.

Although we always knew it would be tough, we went into every game believing we could win. You have to have that attitude. If you don't think you can win, you shouldn't be on the pitch. That mentality led to us enjoying some fantastic results.

In May 1990, we beat Uruguay 1-0 at Windsor Park. I remember that game very well as one of their players spat at me after a fair but meaty challenge. Fortunately, it landed on my shirt rather than on my face. I turned to Keith Cooper, the referee, and asked if he saw it.

"No, I didn't, Dan," he replied, although he could see the spit on my shirt.

We had a throw-in a little later in the game, and as we went up the touchline, I punched the player straight in the face. The South Americans went bananas, but the referee turned a blind eye.

Later that year we drew against Denmark who were the reigning European Champions. That result showed that we were getting better. I wouldn't say we were a great team, but we were improving in the way we played, and little results like that stood out.

The biggest win during my time with the national side was a 5-0 victory over the Faroe Islands. It's safe to say that we were a better team than them! It was a huge confidence boost, even though it was against the Faroe Islands not Brazil. To keep losing by the odd goal, or snatching a draw, can get a bit demoralising, and you need a couple of good score lines to keep morale up. It doesn't matter who it's against, you just need a win every now and then.

I made my final appearance for Northern Ireland on 19th February 1992 in a match against Scotland at Hampden Park. That was a good game between two very committed sides. Joe Worrall, an English man, was the referee, and it was more like a typical British game than an international. We got beat 1-0, although I felt we were very unlucky not to have gotten anything out of the match.

I was thirty-two years of age at the time of that game, and I wanted to prolong my club career. I didn't enjoy getting on aeroplanes all the time and being away from home for long periods of time. I'm not saying that I wasn't committed to my country because I was, but you get to a certain age, and you have to start making things a bit easier for yourself. Billy and I discussed it and came to a mutual agreement that the Scotland game would be my last. I hadn't been fantastic, and there were some younger players, like Jim Magilton, coming through in my position, so it was the right decision for everyone.

I'm proud of every single game in which I represented

Northern Ireland. At twenty-seven you don't usually get an international debut, so it was all a huge bonus for me. I'm incredibly grateful to Billy Bingham for giving me an opportunity that I never thought I'd have.

If you look at my statistics, you'll see that I have twenty-four caps, but that's not quite true. I understand that the English boys receive a cap for every game they play, but we got one each season instead, so I only actually have six caps.

They are all very high quality, with gold embroidery on green velvet. There was a lovely ritual at the end of the season where we were presented with our caps in a little ceremony at the hotel. I couldn't wait to be presented with my first cap, and I treasure every single one.

CHAPTER 7
The underdogs

It wasn't an easy decision for me to make. Oxford had some fantastic players, including Ray Houghton, John Dreyer, and my former Brighton teammate Dean Saunders, who had been transferred earlier in the year.

However, Luton had just finished seventh in the First Division – their highest ever league finish – and with their squad, I felt that I had a better chance of winning something with Luton, so on 1st July 1987, I joined the Hatters for £150,000.

I knew this was an important decision, but I feel I got it right.

Luton were an ambitious club, who weren't in the division just to make up the numbers, they were there to win something. At twenty-seven years old, I didn't feel I had reached my peak, and I found that the older I got, the better I became. Not just physically but mentally too, because I was able to read the game better.

As I've already said, I didn't ever find the step up from one division to another particularly difficult but I certainly had to adapt my game when I joined Luton because we played our home games on an artificial playing surface.

There were a handful of clubs in the eighties who had dug up their grass and replaced the turf with a plastic pitch. Luton were one of those teams. A lot of finesse was required to play on a plastic pitch, and our football took on a different dimension. We adopted a passing style of play to accommodate the pitch. I quickly learnt that I had to be very precise with my passing because if I played the ball into space, it would just roll out of play, so we were told to always play the ball to feet. Teams like Manchester United and Liverpool did well at our place because they played good football, but other sides found it more difficult.

I GET KNOCKED DOWN

The pitch at Kenilworth Road was very close to the supporters and although we didn't get huge crowds – our average attendance was just eight thousand – those fans who did come were very vocal and noisy. Away supporters were banned from our ground for league games during my first season because of a riot that had happened during a match against Millwall in 1985. The atmosphere was unique because you could only hear the home supporters – who were always magnificent, by the way. It's safe to say that none of our opponents liked coming to Kenilworth Road. I suppose our ground gave us a bit of advantage and it's no coincidence that the majority of our victories came at home.

We had to adapt our style away from home where we were able to play balls behind the defence. We certainly had the pace to do so, and we had one of the best centre forwards in the game in Mick Harford. He was a fantastic striker and a great leader. He could link play, get on the end of high balls, had a fantastic touch and the clichéd 'great feet for a big man'.

In midfield we had Ricky Hill, a fairly quiet lad, but what a talent. Playing alongside him was brilliant. He had two great feet, his vision was second to none, and without being disrespectful to Luton, I was surprised he didn't go on to play for a bigger club.

Another midfielder was Darron McDonough, who later became Kevin Keegan's first signing for Newcastle. We called him 'Rocker Biff' because he was a tough boy, almost like a bulldog at times.

Before the season started, we went over to Marbella, and I was rooming with Darron. We'd had a few days of training before we were allowed to go out on the lash on the last night. After enjoying a few pints in the Spanish bars and clubs, we finally got back to the hotel at two in the morning. We had an early flight and hadn't packed our bags before we went out, so we just chucked everything in our suitcases, and off we went to the airport. As I was leaving the room, I noticed Darron had left his passport, so I picked it up and put it in my back pocket. When we got to Customs, he was panicking because he couldn't find it!

Anyway, a day or two later, Karen was doing the washing. I was lying on the sofa watching a bit of television, when she leaned over the seat, dangling a black G-string in my face.

"Whose is this then?" she asked.

"I couldn't tell you, love. I have no idea," I replied, wondering where the hell it had come from.

Things were a bit frosty for a while, as I'm sure you can imagine. About a month later, Karen and I went out for a meal with Darron and his wife, Alison. We were talking as a foursome and Alison was telling Karen how sloppy and careless Darron is. "I brought him a new G-string to take to Marbella, but he's lost it. We can't find it anywhere," Alison said.

"It wasn't a black one, was it?" asked Karen. We all had a good laugh. He was such a tough old brute that I couldn't imagine him wearing a G-string!

Les Sealey, God bless him, was our goalkeeper and a brilliant character. He was like Arthur Daley in the dressing room, with his cockney rhyming slang. "Awight, san," was how he'd greet you. He loved wearing his snide watches. He'd tell us they were the real thing, but he always took them off before he went in the shower, so we suspected they were fake.

Les was absolutely fantastic, a hilarious bloke. To go to Manchester United and win the FA Cup late in his career was a dream come true for him. As a teammate you want it to happen for him because he deserved it, but at the same time, you also didn't because he'd never shut up about it!

Steve Foster had moved to Luton the season before I did, and it was great to join up with him again.

Another player who I remember fondly is Emeka Nwajiobi, a Nigerian boy who was a qualified pharmacist. A very intellectual lad. He was a strong striker who came off the bench quite a lot and was capable of changing games. One of the funniest things about him was his belly button. He had the best belly button I've ever seen – it was like a pocket of air. Every time someone walked past him, they pushed his belly button in, and the rest of us would watch on, waiting for it to pop out again. We had hours of fun doing that. Emeka laughed along with us.

Despite the fact that the bulk of our team were international footballers, I don't think the lads got the credit they deserved because we weren't classed as a big club. But we quite liked being the underdogs and it helped to foster a good team spirit. The dressing room was a fun, happy place to be.

There are so many memorable games during my first season

at Luton, but one that stands out to me was a visit to Upton Park on 2nd January 1988. Paul Ince was just breaking into West Ham's team, and he came on as a substitute in the first half. Billy Bonds, the Hammers captain, was very highly regarded and respected by everyone in football. Incey had a bit of arrogance about his game, even in those early years, and as we walked down the tunnel at half-time, Billy absolutely caned him from pillar to post, giving him one of the biggest bollockings I've ever seen. It upset Paul so much that I could see tears in his eyes.

But what I remember most from that game, was Ince scoring fifteen minutes into the second half – the little sod. He must have been so inspired by the bollocking he'd received. That's when I knew that he was going to become a great player. At the full-time whistle, Billy came over and put his arm around Paul and I thought, *What a mentor Billy Bonds is.*

With Luton's budget, It was tough for us to compete with the Liverpools, Arsenals and Manchester Uniteds on a regular basis, but we kept pulling a little rabbit out of the bag that kept us in there with the big boys. We were sat in the top half of the First Division for the majority of the season which is an incredible achievement. However, I had joined the club to challenge for trophies which is why our cup runs were so exciting.

Our League Cup campaign kicked off with a 5-2 aggregate victory over Wigan Athletic, and we then went on to beat Coventry City, Ipswich Town, and Bradford City, to set up a two-legged semi-final against Oxford United.

The other semi-final was Arsenal against Everton, the League champions, so I think both Luton and Oxford were both relieved to have avoided the bigger clubs. There was a bit of added spice for me because I wanted to prove that I'd made the right decision in joining Luton, and I suppose Oxford wanted to stick it to me.

Our two league games against Oxford had been very high-scoring affairs – we won 5-2 away and 7-4 at home – so I think most people were expecting a very open semi-final. Instead, they were two very close matches, very physical too.

The first leg, played on 10th February 1988, was very tough. They were arguably the better team on the day and possibly should have won it. We took the lead in the first half through Brian Stein, before Dean Saunders equalised from the penalty spot just after half-time. Fortunately for us, Oxford missed some good chances in the second half, and the game finished 1-1.

We were full of confidence ahead of the return leg at Kenilworth Road. The final was in touching distance, and we knew we could beat anyone at our place. Brian Stein opened the scoring after half an hour, and Ashley Grimes doubled our lead ten minutes later. The game finished 2-0.

Luton Town were going to Wembley for a major cup final for the first time in their history. Arsenal, who had seen off Everton in the other semi-final, would be our opponents.

A week after the victory over Oxford United, we beat Swindon Town in the semi-final of the Full Members' Cup to set up another final, this time against Second Division Reading.

We were the overwhelming favourites as we travelled down to Wembley for the Full Members' Cup final on the 27th of March 1988. It was my first ever game at the historic stadium. Walking out of the tunnel in front of sixty thousand cheering supporters was absolutely brilliant. Reading weren't expected to cause us any problems and because of that, we didn't do our homework in terms of preparation. Not the manager, but the players. We thought it was going to be one-way traffic, especially after Mick Harford gave us an early lead, and we became a little complacent.

We were a shambles. Reading came back to beat us 4-1, and we fully deserved the rout they gave us, with Michael Gilkes and my former Brighton teammate Neil Smillie tearing us to bits. As I walked off the pitch I thought, *I haven't even had a kick*. It was a big cup upset. We were awful, but I don't want to take anything away from Reading who were brilliant on the day. People can turn around and say that it was a Mickey Mouse cup, but it wasn't. A lot of big teams entered the competition, and when you're in it, you want to win it. Ray Harford read us the riot act and told us that he expected an instant reaction. The only positive from our point of view was that we now knew how it felt to lose at Wembley in a cup final. We were all determined not to experience the same feelings and emotions after the League Cup final.

We were also performing well in the FA Cup, defeating Hartlepool, Southampton, QPR, and Portsmouth on our way to the semi-final where we faced Wimbledon at White Hart Lane on 9th April 1988.

The Dons, with Vinnie Jones, John Fashanu, and Dennis Wise, were a very physical team with tactics designed to intimidate their opponents, but that was no problem to us at all. We had players who could do that too. We had lads like Brian Stein, little David Preece, and Ricky Hill, who all possessed enormous amounts of skill. Mal Donaghy was like a Rolls Royce at the back. But we could also dig in when needed. You couldn't intimidate Mick Harford or Steve Foster, that's for sure, and we didn't fear anyone. If teams wanted to play football, we'd play football. If they wanted to have a battle – bring it on.

We played well and took the lead just after half-time when Harford finished off a flick-on from Stein. We should have seen the game out, but two moments of madness cost us. First Andy Dibble, our goalkeeper, gave away a penalty that was converted by Fashanu. With ten minutes to go, we switched off, which allowed Wise to slide the ball in from three yards, and the game finished 2-1 to the Dons. It was disappointing to lose that game as we had played so well, and I felt we had done enough to win. I was devastated to miss out on an FA Cup final, even more so when I watched the final a few weeks later and saw the Crazy Gang lift the trophy after a shock 1-0 win over Liverpool.

We'd had a great chance of winning three trophies, but now after two disappointing defeats, the League Cup was our only chance of silverware. It all added fuel to the fire and made us even more determined to beat Arsenal.

Our preparation for the League Cup final was much more professional than the way we had approached the Reading game. We travelled down to Wembley the day before the game and did a bit of light training in the morning, before some team bonding and relaxation in the afternoon and evening.

We had a few injuries leading up to the game. Les Sealey, our first-choice goalkeeper, was definitely going to be out, while Mark Stein, our striker, was only fit enough to make the bench, so Ray Harford waited until the morning of the match before naming the team. I was delighted to be handed the number seven shirt and couldn't wait for kick-off.

The bookies and the public had made Arsenal the big favourites, but not in our mind. We'd had close games against the top teams all season, and on the big stage, you're always going to get a bit more resistance from the underdogs. Although we never classed ourselves as the underdogs. It wasn't a case of thinking that we *could* win the game, we *expected* to win. We went into that match full of confidence. I didn't ever think that they were too good for us, I never thought that about any team.

There were ninety-five thousand fans packed inside the Twin Towers, and every hair on my body was standing on end as we lined up for the National Anthem. I reminded myself how low I had felt the last time I played at Wembley and was determined to be the one celebrating this time.

We were up for the game right from kick-off and took an early lead through Brian Stein, who finished neatly after a clever pass by Steve Foster.

The goal woke Arsenal up and they began to attack us as they searched for an equaliser. We defended well, kept our shape, and Andy Dibble made some fantastic saves to keep the Gunners at bay.

However, in the seventy-first minute, Martin Hayes equalised following a goalmouth scramble, and then just three minutes later, they took the lead through Alan Smith. We didn't give up though. While there was only one goal in it, we still felt we could get back into the game.

With just ten minutes of the game remaining, David Rocastle was brought down in the penalty area, and the referee gave Arsenal a spot-kick. At 2-1 down, we still had a chance, but 3-1 would probably have been game over. Nigel Winterburn – a very good penalty taker – stepped up and hit the spot-kick hard and low to the goalkeeper's left. He couldn't have hit it much better, but Andy Dibble produced an unbelievable save. If that had gone in, it would have been the winning goal, but Dibble's save gave us a big lift, and we pressed forward looking for an equaliser.

Not long after the penalty, Arsenal's centre back Gus Caesar, under pressure from Mark Stein, got the ball tangled up between his legs and stumbled inside the Gunners' penalty area. Kingsley Black took the ball off him and laid it off nicely for Brian Stein. Brian's shot was saved by the keeper, but the ball rebounded back to him, and Stein sent the ball across the face of the goal. Fortunately, I had made a run into the area, and I managed to head it home from about three yards. It wasn't a conscious decision to head it, I was just trying to make enough contact to knock the ball past the goal line.

The feeling I experienced when the ball hit the back of the net was incredible, absolutely incredible. I just exploded, sprinting away, and pumping my fists in joy. I don't know where all that energy came from. It was the quickest that I've ever ran in my life! I think most boys dream of scoring at Wembley in a cup final, and I was no different, so to achieve that dream was just amazing. What a brilliant feeling.

Arsenal were rocked, and we sensed an opportunity to finish them off. With less than a minute left on the clock, Ashley Grimes broke down the right wing. He was a left back, so what he was doing on the right, I do not know, but he played a cross with the outside of his left foot that people would still be purring about today if he'd been a Brazilian. Brian Stein put the ball into the back of the net to make it 3-2 to Luton. It was such a dramatic finish, and the Arsenal boys didn't have time to get back in the game. The match was all done and dusted, and by the time we finished celebrating, the referee's whistle signalled the end of the game.

People look back at that cup final and focus on the three goals that we scored, but Andy Dibble's penalty save was just as crucial, no doubt about it.

It was the first time in our history that Luton Town had won the League Cup, so it was a historic moment. It was also my first major trophy. What a fantastic feeling. The belief and pride that cup win gave us was huge, and all we wanted to do was start the next season so we could have another go at replicating our success. The players' wives and girlfriends had travelled down to London for the game, and we had an unbelievable party that evening, as I'm sure you can imagine.

We still had a few league games left, and the euphoria from Wembley helped us to finish the season strongly. We only lost once from our final seven games, including a 1-1 draw against Liverpool at Anfield.

The final match of the season was at the City Ground, against my former club Nottingham Forest. It was the first time I'd been back since I had left five years earlier, and I was Luton's captain for the game.

Before each game, the managers and captains from both teams went into the referee's dressing room to hand in the team sheet and receive some instructions from the ref. Things like how to approach him if you disagreed with his decision. It was an important meeting because every game, and every referee, was different.

Luton's physio was Dave Galley, who along with his wife Sue, are great friends of ours. They are Godparents to Carrie. Karen and I are Godparents to their daughter Samantha.

Anyway, on this particular day, Dave came with me to the referee's room in place of Ray Harford. Mr Clough was always in there before anyone else to make sure he could put a bit of pressure on. So, Dave and I walked in and shook hands with Mr Clough, Stuart Pearce, who was Forest's captain, and the ref.

"You've got the best left back in the country here," said Mr Clough, pointing at Pearce. "You've got the best manager in the country here," he said pointing at himself. "And you've got the best midfielder in the country here," Mr Clough said, pointing at me. I couldn't believe it. That comment made me feel on top of the world.

"I don't know who you are," he said to Dave, before turning to the ref and saying, "And I'm not sure how good you are so you better have a good game today."

As we walked back to our respective dressing rooms, Mr Clough turned to me and said "Hey young man. I was only joking about you being the best midfielder in the country!" He brought me right back down to earth! That was Clough all over, you just never knew what he was going to say next.

We finished ninth in the First Division in the 1987/88 season, so it was a good season. As a treat, we flew over to Fort Lauderdale for an end-of-season break, determined to let our hair down.

There were some international games taking place during the summer, and within a day of arriving in America, Andy Dibble, our Wembley hero, received a call up to the Welsh national team. When your country comes knocking you answer, so he asked the club to arrange to fly him home. While he was waiting, he decided to make the most of the scorching weather and work on his tan. He stayed in the sun virtually all day, and by the time he left for the airport, he was burnt to a cinder and could barely move. He was as red as a lobster, and the lads were pissing themselves. We were wondering what was going to happen if he was selected for Wales as I don't think he'd have been able to move his arms without being in agony. Fortunately for him, Neville Southall got the nod instead, and Andy got to rest his blistered skin on the subs' bench.

Andy was a great lad and went on to have a fantastic career, not just as a player but also as a goalkeeping coach. It's not easy being a keeper, they are the butt of all jokes and get blamed for every goal, so they have to be tough as old boots. Those boys need to have rhino skin because everyone always vents on them.

Every goalkeeper I've ever met has been mad. I suppose they have to be. They can have a great game but make one mistake and they are cast as the villain, whereas a striker can have a terrible game, miss ten easy chances, but pop up in the last minute with the winning goal, and they are the hero.

Goalies have their own little union, and they always stick together. They'd do their own warm-ups before breaking off with the goalkeeping coach for some specialised training. They'd sometimes join the rest of the group after an hour or so for some small-sided or eleven versus eleven games. They are like a family, and I've never seen any animosity between the number one keeper and the reserve one. They chivvy themselves up and are always full of support for one another.

The close season was always a chance for me to spend some quality time with my family. One evening, Karen and I had arranged to meet another couple for dinner at a Chinese restaurant called the China Garden in the town centre, not far from Kenilworth Road. We drove into Luton, and when we arrived at the restaurant, there was nowhere to park, so we decided to keep driving around the one-way system until we were lucky enough to find a spot.

We'd driven around three times, often slowing down to keep our eye out for a space, when I saw blue flashing lights in my rear-view mirror. Unbeknown to me, the police had been following us.

"What are you doing, sir?" the officer asked when he walked to our car.

"Trying to find somewhere to park, officer," I replied.

"Are you sure? You do know where you are don't you?" he asked me.

"Yes. We're meeting some friends at that restaurant there," I said, pointing to the China Garden.

It turned out that we were in the red-light district, and the street we'd been driving on was notorious for kerb-crawling. That's what the policeman thought we were doing! Karen loved me for that as I'm sure you can imagine! The next time we went to the restaurant, we parked about a mile away!

By the time the pre-season came around, we were raring to go, buoyed on by our success from the previous year. Ray Harford was looking at us and must have been thinking, *Blimey, I don't need to do anything to motivate these boys.*

Unfortunately, we lost Brian Stein to Cannes, who played in the French First Division. He did really well there which wasn't a surprise because he was a terrific player. His departure was a big blow, and we also sold his brother, Mark, to QPR. Ray signed a couple of new strikers to replace them – Iain Dowie and Roy Wegerle.

Iain was an old-fashioned centre forward who joined us from non-league Hendon. He is a very funny man, with a dry sense of humour. Iain is very intellectual too. He must take after his dad, who worked in a very senior position at Concorde. If he didn't give the go-ahead, the Concorde couldn't take off. Iain followed the same path as his father, gaining an MEng Degree in Engineering and took a job with British Aerospace whilst playing non-league football. And then he joined us. He was obviously a clever boy, and you can imagine what he was like coming into a dressing room full of footballers! He'd come out with all these big words, talking down to us, and he loved it! He was a great character and is still a very good friend of mine.

He married Deborah, a gorgeous air stewardess, and we used to tell him that he was punching well above his weight. Iain's mum and dad, Ann and Bob, were so proud of him and used to come and watch every game he played, internationally and domestically.

Roy was a South African-born USA international who we signed from Chelsea. He was a skilful player who knew where the goal was and was a good addition to the squad.

Although we had won the League Cup, we didn't qualify for Europe because English clubs were banned from all European competitions at the time. Whilst it was disappointing not to have the opportunity to play in Europe, it was fully understandable. The Heysel disaster was horrendous, and UEFA came down hard on all English teams. The ban hurt us more than it did the bigger teams like Arsenal or Manchester United, because their chance would come again, whereas it was unlikely Luton would have another opportunity.

The UEFA Cup was a knockout tournament back then which was our speciality, and with our plastic pitch, it would have been interesting to see how we'd have fared against the best Europe had to offer. We always did well against the big boys of the First Division, and I'd have loved to test ourselves against the likes of Roma, Ajax, Sporting, Bayern Munich, and Stuttgart, who all qualified for the UEFA Cup that season. The different style of football would have presented an interesting challenge, but it wasn't to be.

We enjoyed some great results at the start of the 1988/89 season, doing the double over Everton and beating Liverpool, which was always special for me because I had supported them as a boy. The problem was that our League Cup success had raised the supporters' expectations. That was a bit dangerous as we didn't have the squad to compete for honours on a regular basis. Yes, we could beat anyone on our day, but we needed everyone to be at the top of their game and couldn't afford to carry two or three players who weren't performing. That was the difference between us and the very top teams, who have squads full of quality players.

We were never a group who strolled around the pitch, we always played at the same high tempo whether we were playing Bolton or Manchester United, and we never changed our style of play. Even if we were the odds-on favourites, we still knew that we had to be on the top of our game. If we tried to slow it down and be better players than we actually were, our system didn't work. So we played to our strengths as a team and that gave us an edge, certainly in the cup competitions. There was no secret to our success, it was sheer hard work. If our work rate dropped by ten, or even five per cent, we wouldn't win, and we knew that.

Although our style of play was based around aggression and a constant press that required high levels of fitness, believe it or not, we did more work on the technical aspects of the game during training. Ray Harford was a technically astute coach and I think he preferred coaching to management. He didn't enjoy dealing with the issues that managers have, like unsettled or disgruntled players knocking on his door. He was never one for confrontation.

I loved Ray; he was a gentleman in more ways than one. He was a very calm man who didn't flap around and that helped us on the pitch. If you look over and see that your manager is panicking, you begin to panic yourself. He was a real calming influence on us all, but he wasn't afraid to raise his voice a little if he needed to. Never to the extent that he'd be shouting at us or going bananas, though, and definitely no hairdryer treatment! He didn't need to yell at us because we had such a strong dressing room and we sorted things out ourselves. If someone wasn't doing what they were expected to do, we'd dig them out, no problem. We didn't need the manager to tell them which helped Ray massively. He had one or two run-ins with players who didn't understand or like the way he wanted to play, but Ray's attitude was, "This is how I want to play. If you don't agree, you won't get picked."

Ray was definitely more of a technician than anything else, but he made sure we all knew our roles and we knew we had to press when we were out of possession. If I sat off the ball and gave the opposition too much space, I wouldn't be in the team the following week. When we pressed, we pressed as a team. The strikers needed to press the full back and we would get up the pitch as a team to help him out.

We had so much creativity in the side, so when we won the ball back, we knew we'd have a chance to score. We regularly played it out from the back, but in Mick Harford, we had a centre forward who could get on the ball if the goalkeeper launched it long. Mick could hold it up and bring the ball players into the game, people like Ricky Hill, David Preece, and Roy Wegerle.

We got to the League Cup final again in 1989, following victories over Burnley, Leeds, Manchester City, Southampton, and a 5-0 aggregate victory over West Ham in the semi-final. We drew Nottingham Forest in the final (when Mr Clough tried to kiss me in the tunnel), but I didn't feel I had anything to prove to my former club and old manager. I'm not that type of person. We knew that they had some good players, as did we, and we went out there to try and play our best, but unfortunately, we fell short.

Mick Harford gave us the lead in the first half, but we made some costly mistakes in the second half that Forest jumped on. The good teams will capitalise on mistakes, just as we had twelve months earlier. It was a close game for most of the match, and I don't think you could say that either team really deserved the win. The difference was that we made mistakes, and they punished us for it. We lost the game 3-1.

It wasn't a conscious thing, but the cup run was a bit of a distraction and our league form suffered as a result. Going into the final four games of the season, we needed a miracle to get ourselves out of trouble and stay in the division. We should never have allowed ourselves to get into that position.

You can only put it down to the players. Our standards had slipped. Knowing that we had performed against the top teams, the fact that we were struggling meant that we had to look at ourselves in the mirror and question what we were doing. The last thing I did was point fingers at the manager and coaches. They weren't the ones out there putting in tackles or whipping in crosses. They set the team up to win and whether you agree with the line-up or not is irrespective.

Our results between the semi-final and the final were rubbish. We picked up just one point from six matches, and people started to believe that our run in the top flight was coming to an end. We could see relegation looming, and when you're caught up in that downward spiral it's very difficult to get out of. It had taken me so long to get to the top division and I desperately wanted to stay there.

It was hard work, and a little nervy at times. We were on the verge of going out of the league we felt we deserved to be in. We got a couple of good results, beating Derby (3-0) and Charlton (5-2), before losing to West Ham in the penultimate game of the season. That meant that we needed a win at home to high-flying Norwich City in order to stay up. The only positive aspect was that our destiny was in our own hands.

Just fifteen minutes into the game, Mick Harford won us a penalty to give us a fighting chance. I was on penalty duty that season, as I was for most of my career. I didn't miss many. There is a certain technique to taking a penalty, and everyone is different. I very rarely side-footed them, I usually picked my spot and put my laces through the ball so that if the keeper did guess the right way, hopefully the pace would be enough to get the ball past them. I never suffered with nerves because I practised so much that I could usually visualise where the ball was going to go.

So I placed the ball on the spot, as usual, took a few steps back and stuck the ball ... wide of the post!

Shit!

8080The fans were groaning, but I picked myself up and got on with the game. There was plenty of time left, I hoped.

In the second half, we were awarded another penalty when Roy Wegerle was fouled and I once again picked the ball up, ready to make amends for my earlier miss. I knew that if I missed again, we'd probably be relegated, but I never once thought about letting someone else take it. I wasn't one for walking away from my responsibilities. I was trusted to take penalties and because I'd already missed one, I was even more determined to score this time.

There was a lot of pressure riding on that spot-kick, but the nice thing was that as I looked around my teammates, I felt that I had their support. Having the backing of the lads filled me with confidence.

I'm not sure that the fans shared my confidence though, because as I placed the ball on the spot, I heard the Luton supporters moan, "Not fucking him again!" One particular fan behind the goal had his head in his hands, and I could see him thinking, *Anyone but him, please.* It was a good job I was never affected by the crowd! I took a step back and drilled the ball into the bottom corner, past the goalkeeper, and into the back of the net.

Kenilworth Road went bananas.

We won the game 1-0 to stay in the First Division for another season, although my overriding emotion was one of huge relief more than anything else.

I scored twelve goals in all competitions to finish the season as our joint top scorer along with Roy Wegerle, which was a great achievement. I had been given a little bit of free reign to go forward which I thoroughly enjoyed. I was quite a fit lad who could get around the park, and I had a bit of pace so I could burst forward from midfield if we got a counterattack going. I was always capable of getting into the right areas. Whether I could finish the chances or not was another matter. If the ball went in off my face or my arse, I didn't mind as it showed that I was getting into the right places. It didn't surprise me that I scored goals, although it did surprise me that I was the joint top scorer, especially considering some of the other strikers we had at the club like Mick Harford.

CHAPTER 8
The mad Hatters

We had some terrific times at Luton – on and off the pitch. The culprits who always reared their heads were Steve Foster and Mick Harford. Two of the funniest lads I know. They were always in the thick of things and are still big friends of mine.

At the end of the 1988/89 season, we went over to Marbella. I was rooming on my own, and after lunch, I was showing Mick and Fozzie the new clothes I'd bought for the trip. "What do you think to this, boys?" I asked, showing them a shirt I was particularly fond of.

"Oh, yeah. Nice that Danny," they replied. We were going out a bit later, so we said our goodbyes and returned to our rooms to get ready.

A couple of hours later, we were due to meet up in the hotel reception, but Mick had left a message to say that he and Fozzie would see us later, so, the rest of the lads and I walked into Puerto Banus to a bar called the Navy Club.

Halfway through my first drink, I spotted two people walking towards me in the distance. *That's Mick and Steve,* I thought, and as they got closer, I almost spat my drink out.

Mick was wearing my gear, but with his six-foot three-inch frame, none of it fit him. He had my trousers on, but they wouldn't fasten and were halfway up his calf. My long-sleeved shirt was unbuttoned at the front and looked like a short-sleeved one, and because my cowboy boots didn't fit him, he was treading on the sides of the leather as he walked down the road.

The lads were pissing themselves laughing, but I was going mad inside because he was wearing my best gear. The bouncers wouldn't let him into the Navy Club, so he had to go back and get changed. Mad as Hatters they were!

In the late eighties, Marbella was *the* place to be, and we often saw six or seven other teams out there. You didn't go to Marbella if you wanted a quiet holiday! There was always good camaraderie and banter with the other teams, and we all mixed together.

One night we bumped into the Rangers boys: Gary Stevens, Richard Gough, and Ally McCoist, in the Navy Club. I was stood at the bar with Ally and a few other lads when he asked the barmaid if they had any champagne. She opened a bottle of bubbly and put it on the bar along with a couple of champagne flutes. "Hold on, how much is that?" asked Ally. The barmaid told him the price, which worked out at around £80 a bottle, which was an extortionate price back then. Ally said, "You what?"

All of a sudden, two huge bouncers appeared behind him because they thought that he was going to do a runner. Ally looked at the bouncers before turning back to the barmaid and said, "You better make that two bottles then!" He was another really funny man.

After a long, gruelling season, it was good to go and let your hair down. We only went for five days but believe me when I say that was long enough. Especially considering the company I was keeping!

When we returned to England, just before pre-season training began, we were invited down to Stringfellows, a famous gentleman's club in London. The same culprits again, me, Fozzie, Mick, and a friend of ours called Sledge. He was the tik tac man who put bets on for Fozzie and he knew everyone at the race tracks.

We hired a little minibus to take us into central London and our evening began at the Punch and Judy pub in Covent Garden. Mick was swinging from the pipes at the top of the ceiling which didn't go down particularly well with the bouncers, but Mick just shrugged them off. He wasn't intimidated by anyone.

When we finished our drinks, we strolled over to Stringfellows and walked downstairs into the bar. Mick was behind us somewhere. Steve, Sedge, and I ordered our drinks, but before we'd finished them, I got a little tap on my shoulder from one of the doormen. "Put that down, you're going," he said.

"What are you talking about? We've only been here for ten minutes," I asked.

"You and your mates are out. Now!" he said, firmly.

I didn't have a clue what was going on, but I wasn't going to argue with him. I put my drink down on the bar and walked up the stairs, where I saw Mick being carried out by two bouncers. They used his head to open the fire doors and threw him out into the alleyway at the back. I looked at Steve and thought, *wow, I wonder what's going on here.*

It turned out that Mick had been throwing ice at the dancers, trying to get it into their cleavage as they were walking up the stairs, and that's why they kicked him out. I knew it must have been a good fight because Mick wasn't a soft boy. When we met up with him outside the club, he was smiling. "Fair play to them. They grabbed me from behind, and I just collapsed. I never saw them coming," he said, proudly.

I couldn't believe it. We were standing outside the club, having travelled all the way down to London just to go to Stringfellows. We hadn't even managed one drink, and Mick was happy because he'd been thrown out in the manner he had! That was another night curtailed early, but I just had to smile. Mick was never bothered about anything; he had such a carefree attitude. We as a team always looked out for each other. Not that there was ever any big trouble, just little incidents like this one that livened up the night.

You'd think that we'd change as we got older, but we didn't. A few years later, Mick, Fozzie, and Steve Purdew, a big friend of ours and owner of Champneys Health Resort and Spas, went over to Rome to watch England play Italy in the famous World Cup Qualifier when Paul Ince wore a bloodied headband. We stayed at a fantastic hotel in the Italian capital and had hospitality tickets for the game. Our seats were fantastic, right on the halfway line, with a great view of the pitch.

Before the game, a few fights were going on in the city. It was a time when, some of the Italian supporters were going past people on mopeds, holding a Stanley knife, and cutting people open as they rode past. It was quite nasty. During the game, the atmosphere wasn't very nice at all, and we could sense that something was going to happen, so we decided to leave at half-time and watch the rest of the game from the safety of our hotel bar. Sure enough, there was quite a bit of trouble – it was carnage in fact – and it proved that we had made the right decision.

Mick, unlike him, headed up to bed earlier than us. Eventually, Fozzie and I, who were rooming together, said goodnight to Steve and took the lift up to our room. Just as we were about to get into our beds, there was this almighty bang, crash, and wallop. Mick had come through the adjoining room, through the back of the wardrobe, and then through the wardrobe doors. Wood was splintered everywhere, and he stood their bollock naked and said, "Ta-da!" He'd been waiting for ages for us to go to bed. The antique wardrobe was completely demolished! I think Steve copped the bill for that. You couldn't relax with Mick about. He was mad!

By the time we started the 1989/90 season, our team was a very different one to the side who had won the League Cup just fifteen months earlier. Ricky Hill had gone to Leicester City, Mal Donaghy had joined Manchester United, and Mick Harford had signed for Derby County. Brian and Mark Stein had already left in 1988, of course, and then Steve Foster was sold to Oxford United.

Our one major incoming transfer was Lars Elstrup, a Danish boy, who became Luton's record signing. I don't think he expected the First Division to be as tough as it was, and it took a while for him to get going. But as time went on, he struck up a fantastic partnership with Iain Dowie, scored some great goals, and he became a fan favourite. Despite that, and for how good Lars was, he was not Brian Stein, who we hadn't really replaced. We had to change our style of play because Lars preferred the ball behind him to utilise his pace, whereas Brian wanted it played to his feet so that he could manipulate the ball a bit.

The heart of the team had left, and we didn't replace them with players of the same ilk. What we did do was bring in some younger players who had the potential to be as good in the future, but they didn't have the same immediate impact as the experienced guys. When our opponents looked at our team sheet and saw the names Hill, Stein, and Harford, they knew they'd be in for a tough game, and a physical one at that. Having so many youngsters in our line-up gave the opposition the upper hand because although the kids were good, they were still learning their trade. I'm not knocking the youngsters because you have to learn somewhere. They needed a platform which they wouldn't have got if the high-profile players had stayed, but I just feel we tried to change too much too soon.

Don't get me wrong, the kids we brought through the ranks went on to do very well, and they certainly benefitted from the opportunities they were given. Players, like Mark Pembridge and Ceri Hughes, both became Welsh Internationals, Paul Telfer, a midfielder, who went on to represent Scotland, and Kurt Nogan, a striker, who enjoyed a long career in the game, were given chances to shine.

We started the season well, suffering just one defeat in our first five games, but then we struggled with consistency which is bound to happen when you have a young side. With senior players, you generally have a better idea of what their performances will be like as the more experienced you get, the more reliable you become. The younger players needed to play to get that experience. It was frustrating for everyone, getting a great result and following it up with a string of defeats.

Even my little superstitions weren't helping us. If we won a game, I'd wear the same socks, same underpants, same shirt, and tie for our next match. But if we lost, I'd change everything. Sometimes, I'd lace my left boot before my right, other times I'd put my shorts on at the last minute before we walked out of the tunnel. I tried all sorts of silly little things that made absolutely no difference to my performance or the result, but that's what I and most other players did. You think that it'll have some impact on the game, but you forget that the other eleven lads in the dressing room opposite you are doing exactly the same things.

It still happens today. I see players doing the same little rituals that we did – not shaving until you've scored a goal, parking in the same place, etc. Although these things don't directly improve your performance, they can give you confidence which is a massive thing in football. It's all between your ears really, and your legs follow your brain. If you believe these superstitions make a difference, and it puts you in a better place mentally, then there is certainly no harm in trying it.

The mental side of the game is so important. In fact, it's everything. When I moved into management, I always looked at a player's mentality before deciding whether to pick him or not. Obviously, injuries and fitness come into it too, but even if you are in peak physical condition, if you're not in the right state of mind, you won't be able to function. I am a great advocate for psychology in football. When Glenn Hoddle had his problems with the media, and their scepticism, for bringing in Eileen Drewery to help the England players, I was already mindful of the mental side of the game and looking at people to come in and help me and my teams. I couldn't understand why Glenn was ridiculed. Maybe it was because Eileen was a woman but that shouldn't come into it at all. When someone has experience and expertise in a particular subject, they have to be respected, regardless of their gender.

Frank Barlow, my former manager, who later became my assistant, was very receptive to that side of the game. When we were at Sheffield Wednesday together, we brought in Brian Jones to help us. Brian's background was as an explorer in the Antarctic for the government, where he conducted all sorts of studies. He was a professor, although he didn't like to be called one, and later moved into psychology. What he did for me, and the lads, was fantastic, and I worked with him on and off for fifteen years.

The pressure in football is immense and totally unique; to block out the thirty thousand jeering or cheering supporters; to forget about the television cameras and the millions watching you around the world; to forget and block out your private life – marital problems, a child struggling in school, etc. – and to be one hundred per cent focused on the task in hand is very difficult.

As managers we are asked to do all these jobs that we're not qualified for, and we're doing them off the cuff. Managers aren't psychologists, doctors, home help, or marriage guidance counsellors, but you go with it. Players trust managers and at times they want to tell you what's going on in their lives. A lot of the time you don't really know what the answers are, so for me to have someone like Brian around was a massive help. There's not much difference between being a manager and a parent – it's just the age of the child! In fact, some babies are easier to control than some of the players I've managed!

Players will always want to play, even when they're not in the right frame of mind, and the manager has to make a decision for the good of the team.

In October 1989, my son, Laurie, got taken ill. He was only four years old, and we just couldn't get his fever down. We took him to the doctors, who referred us to the hospital. Poor Laurie had to have a lumbar puncture which was painful for him and scary for me and Karen. They admitted him to a room on the tenth floor and it was absolutely freezing. It felt like it was the middle of winter. We had all the windows open, a fan was turned on, and Laurie was lying there wearing his underwear, but we just couldn't cool him down. It was terrifying.

The doctors sent him off for tests and the poor little lad didn't know what was happening to him, but he was so strong, getting up out of bed and running around in a fit – I couldn't catch him! We were there for two nights (Thursday and Friday) before the doctors told us that he had a viral and bacterial chest infection, which was fantastic news as it meant that they could treat him. We all feared Laurie had meningitis at first.

Knowing that Laurie was on the mend, I arrived at Kenilworth Road on the Saturday for a First Division match, feeling knackered as I hadn't slept for two days and had been out of my mind with worry. Ray Harford asked me if I wanted to play and I told him that I did, so I was named in the starting line-up.

I was absolutely shit.

I ran around like Laurie had in the hospital, all over the place with no coordination. It didn't take long before Ray quite rightly took me off. I felt so disappointed in my performance, but it was understandable under the circumstances. As I was walking down the tunnel towards the dressing room, a couple of fans started having a pop at me because I'd been shit. People don't know what's going on in your private life, and as a footballer, you're supposed to turn a blind eye to the abuse you receive. The supporters want you to perform on the pitch every game, which is fair enough, but I think I was allowed an exception that time because of what I'd been through.

The abuse continued and because of the mood I was in, I lost my head a little bit and the stewards had to wrestle me down the tunnel before I could get to the fans. Thankfully, they did, because it was only ever going to lead to me getting punished for that.

I thought that I needed to play, but I was wrong. My preparation was non-existent, I'd hardly eaten or slept, and I wasn't focused like I'd normally be, but I wanted to play. I always wanted to play. Ray was brilliant. He virtually left the decision to me, but in hindsight, it was a selfish decision on my part because when I played like that, I let my teammates down. It taught me a big lesson, and when I became a manager, I always talked situations through with a player to see what frame of mind they were in. Sometimes I took the decision out of their hands.

The most important thing was that my little lad was going to be OK. We honestly thought we'd lost him at one stage. But four days later he was back to his normal self and to look at him, you'd never have known he'd been poorly.

I have to say though, that one incident aside, the Luton fans were always incredibly supportive of me and the team. They'd lost quite a few of their favourites, their heroes, but they could see the youngsters coming through and were excited. They realised that we had perhaps overachieved as a club and they knew that we needed their support behind us, especially with a young side.

We needed all the encouragement we could get because we got drawn into yet another relegation battle, and in January 1990, the board decided to relieve Ray Harford of his duties. It was a huge shock for me and the rest of the lads when we heard that Ray had been sacked. I got on so well with him, on and off the pitch, and we remained friends. We felt that it was a very harsh decision as Ray had been at the helm for the most successful period in the club's history, and it was very sad to see him go.

Jimmy Ryan was promoted to the role of manager. Jimmy was a very good coach, an excellent coach in fact, and he was one of the main reasons why the younger players had started to come through. He believed in them and wanted to help them fulfil their potential. In fairness, the players he did develop went on to have very good careers which is testament to his ability. Jimmy later became a coach at Manchester United, where he helped Sir Alex Ferguson bring through another crop of good youngsters, including David Beckham, Paul Scholes, and Gary Neville, maybe you've heard of them.

Our problem, as I've already mentioned, was consistency.

During the 1989/90 season, we didn't lose to Liverpool, who later became champions, so we were still capable of competing with the big boys, but we couldn't replicate those performances week on week.

With just three games to go, Charlton and Millwall were already down, and the battle for the final relegation spot was between us and Sheffield Wednesday. We were six points behind Wednesday, so we had to win every game and hope that the Owls picked up no more than three points. A tough ask. In everyone's mind, we were dead and buried.

But in the Luton dressing room, we still believed that we could stay up, although we knew it was going to be very difficult. We'd survived the previous season and we had to draw on that experience to drag ourselves out of the mire again. We went back to basics, working hard in training, and the young lads, with their pace and energy, gave us the opportunity to counterattack, something we'd not been able to do before.

We surprised everyone by beating the reigning champions Arsenal 2-0, a fantastic result. Wednesday lost to QPR which meant we had closed the gap to three points with two to play.

Iain Dowie's last-minute winner was enough to secure a 1-0 victory over Crystal Palace in our next game, but as Sheffield Wednesday beat Charlton, we were still three points behind the Owls going into the last match of the season.

On the 5th of May 1990, we arrived at the Baseball Ground for a must-win game against a strong Derby County side. Derby were managed by my old gaffer, Arthur Cox, and featured England internationals Peter Shilton and Mark Wright, with my former teammates Mick Harford and Dean Saunders up front.

Not only did we need to beat the Rams, but we also needed Nottingham Forest to beat Sheffield Wednesday at Hillsborough. The odds were firmly stacked against us. It was such a high-pressure match, but we didn't go there with any fear. Yes, we were the underdogs, but we were used to that. We knew that if we could perform to the best of our ability, like we had against Liverpool and Arsenal, we could win. That's what we focused on.

Our supporters were absolutely magnificent on that day. The thousands who made the journey up the M1 were so loyal and their support made a massive difference to the players on the pitch.

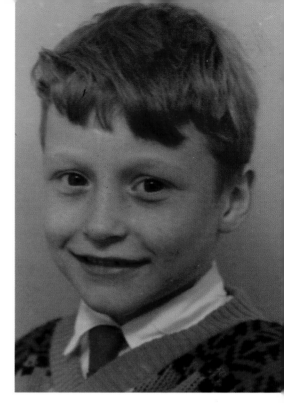

I inherited my footballing ability from
my dad who played for Derry City.

Say cheese! That cheeky smile got
me out of trouble quite a few times!

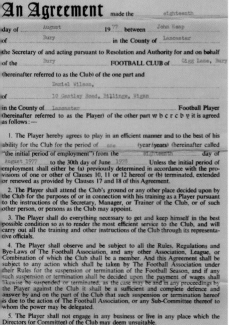

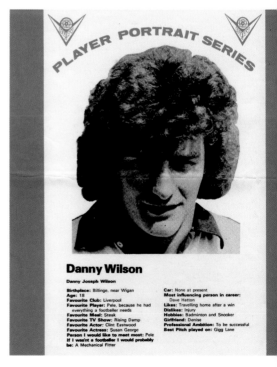

It was an amazing feeling to sign
my first professional contract.

Just look at that hair! I didn't even know
where Bury was when I signed for them.

I learnt so much during my three seasons at Bury. I'm fourth from the right, on the back row.

I played over a hundred
games for Chesterfield.

Winning the Player of the Season award
with Chesterfield in 1981 was a huge honour.

Our victory over Glasgow Rangers in the Anglo-Scottish Cup put Chesterfield on the map.

To win the Anglo-Scottish Cup in my first season at Chesterfield was fantastic.
With that squad we should have won promotion to the Second Division.

My children Carrie (left) and Laurie (right) were both born in Brighton.

With the squad we had at Brighton, we should have won promotion back to the top flight.

Mum and Dad with Laurie. I couldn't have wished for two better parents.

I loved the responsiibilty that came
with being Brighton captain.

I celebrated every goal I scored,
don't worry about that.

To score a goal at Wembley Stadium in a major cup final was the stuff of dreams.

I went to Luton Town to win trophies, so I was delighted to win the League Cup in 1988.

Scoring for Sheffield Wednesday, against Chelsea, in the League Cup semi-final in 1991. We always seemed to do well against Chelsea.

Beating Manchester United to win the League Cup in 1991 was a huge shock – but not to us. Under Big Ron we knew we were capable of beating anyone.

Karen and I holding the League Cup in 1991. She's been my rock.

Playing in the Steel City derby. The atmosphere was always electric.

Carlton Palmer and I tackling Wimbledon's John Fashanu. The Dons had a reputation as a physical team, but that side of the game never bothered me.

We got off to a fantastic start when Tim Breaker, our right back, scored an unbelievable goal in the second minute. He struck the ball from thirty-five yards out, and it flew past Shilton into the top corner. Tim, a very reliable defender, wasn't known for his goalscoring exploits – he only scored three goals in almost two hundred and fifty games for Luton – so we were all in shock!

Kingsley Black doubled our lead in the nineteenth minute to give us a fighting chance. That should have been game over, but we made things difficult for ourselves.

Derby pushed Mark Wright up front, and he pulled one back for the Rams just before the half-hour mark. Then Paul Williams scored a stunning goal to equalise just on the stroke of half-time. It was quite remarkable and must have been an exciting game for the neutrals to watch.

At half-time we heard that Forest were beating Sheffield Wednesday 1-0, but irrespective of that score, we knew that if we failed to beat Derby, we'd be down, so we went back out for the second half determined to snatch another goal.

With fifteen minutes left, the score remained 2-2, and as it stood, we were going to be relegated. But then up popped Kingsley Black with his second goal of the game to regain our lead. The crowd went bananas.

We had people on the bench with a transistor radio, listening to the Sheffield Wednesday game, and the message was relayed to us that Forest were now 3-0 up. All we had to do was not concede and we'd stay up. We grew into the game and professionally saw it through to the end.

When the referee's whistle signalled the end of the match, we were ecstatic. No one had given us a chance, but we'd done it. We'd secured our First Division status for another season, by the narrowest of margins. Our goal difference was two better than Wednesday and that was the difference between survival and relegation.

I didn't know it at the time, but that was my final appearance for the Hatters. During my three years at Kenilworth Road, I played in three cup finals, we had two relegation escapes on the final day of the season and I was thrown out of Stringfellows. It's safe to say that my time at Luton certainly wasn't dull!

CHAPTER 9
On stage with Jasper Carrot

At the end of the 1989/90 season we flew out to Puerta Banus (where else?) where we bumped into Sheffield Wednesday, the team we had sent down. The last thing we wanted to do was rub their noses in it, but there were no problems at all in that respect. I knew a few of the Wednesday players, like my Northern Ireland teammate Nigel Worthington, so the two teams went out and had a few beers together.

Carlton Palmer was a big, big character and a funny boy. He was in the Navy Club one night smoking a cigar and I told him his finger was on fire! A few expletives followed before normal service resumed.

Big Ron Atkinson, the Owl's flamboyant manager, was also in Marbella and a few days into the break, he asked if I'd consider joining Sheffield Wednesday. I'd enjoyed three very good seasons at Luton Town, but the team was being broken up as the club moved towards a more youthful side. I was approaching my thirty-first birthday and could see that my time at Kenilworth Road was coming to an end. Sheffield was much closer to Karen's family in Chesterfield and after years of living in the south, it felt like the right time to move closer to our roots. There was interest from my side, but I told Ron that he'd have to speak to Jimmy Ryan first to see if I was available.

Within a week of returning to England, I received a phone call from Luton to say that they had agreed a transfer fee and I needed to meet with Big Ron to agree personal terms. We met in a hotel, just outside Luton, and Ron asked me what I was looking for in terms of wages. I told him and his instant response was no! But we negotiated for a bit and agreed terms in just twenty minutes. Then it was time for my medical. "Stand on one leg," Ron instructed, so I did. "Right, you've passed."

And that was it. I became a Sheffield Wednesday player. Medicals were very stringent in those days, as you can tell!

I was, at the time, the oldest player Ron had ever signed, but he had no doubts. He was looking for a certain type of player and Ray Harford had recommended me to Ron's assistant Ritchie Barker.

There were no doubts from my point of view either, even though the transfer meant I would be dropping down to the Second Division. When I looked at the size of the club, the fan base, and the stadium, I was very clear in my mind that the move was another step forward in my career.

When I first went into the club and met my new teammates – many of whom I'd played against the previous season – I saw so much quality and I knew we were going to go straight back up, no doubt about it at all. We had a very strong team for the Second Division and fortunately for us, Big Ron was able to keep the majority of the squad together.

The ice had been broken in Marbella, so all the jokes and jibes that I'd received about my part in sending Wednesday down had been watered down when I arrived for my first training session. The lads welcomed me with open arms. The dressing room was fantastic, very strong. Full of leaders and characters.

The supporters were bitterly disappointed with the manner of relegation. The majority of the team felt that they'd let the fans down and it was up to us to rectify it. Ritchie Barker drilled it into us that we were going up and we believed him. Why wouldn't we with the quality that we had?

There was such an array of talent that began with an outstanding back four consisting of Nigel Worthington at the top of his game, Roland Nillson who had played very well at the Italia 90 World Cup and Peter Shirtliff alongside Nigel Pearson in the centre of defence – two lads who would go through a brick wall for you. And on the odd occasions when something did get past them, we had Chris Turner in goal saving everything else.

In midfield, we had John Harkes, an unknown when he arrived at Wednesday from America. John was a funny guy, but he could play too and as the season progressed, there were times when he took my place. I wasn't happy about it, no one likes it when you're not playing, but I could respect the manager's decision because he was such a good player.

We also had Steve McCall who had played for Ipswich during their glory days where he won the UEFA Cup.

Up front we had the legendary Trevor Francis – the first £1,000,000 footballer. Even at thirty-six years of age, Trevor was as fit as a fiddle and still a very good player capable of changing a game. Trevor, or Tricky as we called him, partnered David Hirst who was easily one of the best strikers in the country.

Having David in your side was an absolute dream from a midfielder's point of view because I knew that if we created the chances, he'd finish the vast majority off, especially in Division Two. Not only that, but Hirsty could create a goal out of nothing, he wasn't reliant on receiving the right service. You could play the ball into his feet and he was that strong and skilful that he could hold it up all day long. He could twist and turn to create half a yard from his marker, and he had a cannon ball of a left foot. To top it off he could strike it from anywhere. And boy did he strike it from anywhere, often catching goalkeepers out because he hit the ball so early and with so much power.

If we were moving forward on a counter attack and the ball went to David, it would stick to him. From a midfielder's perspective that was heaven because that gave me the opportunity to make my runs. Hirsty had everything: he could head the ball, was strong, and as brave as a lion. A real all-round striker. Ron loved David, absolutely adored him. Not just the way that he played his football but also the way he was in the dressing room. He was a fantastic character.

And then there was John Sheridan, known as Shez. One of the most technically gifted players of his generation.

When I looked around at the players for the first time I remember thinking, *Crikey, this isn't a bad side.*

We went to Genoa in Italy for our pre-season training camp. We stayed in a beautiful old-fashioned hotel that Trevor knew all about from his five years playing in Italy. Tricky gave us some insights on where to go and what to do, but Ron and Ritchie made sure we worked hard too.

During the trip, Big Ron gave us a night off, so we went to

this fantastic place where there was a pool on the ground floor and a bar upstairs. It was great in there, quite busy, and full of locals.

"I've no problem with you being out, lads, but you all need to be back at the hotel by midnight," Big Ron told us.

"No problem, boss," we replied.

We enjoyed ourselves, had a few drinks and returned to the hotel by midnight. All except John Sheridan who decided to break the curfew and have a couple more beers, for some reason.

At half past midnight, Shez walked in. Ron was waiting in reception and ripped into him big time. John was no shrinking violet either, so he let rip back. I was rooming with Trevor, and we could hear Big Ron sending Shez back to his room. The corridors were so big that we could hear their argument echoing across the entire floor, so we went to see what was going on.

Ron and Shez were shouting at each other. It got so heated that we thought there was going to be a punch up, so we pulled Shez away from the manager and with the help of a couple of other lads, managed to get him in his room where we tried to calm him down. When we thought Shez was OK, we walked back to our rooms. The next minute he was knocking on Big Ron's door, having another go at the gaffer, so we went back to sort it out.

We dragged Shez back to his room, but he was so upset that he told me to fuck off. I warned him to calm down or I'd give him one, not that that would have bothered him anyway. Anyway, we eventually settled him down and went back to our rooms.

We met up for training the following morning, but there was no sign of Shez. This was one of my first training sessions since joining the club. Big Ron addressed us, "Right, lads, we've got a decision to make. Do we send Sheridan home, or should we let him stay?" Then he turned to me and said, "Danny, you'd send him home, wouldn't you?"

"What do you mean, boss?" I replied, thinking, *Why are you asking me?*

"Should we send him home for gross misconduct?" Ron asked.

"Well, you've got to take into consideration that he's one of your best players and you need him if you want to have a successful season," I replied. "Yes, he may have got it wrong last night, but give him a little fine and keep him here, otherwise you'll be cutting off your nose to spite your face."

Big Ron looked at me for what felt like an eternity before saying, "Fucking exactly what I was going to say, Danny." The tension was lifted and Shez joined in training later that day.

By the way, they loved each other, Big Ron and Shez. There was no animosity between them apart from that one little argument between two very strong characters. Ron loved the way John played. Shez knew how good he was and that allowed him to push it a bit with the manager.

By the time the season kicked off on 25th August 1990, against Ipswich Town at Portman Road, we were psychologically in the zone, expecting to win every game. We absolutely played Ipswich off the park. We won 2-0, but it could have been anything, we were that good. Big Ron was a fantastic man manager, who made you feel top dollar, and in the dressing room after the game I reflected that I'd joined a very good side and was about to have a successful year.

My decision to join Wednesday was one of the best I've ever made. Not just on the footballing side, but it was the right thing to do for my family too. Karen and I had no relatives in Brighton or Luton. Karen is such a great mother and wife, and never complained once, but it was much easier for her moving up to Derbyshire where she had all her friends and family close by. With Laurie and Carrie both at school age, it was important to find somewhere they could settle too, so it was a great move for all concerned.

We beat Hull City 5-1 at Hillsborough in our next match with David Hirst scoring an incredible four goals. Everything just clicked and we knew that we'd take some stopping. That was the start of a fourteen-game unbeaten run that ended with a 4-2 defeat to Millwall on 27th October 1990. During that run I bagged my first goal in the blue and white stripes of Sheffield Wednesday against Leicester City in September. I also continued my habit of scoring against my former teams, grabbing the opening goal against Brighton.

Even a bad gambler would have backed us during that run, and everyone connected with Wednesday was very excited. It wasn't just that we were winning games, we were putting goals in left, right and centre. Hirsty was going through a real purple match as was Paul Williams, a striker we had signed from Charlton.

After the defeat to Millwall, we didn't struggle as such, but our form stuttered and that helped bring a few teams closer to us. Although we had a healthy number of points, we certainly weren't walking away with the league. We aimed for an average of two points a game and though we didn't lose many, we drew far too many matches. It wasn't that we'd consciously taken our foot off the gas, it was more that teams knew how good we were going forward so they started to sit back, and we found it difficult to break them down.

In January, Big Ron pulled off a huge transfer coup by signing Viv Anderson from Manchester United. I enjoyed linking up with Viv again. We'd played together at Nottingham Forest, and our friendship went back a few years. Viv is still to this day one of my best friends in football. For what he was done for the game over the years is incredible. He's a real pioneer and best of all, he's never changed. He's a very humble, down to earth man.

Viv's presence added further experience to our dressing room, one that was already packed full of leaders. We were highly respected, disciplined, and although we weren't squeaky clean, we conducted ourselves well and kept ourselves out of trouble. The fact that so many of that squad moved into management – Chris Turner, Roland Nilsson, Viv, Nigel Pearson, Trevor Francis, John Sheridan, Nigel Worthington, and Carlton Palmer – certainly made the manager's job easier.

The gaffer always told us that playing our normal game would give us the best chance of winning. When it came to a Thursday before a Saturday match, Ron would tell us about our opponent's strengths, so we knew who was covering who and what our individual duties and responsibilities were. We didn't have the video watching sessions that are prevalent now, though. That wasn't available to us back then.

Big Ron wasn't a shouter, his assistant Ritchie Barker was the one for the that. You could hear him yelling right from the other side of the pitch! Ritchie was great at that. He'd been a fantastic striker in his day, was trusted by Ron and knew his onions, so if he was shouting at you, you always turned your head and listened.

But Ritchie didn't need to shout at us much as we managed ourselves when we were out on the pitch. If there was a bollocking needed, we'd give it. If a pat on the back was deserved, you'd get that too. It was a brilliant group of players who demanded a lot from each other but had enough respect that no one whinged if they were dug out. It is a dream for managers when the players can do that.

On 19th February 1991, we lost 2-1 to Swindon, a result that left us nine points adrift of West Ham United who were top of the table. We didn't have much time to dwell on that defeat though, as a few days later we were travelling to Stamford Bridge for the first leg of the League Cup semi-final.

I had experienced the joy of winning the League Cup when I was at Luton, but when I joined Wednesday, I didn't expect to have a chance of winning it again.

We had beaten Brentford 4-2 on aggregate in the second round and after that match, Big Ron said, "You're only five games away from Wembley. You've got no one to fear." He still believed that we should have been in the top flight and that it was a travesty that we'd been relegated. Ron kept telling us that we were all First Division players and we believed that too. We had so much belief that we never felt we would lose, regardless of who our opponents were.

After seeing off Brentford, we beat Swindon in round three and then saw off First Division Derby County in round four. John Harkes scored a twenty-four yard thunderbolt that flew past the England goalkeeper Peter Shilton. Derby were a terrific side, but we had enough quality to see them off and that victory gave us a lot of confidence. We knew that we could take on the top teams and were capable of beating them.

Next up was Coventry City, another Division One team, full of talented players such as Cyrille Regis, David Speedie and Terry Butcher. Nigel Pearson's first half goal was enough to give us a 1-0 win and secure our place in the semi-final where we faced Chelsea.

We were to become Chelsea's bogey team as we always seemed to do well against them. Even though they were a division higher than us, when you looked at the teams side by side, I felt we were evenly matched. In fact, I'd say that we had the better players. We beat them 2-0 at Stamford Bridge, a result that wasn't lucky at all it was fully deserved.

Three days later, Chelsea arrived at Hillsborough for the second leg and the ground was absolutely banging with over thirty thousand Wednesday fans in full voice. They were magnificent and when you've got that kind of support driving you on, you cannot let them down.

Nigel Pearson gave us the lead in the thirty-fourth minute and I doubled it just before half time to wrap the game up.

Graham Stuart pulled one back for Chelsea in the second half, but we defended stoutly and when Paul Williams made it 3-1 on the night, 5-1 on aggregate, all hell broke loose with our fans. They knew then that we were on our way to Wembley for our first ever League Cup final.

Sheffield Wednesday is a proud club with a rich history, although their last cup final was in 1966 when the Owls lost to Everton in the FA Cup final. You had to go all the way back to 1935 for Wednesday's last trophy.

Our cup run gave the city a huge lift, well half of it anyway. No matter where we went, people were talking about the final. It might have been different if we'd gone to the other part of the city, the United part, though. People were getting excited, and our story was all over the press, especially because we were a Second Division club taking on one of the best teams in the country. It was a major talking point on football shows and in newspapers up and down the country. We had to try and keep level heads.

Although we were confident that we could win, we also knew that it wasn't going to be easy as we would be facing Manchester United in the final. United had won the FA Cup the previous season and were on their way to winning the European Cup Winners' Cup. We were very much the underdogs in everyone's mind, so Big Ron's approach in the build-up was about keeping us relaxed.

We went down to Bisham Abbey in Berkshire, a beautiful grade one listed manor house that has outstanding training facilities, for a few days training. We did all our preparations at Bisham Abbey, so we knew what our duties were and what United's strengths were. And they had loads of strengths, by the way, not just one or two.

After that we moved on to the Royal Lancaster Hotel in London where it was just laugh after laugh.

It was Trevor Francis's birthday on the Friday before the final and Big Ron let us have a party to celebrate. The wives and girlfriends came down too. We had a few drinks and a lot of laughs. It was the kind of thing that Brian Clough would have done.

The next morning we went to Hyde Park, and we just pissed about with the football for a couple of hours having fun. We then headed back to the hotel where we were joined by Stan Boardman, the comedian, who was a big mates with Ron. Stan joined us for our evening meal and the next morning he came along on the coach with us to Wembley. We didn't stop laughing for two days – we didn't even think about the game. We were still cracking jokes as the coach drove up Wembley Way. We were laughing in the dressing room.

About half an hour before kick off we began to settle down and focus on the match. Big Ron's genius put us the right frame of mind. If the game had been too hyped up, we could have been intimidated or felt the pressure. Manchester United had sacked Ron a few years earlier, and although we never heard him speak about it, we knew that deep down he would love to go to Wembley and beat them. It was a chance to put him back on the map as a top manager, which he was.

We took the lead in the thirty-seventh minute through a stunning strike by John Sheridan. It's a good job Big Ron didn't send him home from Italy after their earlier argument, that's for sure!

United were a good team with some fantastic players in their side and 1-0 is a very slender lead to hold, but we defended admirably. Manchester United missed some good chances, but Chris Turner had a brilliant game and made one amazing save from Brian McClair. I still don't know how he managed to keep it out. While you do need to have a certain amount of luck to win a final, it wasn't one way traffic by any means. It was a great game for the neutrals and an even better one for us.

When the referee's whistle signalled the end of the game my overriding emotion was one of sheer joy. Like most teams who have lost a cup final, United's fans left not long after the final whistle. All I could see when I looked around Wembley was a sea of blue and white. For that hour after the game, the stadium belonged to us. It was brilliant, a very proud moment for me and even more special because my family were there in the stands. They are memories that you cannot buy, and you just have to make the most of them.

After the game we celebrated hard. We had a huge party at the Royal Lancaster with family and friends. A few lucky supporters even managed to sneak in too. We danced, we hugged, we drank – I even got up on stage and sang a duet with Wednesday fan Paul Carrack, Mike Rutherfood, the lead singer of Mike and the Mechanics, and Jeff Lowe, while Jasper Carrot, who was friends with Trevor, played the guitar. It was such a surreal moment.

I'm not sure what time the party finished, but I do know that most of us were still pissed when we travelled back up to Sheffield the following morning, just two days before our next league match.

It's always important to get a win after a piss up, but we could only manage a 0-0 draw with Leicester City at Hillsborough which was disappointing. Not that the fans seemed to mind though, as they were still celebrating our cup win! We beat Barnsley 3-1 in our next game which was a huge result as defeat would have seen us drop out of the automatic promotion places.

We beat Bristol City 3-1 at home in the penultimate match of the season to secure promotion back to the First Division. We lost our final game 3-2 to Oldham, who went up as champions, so we had to settle for third place. It was disappointing not to get the top spot, but there was a still a lot for us to be proud of. It had been a long old season and the expectation levels from our supporters was very high. To win the League Cup, but not be promoted would have been devastating, so to finish third was such a relief. It would have been much sweeter to go up as champions, but we still enjoyed our achievement. No team outside the top division has won the League Cup since.

Our celebrations were short lived, though as not long after the season finished, Big Ron announced that he was leaving us to become manager of Aston Villa.

CHAPTER 10
Hold my hand please

Ron had grown up in the Midlands, so we understood his decision to join Aston Villa, even though we didn't feel Villa were a bigger club than us. The Wednesday fans, however, were furious and felt he had let them down.

Trevor Francis moved into the manager's office as Ron's replacement. A good appointment in my view as Tricky knew the club inside out. He also had a different perspective on the game from his time playing in Italy. Whereas Ron was outstanding at man management, Trevor was quite shy – certainly not one to shout from the rooftops – but he was fantastic technically.

I'd roomed with Trevor for a year, so knew him pretty well, and I found it difficult to start calling him boss or gaffer instead of Tricky. Occasionally, I'd forget, but he was OK with that. He had his own ideas and thoughts on how we could improve both individually and as a team, and he put his own stamp on the club. Trevor was a popular choice with the players.

We went to Puerta Banus (again!) for our end of season break. As Trevor was now the manager he got his own room, and I shared with Viv Anderson. One day, we'd been out for a bit of lunch and few pints, and had returned to the room to freshen up before going out again in the evening. Viv took the first shower, so I was relaxing on my bed, watching TV when I heard a bang coming from the bathroom. Viv had been washing his hair and the shampoo had gone in his eyes. He couldn't see a thing, so he rubbed his eyes and because he'd had a couple of pints, he completely lost his balance and fell out of the shower. He ripped the shower curtain off when he grabbed it as he fell.

When I opened the bathroom door, all I could see was Viv

covered in soap and shampoo, wedged between the bidet and the bath. The shower curtain was wrapped around him, and he couldn't get up. I nearly wet myself laughing. It was one of the funniest things I've ever seen. When I tell this story, I'm asked if I helped him up. I didn't. I was laughing too much to help him. He eventually dragged himself up, rinsed the shampoo and soap off, and we went out again.

Paul Warhurst became Trevor's first signing, joining us from Oldham for £750,000. We called him Albert after Albert Tatlock, the *Coronation Street* charector, because boy could he moan! Paul was an excellent centre back. He was quick, good at reading the game and could step out into midfield because he was so good on the ball. If he was playing today, he'd be worth an absolute fortune.

Next to come in was Chris Woods, a talented goalkeeper who had just Peter Shilton as England's number one. Woodsy was a great team player and a really nice guy, but he was also a bit gullible. We went to America for our pre-season tour and when we arrived at the airport I said to Viv, "I bet you £20 that I can get Woodsy to hold my hand while we take off."

"You're on. No chance he'll do that," replied Viv confidently.

As we boarded the plan, I sat between Chris, who had the window seat, and Viv, who was sitting on the aisle. As the plane began taxiing, I jumped up and down every time there was a little bump.

"Are you alright, Dan?" Chris asked.

"I just don't like flying, mate," I replied. As the plane made another little bump, I almost jumped out of my seat. "I don't like it at all. Are we taking off now?" I asked Chris.

"Not yet."

"I don't know if I want to stay on this flight, Chris," I said, panic building in my voice.

"You'll be alright, Dan. Safe as houses these planes. Never any problems."

As we started to pick up speed, I grabbed Chris' right hand and he held mine back. I could see Viv out of the corner of my eye, looking over shaking his head.

Chris held my hand the whole time while we took off. When we were up in the air, and the seatbelt signs had gone off, Viv handed me a crisp £20 note. Woodsy was that kind of lad. A top keeper, and a pleasure to play with. Chris was very unfortunate for England. He had Shilton ahead of him for a number of years and then when it looked like he'd finally get his chance David Seaman came along. Chris was never bitter about it though, he wasn't that kind of person, although I'm sure he'd have liked more caps.

When we arrived in America, we played some friendlies, including one against the US national team, and another in Philadelphia. One night, we were invited to a promotional party in a multi-layered nightclub, with different themed bars on different levels. A liaison officer took us around and introduced us to various dignitaries who had our photos taken with. I had four pints of Guinness and it was a good night.

When we got back to the hotel, Viv told me that it was his birthday and asked if we should go out again.

"No, Viv, we've only just got back. We'll get in trouble if we go out again," I replied.

"Come on, Dan. It's my birthday. Let's go back to that place we went to tonight. It was good in there."

"Alright then," I said. I didn't need too much convincing, as you can tell!

So we climbed out of the window, walked down the fire escape, and caught a taxi to the nightclub. When we walked in, the barman asked where the rest of the lads were.

"It's just us this time," I told him. "It's Viv's birthday."

"I've got just the thing for you then," said the barman, lining up Tequila slammers and more pints of Guinness.

I can honestly say that I've never been as squiffy in all my life as I was that night. When we arrived back at the hotel, we discovered that our room had been raided. Viv's watch had been stolen and bizarrely, so had my shell suit. Viv, who stood at just over six feet tall and always used to take the piss out of my height, quipped, "The perpetrator will be easy to find. We just need to look for a dwarf walking around Philadelphia in a shell suit wearing a nice watch!"

We had to train the next morning and I've never played as bad as I did that day. Viv and I were running into each other and tripping over the ball. The other lads asked what was wrong with us. "Must have been that Guinness last night," I replied.

How they put the fixture list together, I do not know. Maybe someone had some cheekiness in them, or maybe it was jusr random, but we played Aston Villa at Hillsborough on the first day of the season. The build up to the match was dominated by the return of Big Ron and the fans let him know exactly what they thought of him when he took his seat in the visitor's dugout.

With all the animosity surounding the game, we wanted to win for the fans and we got off to a great start, going two up with David Hirst and I both getting on the scoresheet. But Villa came back to win the game 3-2 with goals from Cyrille Regis, Steve Staunton and Dalian Atkinson, God rest his soul.

We never expected to become embroiled in a relegation battle, nor did we think we'd be challenging for the title. If I'm honest, we thought mid table was a realistic target. We were a group of players who felt we belonged in the First Division, but we had to prove that to everyone else.

We did just that.

After the defeat to Villa, we went on a pretty good run, drawing to Leeds United and Liverpool, and beating Everton, Nottingham Forest and Manchester City. Those results gave us a lot of belief. When Manchester United came to Hillsborough on 26th October 1991, we felt no fear, and beat them 3-2 thanks to a brace from Nigel Jemson, a striker we had signed from Forest. After that game we realised that we were in the running for the league title. We never went public by telling everyone how good we were, but privately we knew that we had a chance if we did our jobs properly. We didn't get beaten by United that season.

We knew were never going to be a match for the big clubs in the long term because we didn't have the same financial backing as they did, but for a short period of time, we knew we could compete with anyone. When you have someone like David Hirst, who couldn't stop scoring goals, you've always got a chance. We went into games not just knowing that we could win but expecting to.

We knew the big boys saw us as a threat because Manchester United came in with a £4,000,000 bid for Hirsty. That was a huge statement. United were doing what Liverpool had done in the eighties which was to try and buy the best players from their rivals and at that stage, we were rivalling them. To lose our top scorer would have really hurt us, but Trevor rejected the offer which was absolutely brilliant from our point of view.

Was that the right decision for David? Maybe not. I suppose when you look back and think that he had a chance of playing for Manchester United, winning the trophies they went on to win, maybe he wishes he'd gone. I don't know. If it wasn't for injuries, Hirsty would have been up there with Alan Shearer, no doubt in my mind.

On 17th November 1991, I played in my first Sheffield derby at Bramall Lane. I had no idea how big the rivalry between two two clubs was before that game. The atmosphere around the whole city was electric, never mind inside the ground. No matter where we went in the week leading up to the match, we were reminded of how intense the rivalry was. I can't imagine how difficult it must have been for families containing both Blades and Owls fans.

Sadly, we lost 2-0 giving Sheffield United the bragging rights which was really hard for us to take. The result also put a dent in our title ambitions. That defeat to our local rivals really knocked the stuffing out of us, but the one thing that we never did, and I say this with pride, was feel sorry for ourselves. We weren't the kind of team to sit down and lick our wounds. We picked ourselves up and got back to winning ways. Maybe it was the kick up the backside that we needed.

To improve the depth of the squad, Trevor brought in Chris Bart-Williams, a young kid from Leyton Orient with enormous potential. Chris was a talented midfielder with terrific feet, such a skilful player. He never tied his shoelaces for some reason. When he first arrived at the club, his pre-match meal was bacon and egg sandwiches, so we had to straighten him out! It amazes me that he didn't play for longer at the very highest level. Great things were expected of Chris, and we all thought he would become a mainstay of the Premier League. Don't get me wrong, he had a very good career, but he could have been a world beater.

In January 1992, Eric Cantona came to Wednesday on trial. Eric was looking for a fresh start after receiving a lengthy ban for throwing the ball at a referee during a French league game. We didn't know too much about him when he arrived, although we knew he had a reputation as a hot head.

At the time, our training ground was frozen, so we were training on a 3G pitch on the outskirts of Rotherham. As soon as we saw Eric on the pitch, we realised that he was quality, absolute quality. When the ball was at his feet, he was magnificent. He was so strong that you couldn't get the ball off him. On that 3G pitch, your passing had to be so accurate and if the ball went beyond him, Eric just stood there pointing to his feet, showing you where he wanted it. He didn't speak a lot at the time, and we assumed it was because he couldn't speak English.

We usually trained in the morning, ate some lunch in the canteen and then trained again in the afternoon. One day, we went upstairs to the canteen and Eric wasn't wearing his training kit. He'd changed into his normal clothes. *Strange,* I thought.

We placed our orders and then found a table. Eric sat next to me, and I asked him what he'd ordered for lunch.

"Fish and chips, and a pint of lager," he replied.

"You can't have that, Eric," I said. "We're training again this afternoon."

"No, I'm not," he replied. For whatever reason he decided he'd had enough for the day, and nobody was ever going to change his mind. That was Eric. He was always his own man.

Eric only stayed with us a week or so before joining Leeds United. Trevor has been heavily criticised for not signing him which I think is a bit unfair. I understand that Eric was asked to stay for a few more days, but there was a breakdown in communication and Eric joined Leeds instead. Trevor didn't ever say that he wasn't good enough. That never happened.

On 12th January 1992, we lost 6-1 at home to Leeds. I didn't play in that match, I was on the bench, and didn't enjoy being left out of that one. Tony Dorigo, the Leeds left back, was outstanding and I would have been up against him. I was fairly quick, and I don't think he'd have had the same joy had I been playing, so I was pissed off not to have been included. Trevor picked the team, and I accepted his decision, but I felt myself becoming more and more angry as the goals kept flying in.

We didn't wallow though, and we redeemed ourselves to the fans by beating Aston Villa – and Big Ron – at Hillsborough. We followed that up with a win over Luton, and a draw against Manchester United at Old Trafford. Things were looking up again, but then we went to Highbury and got beat 7-1. I don't know where that result came from. We were always strong at the back, so to concede seven was unusual. I can't remember anything at all about the game. I've wiped it out of my mind completely!

Once again, we rolled our sleeves up and only lost twice in the final fourteen games of the season to finish third in the league, seven points behind Leeds United who were crowned champions. To come so close to being crowned the best team in the country was a huge disappointment, but we had exceeded everyone's expectations and when I look back, I think it was a very successful season.

Best of all, the European ban on English clubs had been lifted which meant that we had qualified for the UEFA Cup.

CHAPTER 11
Wembley, Wembley

The 1992/93 season saw the birth of the Premier League. Football as we knew it was changed forever.

There was a lot more razzamatazz: cheerleaders entertained the fans during the half time break, and there was often a firework show taking place on the pitch before the game. We'd hear the explosions while we were receiving our pre-match instructions! It was all totally new, something none of us had experienced before.

Branding and advertising became huge. We were told that when we drank on the pitch, during the game, that we had to hold up the bottle with the logo facing the front, so the cameras could pick out the drinks brand.

I had a boot sponsor, Puma, for virtually my entire career, but not to the extent that you see now where players receive millions. I was given free boots and the occasional pair of free trainers that I'd try and scrounge for my family, but it certainly wasn't as lucrative as it is now.

Games kicked off at different times to accommodate Sky. It felt strange at first, but we adjusted. There were so many changes to kick off times, but we didn't complain, we just had to get used to them. There were more games on television, more interviews needed and that led to greater media attention. We the players became known all over the world.

We were allocated squad numbers and had our names printed on the back of our shirts. For the first time, fans could buy a replica shirt complete with the name and number of their favourite player. Waddle and Hirst were the big sellers, but I'm sure I saw at least two people who had 'Wilson 7' on the back of their shirts - my daughter Carrie and son Laurie! It was strange to see at first, but that's the way football was going. It was good for the fans though, and good for the people watching on television. If they didn't know who you were before the game, they could see your name during it. It made things easier for visiting scouts too, and of course, clubs made more money from merchandise.

The biggest change was the enormous sums of money that suddenly surrounded the game. Money that I believe changed football for the better in most respects.

We tried to push on after our third placed finish and Trevor Francis bought Mark Bright from Crystal Palace for £1,300,000. Brighty was a very robust centre forward, great to play up to, excellent aerially, and a great foil for Hirsty.

We also signed Chris Waddle for £1,000,000. What a player Waddle was. Trevor used to tell us that if we wanted a rest to give it to Chris and he'd take it up the pitch where no one could get it off him. It was the same thing Brian Clough used to say about John Robertson.

Waddle possessed fantastic skills. His body swerves and feints were magnificent, pretending to go one way before going the next. He could produce goals and create opportunities from nothing. He is without a doubt one of the best players that I've ever played with. Chris had worked in a sausage factory in Sunderland before he became a professional and he was a grounded lad. Always one of the boys. Even after all the success he'd enjoyed in his career, he never let it go to his head.

For whatever reason, we got off to a poor start to the season, winning just two of our first eight league games. There was, however, the added bonus of European football. I'd missed out on Europe after Luton and Wednesday won the League Cup in 1988 and 1991, and although I'd made a cameo during my brief spell at Nottingham Forest, I thought my chance might have gone.

I came on as a substitute in our 8-1 victory over Spora of Luxembourg and played the full ninety minutes in the return leg a fortnight later.

I started again in the next round against the German club Kaiserslautern. The first leg was held in Germany, and it was a disgrace out there. The referee was awful. David Hirst gave us an early lead, but then he was terrorised by their defenders who were booting him all over the place. The ref gave him no protection and in the forty-third minute, Hirsty retaliated to yet another bad tackle and the ref sent him off. It was a ridiculous decision that hurt us as we lost the game 3-1.

To chase a result like that was going to be tough. Our fans made the second leg a very special night. Hillsborough was banging. It was a packed stadium, full of supporters singing their hearts out, some had even brought flares.

We had a glimmer of hope when I gave us the lead in the first half with my first European goal, but we couldn't break them down and we ended up drawing 2-2 on the night. Had Hirsty not been suspended, maybe the result would have been different.

Paul Warhurst had been signed as a centre back the season before, but when David Hirst began to suffer with injuries, Trevor decided to move him up front for a game against Chelsea. Paul scored the opening goal and then just couldn't stop scoring. In the next twelve games, Paul hit the back of the net twelve times. Incredible for a striker, unbelievable for a defender!

Hirsty missed almost two months of the season and his absence was a big blow to us. Our league form was steady throughout the season, with some good wins over teams like Spurs, Chelsea, and Manchester City, but we lost games to Norwich and Coventry. Those results, combined with the loss of our top striker, cost us the points that we needed to finish higher up in the table.

The Chelsea game brings back a few memories. They were always physical games and I don't think this one was any different. I had a little altercation with a certain Dennis Wise ,as we were going down the tunnel, that left me with a beautiful black eye after our heads met.

That weekend Karen and I staying down in London as treat with Dave and Sue Galley. I arrived at a really posh hotel with a big shiner and wearing a lovely silky tracksuit! Not a particularly nice sight for a five star hotel in the capital. We got lots of tuts and eye rolls from the guests!

On 10th April 1993, we played Manchester United at Old Trafford. United were seeking their first championship for twenty-six years and we went there to be party poopers. John

Sheridan scored a second half penalty and with just four minutes left on the clock, it looked like United would have to wait a little bit longer for their elusive title.

Steve Bruce equalised in the eighty-fourth minute, so we thought we'd have to settle for a draw. But Sir Alex Ferguson was a master of psychology, and he was great at letting the fourth official know how much time to add on. We couldn't believe it when the clock showed ninety minutes and the game continued. In our minds there hadn't been any noteworthy delays that warranted any additional time at all. Maybe there could have been a minute or so for substitutions, but no more than that.

We had the ball for so long, willing the ref to blow his whistle, but it looked like he was waiting for something to happen first.

And it did, unfortunately for us.

In the seventh minute of stoppage time – yes, the seventh minute of stoppage time – Bruce scored his second goal of the game to give United a 2-1 victory. We were really pissed off as we couldn't understand why the game hadn't finished at least five minutes earlier. The term 'Fergie Time' was coined. That win cemented their championship, so it was a huge victory for them. The scenes of Sir Alex and his assistant Brian Kidd jumping up and down on the pitch are iconic.

We had to settle for seventh place, a decent finish, I suppose. But that season wasn't about the Premier League for us. It was all about the cups.

In the FA Cup we beat Cambridge United, Sunderland, Southend United, and Derby County, before facing Sheffield United in the semi-final at Wembley.

The buzz around Sheffield was incredible and it felt like the entire city had travelled down to Wembley. It was one of those games that I will never ever forget. The noise as we walked out of the tunnel was deafening, I'd heard the Wembley roar before of course, but this was on another level. I couldn't hear the person standing next to me it was that loud. The hairs on the back of my neck were standing on end. It was unbelievable.

The game itself was so tense, but we managed to overcome the Blades in extra time. Mark Bright's late goal gave us a deserved 2-1 win. To get through to the FA Cup final was an incredible feeling, a dream come true.

But before we played Arsenal in the FA Cup final, we had to play them in the League Cup final!

We'd already seen off Hartlepool United, Leicester City, Queen's Park Rangers, Ipswich Town, and Blackburn Rovers to reach the final for the second time in three years.

In the final, John Harkes gave us an early lead, but the Gunners came back to beat us 2-1. It was so disappointing that we didn't finish Arsenal off. They were tough team to beat once they got their noses in front, as George Graham instructed them to shut up shop. That made it difficult for us to get back into the game.

Ahead of the FA Cup final, we went to get our suits measured up. They were nice suits, but very down beat compared to Liverpool's famous white Armani suits. We didn't do a song, though. It would have been a waste of money for any producer to put our voices on vinyl or CD!

Trevor's preparation was very different to Big Ron's, but he wasn't intense. He knew that we needed to be relaxed going into any game, especially a cup final. Trevor trusted us to have a drink, but he shied us off the beer and encouraged us to have a glass of wine with our meal instead because that was what they did in Italy. Mind you, the Italians were also notorious for having twenty fags before a game! We were used to drinking pints, so wine was considered posh!

Unfortunately, I suffered a calf strain so I alongwith Peter Shirtliff missed the game through injury. I was disappointed not to play in the FA Cup final, as it's every boy's dream, but fortunately for me, the game finished 1-1 and went to a replay, and I was delighted when Trevor told me I would be starting.

On the morning of the replay, the players' families were supposed to catch a train down to London. Karen, along with my teammates' wives, and our chairman, Dave Richards and his family, were all stood on the platform, but the train didn't slow down. The driver must have forgotten to stop as the train sped through the station and left everyone stranded on the platform! They had to get onto the next train which meant they missed the coach that was supposed to take them from Kings Cross to Wembley. It was a catalogue of disasters.

To play in the FA Cup final was amazing. It fulfilled a

boyhood dream of mine. In those days, the FA Cup was *the* cup and as a boy I would sit down on cup final day and not move. I'd watch the bus travelling up Wembley Way, see the fans lining the streets. It was great. So to be a part of it was an absolute dream. You really can't explain it unless you've been there.

But Wembley is for the winners and unfortunately for us it wasn't our day. Arsenal's Andy Linighan scored the winning goal in the last minute of extra-time to break our hearts.

Over the three games, there was very little between the two teams. Player for player, we were similar, but we were a little more expansive than Arsenal who were very strong defensively and rarely conceded.

Going to Wembley three times was great, but to come away with nothing was bitterly disappointing. Looking back now, I suppose that two cup finals and finishing seventh in the Premier League wasn't a bad season.

Unbeknown to me at the time, the FA Cup final replay was my last match for Sheffield Wednesday. I was about to embark on a new chapter in my career.

CHAPTER 12
Hanging up the boots

In the summer of 1993, my contract was up for renewal. I was enjoying my football at Sheffield Wednesday, playing in a successful team, and I got on really well with Trevor Francis. I was approaching thirty-four, so didn't expect to start every game, but I felt as fit as I'd ever felt. Trevor Francis offered me a contract extension, and I was ready to sign it until Viv Anderson left Wednesday to become player/manager at Barnsley. He offered me the job as player/assistant manager.

It was a tough decision, and had it not been for Viv, I would have stayed at Wednesday. But I knew him well, knew what he was capable of, and I was intrigued. People had always told me that I would make a coach or a manager, so I decided to have a little dabble and dip my toe into the coaching side of the game.

I didn't know what to expect, if I'm honest, and it didn't help that I didn't have any coaching badges because you didn't need them in those days. Looking back now, I think it's important to have your badges. You need to know what you're getting into, and you need to be ready. I can't speak for Viv, but I wasn't ready in 1993. I did everything off the cuff and was learning on the job. I'm lucky that I got away with it.

Barnsley were a mid-table Championship club at the time, and John Dennis, the chairman, wanted us to build a team to start challenging for a playoff spot. We knew it wouldn't be easy as we had very little money to spend.

I was going to be playing for Barnsley, but I had to make that transition from player to part of the management team, so I immediately laid out the boundaries. I didn't get changed in the dressing room with the other lads. Instead, I used the coaches changing room with Viv because I knew there could be problems with me having a foot in both camps. I didn't want the lads to clam up every time I was around, so I made that decision very early on.

We still had a bit of fun and enjoyed the banter, but I had to accept that I was no longer one of the lads. I couldn't afford to be. I don't think there was any reason why I couldn't have a good relationship with the players, but there had to be that line drawn in the sand from the start. I had to be authoritative and earn the lads' respect. My coaching role required me to make big decisions, and I had to be brave enough to do so, even if that meant upsetting people. For want of a better term, I became a little twat.

The 1993/94 season was a huge transition. Viv and I were very much finding our feet. Everything was new to us. During the week, I took the training and coached the lads, but come matchday it was hard. You can't see the wood from the trees when you're playing. I'd spot a few things, but Viv did the team talks and gave us feedback. If I thought someone wasn't doing their job, I'd point the finger, but equally, if I wasn't performing, I'd expect to get a bollocking myself. I still believe that the best teams sort things out in the dressing room and aren't afraid to dig each other out if needed.

I developed a mindset of not trying to compare players. The previous season I'd played with Chris Waddle and David Hirst – two top players – and it would be very unfair for me to expect the Barnsley lads to do what my former teammates were capable of, particularly in the Championship. I'd experienced that league before and I knew the level wasn't anywhere near the same as the Premier League, so it would be foolish to expect the same. That doesn't mean that you can't be demanding and have high standards, though. Viv and I had to get the best out of the players we had at our disposal to help them reach the maximum level of their capability, and I think we did that.

Football is a result-driven business, but we always wanted to play football in the right way. As Mr Clough used to say, "You play football on the green stuff, not the blue stuff in the sky." That was the philosophy we adopted. We wanted to play attacking football and entertain the fans. But it takes time to implement a new style of play; you have to have the right players who are capable of playing the way you want them to, so it's understandable that results suffered while we all adapted.

We finished the season in eighteenth place, four points clear of the relegation zone. The league table doesn't always show the full picture though, as I felt we'd made a certain amount of progress with our style of play, and we'd enjoyed one or two good results playing a nice brand of football.

Viv wasn't managerial material; he'll say that himself. He liked the coaching side but didn't particularly enjoy management, and at the end of the 1993/94 season, he left to join Middlesbrough to become Bryan Robson's assistant.

I was the opposite. I liked the coaching side, but I *loved* management. I liked the weight of expectation that was placed on my shoulders, the responsibility – even the pressure. I knew early on in my Barnsley career that I wanted to become a manager, so when Viv left, I was hoping to get the job, although I didn't really expect it.

John Dennis was impressed with the positive strides that we'd taken, and when he asked me if I'd become the manager, I jumped at the chance.

That first year as a coach taught me a great deal. Although we had tried to get on with the squad that we had, I didn't feel we were going to go anywhere with the players who had finished mid-table for the last few seasons, so we needed some fresh impetus and new faces. All football clubs, in my opinion, need a bit of stimulation each year, and we were no different.

I had to tell players that I'd played with for a season that I was letting them go because, in my opinion, they weren't good enough. It certainly wasn't the most pleasant experience, that's for sure, but it had to be done, and as manager, I was the one who had to do it. It wasn't easy, but it's part and parcel of football.

Another thing I had to get used to as a manager was attending board meetings, something else that was completely new to me. It's a funny thing, sitting in the boardroom having to justify a team that I'd selected or a performance that wasn't great. As a player, if you have a bad game, you dust yourself down and aim to put it right next time. But as a manager you have to explain every decision to the board of directors, the fans, and the media. It's not easy. I never wanted to sound too apologetic, but some things were completely out of my hands. I didn't know how every player was going to play – I didn't even know how I was going to play myself sometimes. I had an idea from watching the lads in training, but it can be hit and miss, so to try and explain your decision after a game was very hard.

Boardroom meetings, media interviews, taking the training, actually training myself and keeping fit, holding team meetings, scouting players – there just weren't enough hours in the day to do everything properly. Not the way that I wanted to do it. And that's where Eric Winstanley came in.

A club legend, Eric was born in Barnsley, grew up in the town, and made over four hundred appearances for the club, many as captain, before he became a coach. I had no hesitation in appointing him to be my assistant. He was absolutely brilliant.

He was a fantastic confidante, and he'd often notice things that I didn't. Eric could put his finger on things very easily, and with his big presence – six foot three inches – he scared the life out of the players, although I never saw him get angry. He didn't need to. The lads hung on his every word because of the sheer amount of respect they had for him. I respected his judgment one hundred per cent, so if he told me something wasn't right, I'd go with him every time.

Eric knew the club inside out, and he introduced me to the young players that he'd been working with. He was so passionate and trusted them implicitly, so I started to give them a chance, injecting some more energy and younger legs into the team.

Dave Watson, a Barnsley-born goalkeeper, became our number one. Nicky Eaden established himself as our first choice right back, and Martin Bullock, a winger we'd signed from non-league Eastwood Town, broke through into the first team. Andy Liddell, a centre forward who'd been on the fringes, took his opportunity with both hands, scoring thirteen goals during the 1994/95 season.

As you will read later on in the book, two of the saddest moments I have ever experienced were indirectly football related. A young player, by the name of Chris Jackson, was coming through the ranks at a rate of knots at Barnsley. Eric and I loved him. Nineteen years old, he had the world at his feet. Unfortunately, he was involved in a car accident, and we were later told that he was going to be confined to a wheelchair for the rest of his life. What a shock. Not just for Chris but also for his loving and caring family.

I will always remember the diving header he scored at Bolton when we played together. Such a sad loss of an up-and-coming talent.

*****

We had to develop players ourselves because we had very little money available to spend on transfers. John Dennis, whose father had also been Barnsley chairman, was a fruit and veg merchant and Barnsley supporter, and he ran a tight ship. John was a down-to-earth Yorkshireman and was very direct in board meetings.

"Can I have some money to sign a player?" I'd ask him.

"Fuck off, you. We've got no money," was his typical reply. That's how he spoke, but in a nice way. John is a lovely bloke and was a major influence on my formative years as a manager. I still play golf with him all these years later.

John deserves a lot of credit for what he did for Barnsley. The infrastructure he put in place, the ground improvements. He left his legacy on the club and is a very proud man. Rightly so. The success that we achieved on the pitch was down to the way he ran the club off it. He didn't splash money here, there, and everywhere. He was frugal and always looked at the long-term interests of the football club.

The board didn't put any pressure on me or set any targets. They were very relaxed from that point of view. Barnsley had struggled for a period of time, mainly languishing in and around the lower half of the table, and the board just wanted to get to the stage where they weren't looking over their shoulder all the time.

When the Taylor Report was published in 1990, it required all teams in the top two divisions to have all-seater stadiums, so we had to change our standing areas to seating, and that had a major impact on us. We built a big, new stand that was lovely, but that was the only one that was open because we had to redevelop the other three. We already had financial constraints, so to close three sides of the ground was a major blow to the club and to the fans. The crowds were dwindling, and we were only getting crowds of four thousand, which wasn't ideal. In fact, it was a struggle. But in many ways, it bounded us together. We dug in and became stronger. As a team, we got stronger and stronger, and by the time we were able to reopen the stands, the crowds came flocking back to Oakwell. John and the board made all these ground improvements without going into debt, so I fully understand why I didn't always get the funds I wanted to improve the playing side.

The club secretary was called Michael Spinx. He was one hundred per cent committed to Barnsley, had been there for years, and did a great job. He'd do anything for the club and was always looking for ways to raise additional revenue. One example is our game against Bradford, which was a sellout. Karen, Laurie, and Carrie arrived at Oakwell but discovered that someone else was sitting in their normal seats. Michael had sold them to bring in some additional funds, so Karen, Laurie, and Carrie had to sit on the steps! You couldn't make it up, but that was Michael, anything to make the club a few extra quid.

I recognised the importance of building a good relationship with the media, and I respected that the journalists had a job to do. There was the club's programme editor, then two or three newspaper and radio reporters, and then depending on the importance of the game, there might be one or two others attending press conferences too. I made a conscious effort to do my interviews within twenty minutes of the final whistle. I knew they had families to go home to and they didn't want to be sitting around for two hours waiting for me. That wasn't fair on them.

Journalists have people above them, and if they didn't ask the difficult questions, they'd get a short shrift from their management, so I rarely got upset with their questions. One or two ruffled my feathers, but that didn't happen often. The questions I was asked were quite mild compared to the interrogations managers receive nowadays. Generally, I got on well with the press and they treated me with the same respect that I treated them with.

You do have to be guarded with the media, though, and I always protected the players. If we had a poor performance, I'd give them a bollocking behind closed doors, but I never hung the lads out to dry in public. I needed the team on my side. Even those who were out of form, I knew I'd need them further on down the line because we had a small squad. I received a few loaded questions, sometimes the same question worded in a different way, but I never fell into the trap. In public, I always praised the lads. Eric and I would give them stick on the training ground or in the dressing room, don't worry about that, but anything we had to say to the players was said face-to-face, never in public.

The coaching, tactics, and team selection; I found that easy. I enjoyed that side of the job. For me, the hardest part of those early days in management was speaking to a group of twenty-odd players and trying to keep their attention. They didn't all agree with me, and not all of them listened. Some may have played against me and didn't like me. Dressing rooms are full of egos and different personalities.

Carlo Ancelotti said, "Everybody has the will to win, but only the best have the will to prepare." I love that quote because it's so true. Eric and I were very thorough in our match day preparation, never leaving anything to chance. Players like to have responsibility; they like to be told what you want them to do and how you want them to do it. As a manager, you can give the players all the information they need, but on Saturday it's up to them to put it into practice.

I liked to name the team as late as possible, usually on the morning of a game, sometimes even in the afternoon, to make sure there weren't any last-minute mishaps that meant I'd need to change the line-up. As a player, I'd witnessed managers announcing the team the night before a game – someone got injured overnight and the manager had to ask the player he'd previously dropped to play. I didn't want to do that. I wanted everyone to be in the right mindset, and it's hard to motivate a player when he's been pissed off all night because he thinks he's not playing.

Brian Clough used to put the team sheet up on the wall and then walk away. If you weren't in the team, he expected you to just get on with it. That might have worked for him, but I always sat players down and explained to them why they weren't in the line-up.

I've mentioned the importance of having a strong dressing room, and that's achieved by having strong leaders. At Barnsley, Neil Redfearn and Gerry Taggart were fantastic. Gerry loved a pint, but he was great for the team because he was good at getting the lads together and making sure there was unity. Redders was a little different, quieter off the pitch, but a general on it, and his performances for us were brilliant.

At first, I found it quite hard to play and manage. I was a bit blindsided by trying to do everyone else's jobs, rather than focusing on my own, and my performances weren't as good as they should have been. I got to grips with it after a few games when I started to concentrate on my own performance, and I ended up playing some of the best football I'd played in a long time. I had a lot of experience, so I understood what was going on around me.

I played in the majority of our games during the 1994/95 season, as we exceeded expectations and finished sixth. In any other season, that would have been enough to qualify for the play-offs, but because the Premier League was being restructured to reduce the number of teams, we missed out. We were very disappointed. We wanted to go one step further, and we had great belief in ourselves, although I don't think anyone outside the club thought we were capable of winning promotion.

The fans were turning up in their droves, and bear in mind that at the time, Barnsley wasn't an easy place to live in. The mines were closing, people were being made redundant, others were on benefits, and money was tight. The football club were giving them a little bit of relief. The whole town got behind us, which was brilliant. The supporters were absolutely fantastic, getting behind me and the team, which was a big weight off my mind. Throughout my career, I set up my teams to entertain the spectators. Even though we didn't get the promotion the fans wanted, they believed in the players and what we were trying to achieve, and this was evident in season ticket sales for the following season.

I was as fit as I'd ever been, but I made the decision to hang up my boots. I thought it would be tough, but it was actually quite an easy decision. I just couldn't continue with the heavy workload; I wanted to focus on the coaching side and watch the game from the touchline to gain a different perspective.

I certainly can't complain about my career: nearly eight hundred appearances, over one hundred goals, twenty-four caps with one goal for Northern Ireland, three League Cup winners' medals, and one Anglo-Scottish Cup winners' medal. I achieved a lot more than I'd set out to, but it was time for a new chapter in my career, even though, at thirty-five years of age, I was still capable of performing in the Championship.

I also had to consider my family. As a player, I'd finish training and be home in the afternoon, so I got to see my children grow up. As a manager, I was never at home. I was either at the football club or on the road, and it was too much. Sometimes I wouldn't come home until bedtime, other times I might pop back for some tea before heading out again. It was full on, and if Karen hadn't been so understanding, it could have put a strain on our relationship. But, as always, Karen was fantastic and supported me in everything I did. I've been blessed with a great partner, and we managed things very well.

Even though it was the right thing to do, my retirement left a bit of a gap in the team that needed filling, and that's when Neil Redfearn came to the fore. He'd been a good player before, but he certainly took on the mantle in midfield, bringing everyone together. Redders scored goals on a consistent basis, was a real playmaker, and I was fortunate that we already had him in the squad to step up another level.

Andy Payton was another who stepped up, scoring twenty goals during the 1995/96 season. He played on the shoulder of defenders, was quick, sharp, and always in the box looking to get on the end of crosses. He scored a lot of scruffy goals, as all good strikers do, and he was good as gold for us. He had a little bit of a reputation off the pitch, but he never caused us any problems. We knew he was one of the lads, but we turned a blind eye to a certain degree because it didn't affect his football. While he was in a rich vein of form, and scoring goals, we let him do his own thing.

We had a few departures and I brought in some new players to give everyone a lift. New players are more receptive to feedback; they listen more than the players who have been around for three or four years, and have sometimes developed a deaf ear.

The new arrivals were exactly what we needed; solid pros with a wealth of experience to help the young lads.

Jan Molby came in on loan from Liverpool. Everyone knew about Jan, but no one knew how good he actually was until his first day at training, when he was absolutely magnificent. The lads were in awe. He was jaw-dropping at times, capable of putting the ball on a sixpence. He didn't run around a lot, but he was like a magnet at times, drawing the ball to him. His arrival gave everyone a massive lift, even though he was only with us for a short amount of time.

Peter Shirtliff came to us from Wolves. I'd played with him before when we were at Sheffield Wednesday together, so I knew exactly what I was going to get from him. He wasn't flash, he fit into the dressing room and just got on with his job. Shirty was so reliable – a seven out of ten every week – and was a massive help to the youngsters.

Unfortunately, we lost Gerry Taggart to Bolton Wanderers. He'd forged a reputation as a terrific left-sided centre half, and they were few and far between. He was good at what he did, and his departure left a huge hole, but we turned to Arjan De Zeeuw, a dutchman we'd had our eye on for a while.

We'd heard about Arjan, and he'd impressed me when I watched him on videos, so we brought him over to take a closer look. As soon I saw him up close, I decided to sign him. He was strong, although not brilliant on the ball, with all due respect. But he played it simple, and that's all we wanted. He was a terrific defender.

Arjan and Shirty hit it off straight away, even though they were chalk and cheese, and they formed a great partnership.

We finished tenth in the 1995/96 season. We played some great football, but we ran out of steam towards the end, and only won one of our final ten games as our promotion bid faltered. It was a long season, and with a small squad, it just caught up with us. We'd shown we were on the right track, though, and I knew that with one or two additions we could mount another promotion charge.

CHAPTER 13
Just like watching Brazil

Finishing tenth and missing out on the play-offs turned out to be a blessing in disguise. It endorsed the fact that although we were close, we still needed one or two new players. In fairness to the board, they were football people as well as businessmen, John in particular. They understood that we were short, so I didn't have to bang the chairman's door down, which was a big, big help. I was given some money to sign some new players, and it was crucial that I spent it wisely.

As part of the rebuilding process, I had to move a few lads on, including Owen Archdeacon, Brendan O'Connell, and Charlie Bishop. It's always difficult to tell someone they aren't in your plans, and it's understandable that they aren't happy. I'm sure the departing players thought I was in the wrong, but I had to make the decisions I thought were right for the football club.

When it comes to signing a new player, it's important to do a bit of research. I know that Sir Alex Ferguson employed people to look into every aspect of a potential signing's life before making an offer. That would have been nice, but we didn't have that luxury. We were shopping at Tesco, while Sir Alex was shopping at Harrods!

I'd always do a bit of homework when I'd identified a player, and I'd ask around: Is he a good lad or a bad lad? Will he cause any problems? What's he like in the dressing room? We brought in players we'd watched ourselves or lads who'd impressed us when playing against us. Sometimes some of our players recommended a former teammate, so we'd take a look at them, although they aren't always the most reliable of sources as they tend to look after their mates.

A lot of the time, it was a case of keeping my ear to the ground. Whether that was managers giving us a player on a free or allowing us to take a promising youngster on loan – sometimes other managers gave me a tip, and that's how we found out about Clint Marcelle.

Sir Bobby Robson, as manager of Porto, had identified Clint and Jovo Bosancic as two talented players. But when Sir Bobby joined Barcelona, he didn't think they were Barcelona quality, so he rang me and suggested I take a look at them. We'd never have known about Jovo and Clint had it not been for Sir Bobby, bless him. Those two boys turned out to be absolutely paramount to our future success.

Clint was excellent running with the ball, tricky, small, and very elusive to the opposition. Along with Neil Redfearn, he gave us an attacking threat from midfield. Clint was born in Trinidad and had played in Portugal, so coming to Barnsley was a huge culture shock for him. I remember him sitting in the changing room wearing a duffle coat because he was that cold – and that was in August!

He was brilliant, though, and settled in very quickly, as did Jovo, and that's down to the players in the dressing room. They were a social group, and everyone was involved. When you've got that kind of environment, new signings are able to relax and acclimatise straight away.

Eric and I decided to play three at the back – an attacking formation – and we wanted players who could fit into that system.

When Jose Mourinho went into Chelsea and played three at the back, everyone was saying, "Crickey, this is good." We'd played that system at Barnsley a decade earlier!

We brought in Neil Thompson, a thirty-three-year-old left wing back. He was absolutely brilliant, and his arrival gave Nicky Eaden a new lease of life on the right-hand side.

We wanted to pass the ball out from the back, so we needed defenders who wouldn't give the ball away. It was important that we retained possession when we won the ball back, not just boot it anywhere, so I looked for defenders who could play. Matty Appleby joined us from Darlington as a midfielder, but we played him in defence as he had the ability to step out from the back and start an attack.

Our midfielders needed to be good on the ball but also be

prepared to do the dirty work and turn defence into attack very quickly. Our system required footballers, but they all needed to put a shift in too.

Our final two signings were strikers John Hendrie and Paul Wilkinson, who both arrived from Middlesbrough to give us the firepower upfront.

It was a great transfer window for us; a good mixture of experience and youth, British and foreign players, and they all clicked from day one.

Pre-season training, for me, was about getting the lads together and building a good team spirit. We didn't have the money to go to all these glorious destinations that the Premier League clubs visit these days, so we often went to Devon or Scotland to train and play a few games. We let the lads have a bit of freedom and allowed them to do what they were going to do, as long as they were ready to work when we needed them to.

I understood that the players were young lads, and I had to trust them to a certain extent. We didn't put restrictions on them; we trusted them to make the right decisions. If one or two had a pint on a Friday night, we let them. We drew the line at certain things, of course. We didn't expect them to go out and get pissed out of their minds the night before a game, but a glass of wine or a beer was quite acceptable – as long as they performed.

Everyone likes to prepare for a game differently, so we encouraged them to do what they needed to do to make themselves comfortable and get their heads in the right place for matchday. As long as players played to their maximum, that was good enough. I set very high standards, but I didn't ever want anyone to feel that they'd let anyone down. Players play better when they are confident, so I never yelled at anyone for an honest mistake or a stray pass. Mind you, I was never afraid to dish out a bollocking if one was needed.

Darren Sheridan, John's younger brother, was a great lad with a fantastic sense of humour. He was packing boxes in a warehouse until Viv and I brought him to Barnsley and turned him into a professional footballer. We'd known about him for a while. Shez was a very aggressive player, despite his short stature, and he had a good left foot. I loved him to death.

Shez couldn't drive, so had to rely on lifts to get to the club.

Andy Payton often picked him up, but Andy could be unreliable. If Darren wasn't where he should have been by a certain time, Andy would drive in without him, so Shez was often late. There was always an excuse too. If he travelled in by train, the train would break down on the way. So many excuses, and in the end, I'd had enough.

"The next time you're late I will fine you a week's wage," I told him one day.

"Oh fucking hell, gaffer. It's not my fault, it's Payton. He's a nightmare," Darren said.

"I'm telling you, Darren. It's your responsibility to be here on time for training."

A few days later, I got a call while I was sat in my office. "Gaffer, it's Shez. I'm sorry, but I'm going to be a bit late today. Payton didn't pick me up."

I went mad. "What have I fucking told you? It's every day. You're fined a week's wage. I'm finished with you now, that's it, done."

And then there was a knock on the door. "Yes," I yelled, still fuming. Shez popped his head around the door. He'd been standing in the corridor when he rang me from his mobile phone. He was winding me up! That was just the way he was, such a great kid. I wish I could have got him earlier in his career because I think he could have gone on to achieve a lot more.

That was the kind of relationship I had with a lot of players. We could have a laugh, but there had to be a level of authority too, and I hope I struck the right balance between the two.

Eric and I had been telling the players how good they were, and they started to believe in themselves. We felt we'd got everything right during pre-season, but no matter how well you prepare, you never know, for sure, how the players will react until they take to the field.

Our season kicked off on 17th August 1996 at the Hawthornes, and we beat West Brom 2-1 with a debut goal from Clint. It was incredible, a real eye-opener. Towards the end of the match, I turned to Eric and said, "Blimey, we've got a chance of going up here."

"Calm down, Dan. It's only one game," he replied. But I wasn't bothered if we'd played one game or ten; I'd seen enough to know that we were capable of beating anyone. You can't turn off that sort of quality; you can only build on it.

And build on it we did, winning the next five games, including a 2-1 win against Manchester City at Maine Road. City were everyone's favourite for promotion, so that was a huge victory. The only concern I had was whether we had peaked too soon, but when I looked at the players, their energy was fantastic, even in training. Players like Neil Redfearn performed in training like he did in a match. It wasn't about how good we were; we knew we were good enough. The question was could we be consistent enough?

After a blip in October when we didn't win once, we picked ourselves up, played some fantastic football, and were always in and around the promotion places. A big factor in our success was Neil Redfearn, who scored nineteen goals from midfield that year. He was unbelievable.

Redders covered every blade of grass, and he had so much confidence that he'd shoot from anywhere, even when he should pass. I'd stand on the touchline shouting, "Redders, pass it, pass it – great goal!"

He was a terrific striker of the ball with both feet, and his goals from midfield were a huge bonus. If your midfielder is scoring almost twenty goals a season, you're not going to be bottom of the league, that's for sure.

Towards the back end of the season, as we chased promotion, it was important we took the pressure off the players and tried to relax them. It helped that I'm a very relaxed person anyway, never getting too ahead of myself or too down.

We were very close to going up. I knew it, the fans knew it, and the board and chairman knew it. They were all excited, giddy as hell was John Dennis, but they were also nervous. I couldn't let the players feel those nerves or get too carried away.

I started to give the lads a day or two off to spend time with their families, to get away from the football club and the constant talk of promotion. When they came back, we focused on the following game and how we could win it, never getting further ahead of ourselves than our next opponents. The day before a match was spent having fun on the training ground, again trying to keep everyone nice and relaxed.

The only game where we allowed ourselves to think about promotion was at home against Bradford on 26th April 1997, the match where Michael had sold Karen, Laurie, and Carrie's seats. Before then, it was all conjecture; if Wolves do this, and we do that, etc. It wasn't in our hands until then. But suddenly, the Premier League was within our sights. Our destiny was in our own hands. Beat Bradford, and we're up. The Holy Grail was right there in front of us.

The players knew what was at stake, so I didn't need to sit them down and build the match up. Quite the opposite, in fact. The night before the game, we got fish and chips for the lads to keep their feet on the ground. Everyone else – the fans, the press, the staff, the whole town – were all talking about promotion, but we didn't mention it once. When we finished our meal, we sent the lads home with instructions to put their feet up and stick a film on or listen to some music. Anything but tune in to the local radio station or look at the league table. I'm sure some of them did, which may have helped them, but we wanted everyone to be relaxed.

On the day of the game, there were a few butterflies and nerves, especially when we walked out onto the pitch and heard the supporters. They were magnificent, getting behind the lads during what was a difficult time for the town. As I sat in the dugout and saw the eighteen thousand fans packed into Oakwell, that's when I realised how much progress we'd made. There were only eight thousand in attendance for my managerial debut just two and a half years earlier.

There were a few scary moments at the start of the game, where we almost conceded, but our nerves were settled when Paul Wilkinson put us in front in the twenty-first minute. As soon as the ball hit the back of the net, I knew we weren't going to lose.

However, it wasn't enough not to lose, we had to win, and one goal is never enough, even though we were a good defensive unit. Bradford had some good players, and there were some very near misses. John Dreyer, who I'd played with at Luton, squandered a big chance, hitting the post when it was easier to score. At that moment, I turned to Eric and said, "That's us in the Premier League now."

Three minutes from time, Clint Marcelle scored our second goal of the game, and there was a collective sigh of relief before reality kicked in, and we realised we'd been promoted. That's when the celebrations really began in the terraces.

There was a pitch invasion when the referee blew the final whistle. It took us an age to get off the pitch because the players were being mobbed by the jubilant supporters. We did well to make it back to the dressing room, where a lot of the lads were bollock-naked as everyone wanted their kit, a piece of history.

I'd won promotion to the Premier League as a player, and I'd won trophies at Wembley, but promotion with Barnsley was the finest moment in my career. When you're not playing, you aren't able to change the game on the pitch, and I always felt a little helpless standing on the touchline. So to see the players put into practise everything Eric and I had been doing with them, day in and day out, was so satisfying – particularly because we'd taken Barnsley up, a club who'd never before graced the top flight. It was fantastic for everyone.

The town was alive, and everything that had gone against the supporters with the mines closing was forgotten about for those few seasons. They were so proud of the team, and I know I've already said this, but I need to repeat it – the fans were magnificent.

The celebrations continued for a week; I don't think the lads were sober for a long time. We went to Oxford United for the last game of the season . . . and lost 5-1! The lads were still pissed! The fans were too, in fairness. So many of them made the long trip down to Oxford, and they were laughing and joking throughout the match, even when we were five down, which isn't normally the case.

The supporters understood, though. The discipline that we'd instilled in the players all season went out of the window and they just went out there to enjoy themselves. A few lads were showboating, playing up to the fans, but I think they deserved those ninety minutes. I don't think they were particularly bothered what the score was, and I have to say, neither was I! I wanted to win the game, of course, but deep down I wasn't really bothered. We'd done our job, completed our mission.

To top it all off, I won the League Managers' Association (LMA) Manager of the Year award. Every year I attended the awards ceremony, so I travelled down to London as usual and was sitting at my table, feeling a bit squiffy because I'd had a few by then, when I heard my name read out. Manager of the Year! It was a massive surprise. I felt very emotional and overwhelmed. I couldn't really speak. Whatever I did say during my acceptance speech was said through tears. My staff were sitting with me at the table which was great as they got to share the success.

It is such a special award because the winner is voted for by the managers of all ninety-two football league clubs, and the nominees included people like Sir Alex Ferguson, who'd won the Premier League; Ruud Gullit, who'd won the FA Cup; and Martin O'Neill, who had won the League Cup. So to come out on top was huge. It's a great privilege to be given that accolade and something I'll never ever forget.

CHAPTER 14
We are Premier League

When the celebrations eventually died down, we had Premier League football to look forward to, and for most of the lads, it would be their first time in the top flight.

Winning promotion put me in a tough position because, in my mind, I wanted to give the lads who took us up a chance to play in the Premier League, but the reality was that they perhaps weren't going to be good enough to keep us there. I needed one or two new players, but my hand was forced in a way because we didn't have many pennies. The training facilities needed a massive upgrade, the infrastructure at Oakwell had to be improved to meet Premier League standards, and that all came at a cost. The board were very frugal, and as a result, the club are still reaping the rewards of the Premier League money.

The ground had to be tarted up and the dressing rooms had to be redesigned. What they did in the away changing room – and this was nothing to do with me, by the way – was have the heating switched on and turned to its maximum setting all the time. The thermostat was boxed in underneath the seats, so you couldn't turn it down, and the window was nailed shut, so you couldn't open that either. It was on all year round and must have cost us a fortune – even we couldn't turn it off! The temperature was set to the same heat in the middle of winter as it was in summer.

I suppose the groundsman thought it would give us an advantage, but I always found things like that gave the opposition an incentive to stick one on us. There was one game against Spurs in the FA Cup when David Ginola was getting changed in the corridors, swearing like anything because it was too hot in the dressing room. The rest of the Tottenham players came out and gave us stick in the tunnel. Although we won the game, Ginola was so fired up that he scored a great goal, so it could have backfired.

As a result of the redevelopment work – and probably the heating bill – the transfer funds available to me weren't as high as I would have liked. Maybe it was a blessing because we could have squandered it and not had anything to show for it like Bradford City did a few years later.

When you look at the clubs who were also in the Premier League at that time, our squad couldn't compete. We brought in a few lads for a couple of quid, but it was always going to be tough. Especially when you consider that we spent a total of £5,750,000, while the other two promoted clubs (Bolton and Crystal Palace) spent £9,000,000 and £14,000,000 respectively.

More than anything, I wanted us to continue to play in the same style that had taken us up. We knew that we'd have to defend more, but we wanted to continue with the attacking philosophy that the fans loved. We always went out to win games and to entertain people, so we never set up negatively. Maybe we could have sat back, but I wanted us to have a go.

When we were out of possession, we needed the whole team to defend, and when we won the ball back, that first pass out of defence was crucial so we could counter. That's where the strikers came into their own. We needed to have an attacking threat, and that's why we made Gjorgji Hristov our record signing.

Gjorjgi was a Macedonian international striker, and we'd been tipped off about him. We needed someone with pace, strength, and an eye for goal. We sent our scouts out to Serbia to watch him in action for Partizan, and they said he did very well, so we paid £1,500,000 for him.

He upset the locals straight away when he said that the girls from Barnsley were all ugly! He got caught up in a conversation that he shouldn't have been having when a local reporter asked him to compare ladies from Macedonia to Yorkshire lasses. He took a bit of stick from the fans for that.

He was a good player, although he lacked the experience of English football which meant he struggled for consistency. At times he was unplayable, in other games he was a passenger, so he had mixed fortunes for us. That's the risk you take with players; you could find a real gem, a duff, or something in between. Beggars can't be choosers, and sometimes we had to sign a player who was tenth in the pecking order.

Eric Tinkler, a South African international midfielder, was another new signing. He was a big lad, a good unit, though not blessed with pace. But he was a good footballer, comfortable on the ball, and could spray passes around the pitch. Eric very rarely gave the ball away, which was so important for us because when you're out of possession in the Premier League, you can be chasing shadows. Eric is definitely up there with my better signings.

Another good addition was Darren Barnard, a left wing back who we signed from Bristol City. He was a Welsh international who'd spent five years at Chelsea. He had plenty of experience, but aged just twenty-five, he was also one for the future.

Darren was a very good player, great going forward, pacy, and fit perfectly into our system. He could also play left back in a back four, which gave us options. Barnard was one of our most consistent players, and I felt we were very fortunate to get him.

Paul Wilkinson left in the summer, and we replaced him with Ashley Ward, an experienced centre forward who was playing for Derby reserves at the time. Despite the fact he was a proven goal scorer, no one else had taken a chance on him, so as soon as we knew he was available, we swooped. We needed a striker who would work hard out of possession, not just stand-up top waiting for the ball. Wardy had a fantastic work ethic. He had Premier League experience and we knew he'd settle in straight away. He was a good lad, a great team player, and fit into the dressing room well. Oh, and he scored goals for us too!

Our recruitment method was based on signing players with the attributes that suited our system, but some of our targets demanded ridiculous wages that we just couldn't afford. If we could have guaranteed that we'd stay up, we might have paid a bit more, but we knew it was going to be a long, hard slog of a season, and if we did go down, we didn't want to be saddled with massive wages. There was no way John, the board, or I, would put the future of Barnsley in jeopardy. The board were the custodians of the club and had a responsibility for our financial future. Again, if I went to John to ask, "Any money?"

"Fuck off, Dan. You've had all you're going to get," was the inevitable reply. I expected that, and it didn't upset me at all. We just had to get on with what we had and make the best of the players at our disposal.

Before the season began, we broke the fixtures down into chunks of four, five, or six games over a month and calculated the return we'd need from those games. It didn't matter who we were playing; we looked at how many points we needed from each chunk. We got it wrong at times, of course we did, but that's how we worked it out.

Our campaign kicked off at home to West Ham. The Hammers hadn't had a good season the year before, and everyone looked at that match as a winnable one for us. *West Ham aren't a good team, so we've got a good chance of getting off to a winning start;* we thought. Maybe that was naivety on our part, because we'd never seen them live, and neither had the fans.

As we lined up in the tunnel before the game, we realised they were huge. The size of our players compared to theirs was unbelievable – they were like giants.

Neil Redfearn gave us an early lead, but John Hartson and Frank Lampard both scored in the second half, and we lost 2-1. It was a real eye-opener for us. If they weren't considered a good Premier League team, we wondered what else was ahead of us. At that point, we knew we had to roll our sleeves up and do better.

Our next match was against Crystal Palace, and Redders (who else?) scored the only goal of the game to give us our first win of the season. It was a big relief to get our first points on the board, away from home too. Selhurst Park was not an easy place to go, so I was pleased with that result. No matter who you play in any season, you always want to get an early win to settle the nerves. Nowadays, you see league tables after the opening match, so you can find yourself sitting bottom of the league on day one, which can affect you psychologically.

After the victory at Palace, we were brought crashing back down to earth against Chelsea at Oakwell. They were outstanding, and showed us what the teams in the upper echelons of the Premier League were like. We knew there would be a gulf in quality, and we saw it for first-hand in that game.

Chelsea ran riot and beat us 6-0, with Gianluca Vialli scoring four. To be honest, it could have possibly been even more.

Welcome to the Premier League!

Victory over Bolton in our next match was a good way to bounce back, but we followed that up with six defeats before getting back to winning ways with a 2-0 victory over Coventry on 20th of October 1997. So after eleven games, we had just nine points which was below the target we'd set. Very disappointing, especially as most of the games we'd played were against teams we felt we should have got something from.

Five days later, we suffered a 7-0 defeat at Old Trafford to Manchester United. You can't do much about a rampant United and you're always going to get the odd result like that. Although on the day it's embarrassing, you can't let it get you down. The supporters certainly didn't. When Karel Poborsky scored United's seventh, our fans were singing, "We're gonna win 8-7!" They were enjoying every moment of our inaugural Premier League campaign, and the score line wasn't going to wipe the smile off their faces.

Our supporters were fantastic. No matter which stadium we were playing at, they always outsang the home crowd. They followed us up and down the country, and they endeared themselves to the opposition fans.

After most games, managers get together to have a chat about the match, and this one was no different. Sir Alex Ferguson offered me a drink and I took it, but I didn't want to be there. We'd just been stuffed 7-0; I didn't want to see his face. I didn't want to see anyone, but I went in, shook hands, and we discussed the game. It's quite uncomfortable as you don't know what to say. I've been on the other end of that situation, where we've battered someone, and it's no more comfortable then. Sir Alex was great; he was very humble and respectful about Barnsley.

I just wanted to go home, but Karen and I had arranged to meet some friends for dinner in Manchester that evening, so we were staying in a hotel. We went to an Italian restaurant we'd been to before, and as we walked through the door, the owner quipped, "Good evening, Danny. Table for seven?"

Sir Alex is a manager whom I have a lot of respect for. Roy Hodgson is another. I'd bumped into him on the circuit but hadn't ever properly met him, so I was looking forward to talking to him after our game against Blackburn on 1st of November.

We drew the game 1-1, and before I went off to do the television interviews, I told Roy to meet me in my office, where we'd have a beer or a glass of wine. So I did my interview, and when I got back, he was sat in my office with a friend of mine, little Chris Colton. Roy said, "Dan. Sky tried to come in here to set up an interview. Did you know about that?"

"No," I replied.

"Good," he said. "Because I told them to fuck off and to not ever come into a manager's office again without their permission."

Chris turned to me and said, "Don't worry, Dan. It was much worse than that!"

Roy is someone people think of as very calm and placid, and people underestimate him; I think that's why he's done so well over the years. He went up a lot in my estimation that day, and he taught me that I needed to have that ruthlessness in my back pocket.

On 22nd of November we turned up at Anfield on the back of a heavy defeat against Southampton. I knew the lads were looking a bit nervous, so I took a leaf out of Mr Clough's book and took the lads to the pub the night before the game for a couple of pints of Guinness.

Anfield is a bit of a cauldron, and they had some wonderful players like Michael Owen, Paul Ince, Jamie Redknapp, and Steve McManaman. We had Lars Leese in goal, a German we'd signed in the summer, because our regular goalkeeper, Dave Watson, was injured, so we knew it wasn't going to be easy. It was a tough game, and they had a whole host of chances, but fortunately for us, their striker, Karl-Heinz Riedle, had one of those games where he just couldn't score. He kept getting into good positions but missed the target every single time.

In the thirty-fifth minute, the ball fell nicely to Ashley Ward, who put it into the back of the net to give us a lead against the run of play. Liverpool came at us with everything they had, but we rode our luck and held on for a famous victory. If I'm honest, we had a bit of a pasting, but we got away with it, and it was a great confidence booster. Whether we got battered or not, the score printed in the newspaper the next day said 1-0 to us, and that was all that counted.

It didn't matter who we were playing, we never went in thinking our opponents were better than us. We had the mindset where we felt we could hold our own against anyone, and on certain days we could. Anyone, even if it's the Dog and Duck against Manchester United, will likely get one chance in a game. You just have to make sure you take it. At Anfield that day, we took our chance. We celebrated to a certain degree – beating Liverpool is a fantastic achievement – but we couldn't get too carried away as there was still a lot of work to be done.

By the time January 1998 came around, we had started to get to grips with the Premier League. I felt we still lacked a bit of firepower, so I signed Jan Åge Fjørtoft from Sheffield United for £800,000. Jan had scored goals in the top flight for Swindon Town and Middlesbrough, and he hit the ground running, not just with the goals he scored, but also with the way in which he led the line.

Whilst survival was our priority, we were enjoying a decent run in the FA Cup, which started with a 1-0 win over Bolton in the third round before we saw off Spurs 3-1 in a replay to set up a fifth-round tie against Manchester United away. We'd lost 7-0 the last time we played at Old Trafford, but we'd learnt from that game and more than held our own this time. John Hendrie gave us the lead in the first half before Teddy Sheringham equalised a few minutes later.

In the last minute of the game, we were denied a stone wall penalty. Gary Neville wiped out Andy Liddell in front of the Stretford End, but the ref didn't give it. I couldn't believe it. Neil Redfearn was our penalty taker, and he didn't miss, so I'm convinced that would have been the winning goal.

Instead, we had to settle for a replay in front of a packed Oakwell. What a game!

We won 3-2 thanks to an early goal from Hendrie and two goals from our young full back, Scott Jones. Scotty's heading ability was underestimated because he wasn't the biggest lad in the team. The bigger players are always the most prominent and tend to be marked at set pieces. Scotty just snuck up and scored two great headers, and the fans went absolutely bananas.

Scott was also a very talented cricketer, and when I found out that he was playing for a cricket team during the summer, I had to try and reign him in, although I'm sure he took no notice of me. He just had a love for both sports. He was a cracking lad and a joy to be around.

We lost to eventual finalists Newcastle United in the quarter-final, but the results in the cup showed that we could beat anyone on our day. The problem was that we had to have our best team available each week. I didn't have the luxury of a squad that I could rotate, so if our best eleven weren't available we knew we'd be in for a struggle.

When Liverpool came to Oakwell on the 28th of March 1998, we had won three games in a row for the first time all season, and although we were eighteenth in the league, we were only two points behind Everton in sixteenth, with a game in hand, so we remained confident that we could do enough to stay up.

Liverpool felt they had a point to prove, having lost to us at Anfield, and they were in the title race along with Arsenal and Manchester United, so again, we knew it was going to be a very tough game.

We started the match very well, playing some great football, and took the lead in the thirty-seventh minute when Neil Redfearn finished off a great move. I could see that the lads were up for it, but then Liverpool equalised bang on halftime with Karl Heinz Riedle making amends for his misses at Anfield.

Although 1-1 at the break was pleasing, I felt a little deflated as we'd been the better side, and I felt we deserved to be in front. Still, I knew that if we carried on playing like we had, we would have a chance of coming away with the three points.

Unfortunately, in my opinion, the referee, Gary Willard, had a horrendous game and sent off three of our players in the second half. He got so many things wrong and was too quick to give decisions against us. It's not small club syndrome; even Roy Evans, Liverpool's manager, couldn't believe his eyes. Willard was very quick to send players off for little offences.

The first red card was given to Darren Barnard in the fifty-third minute. Liverpool had a breakaway, and Michael Owen got across Darren and went down, forty yards from goal. It shouldn't have been a yellow, let alone a red, but the ref sent him off immediately. Owen went down far too easily for my liking, but even if the referee thought it was a foul, Owen was still forty yards away from goal. There is no way that was a clear goal scoring opportunity.

Five minutes later, Riedle scored his second to make it 2-1, and then Chris Morgan was sent off. Owen was running away from the goal towards the touchline when Morgan, a very strong boy, tackled him and the Liverpool striker went down holding his face. It wasn't violent conduct by any means. Willard was miles away, so he could hardly have seen anything, but once again, he didn't hesitate to bring out the red card.

With five minutes to go, Hristov won us a penalty, a definite one that the ref couldn't ignore, and Redders brought the scores level again.

In the last minute of the game, frustration boiled over, and Darren Sheridan had an argument with Jamie Redknapp and stupidly pushed him away with his hands. If you raise your hands, you have to suffer the consequences, and that was possibly one that the ref got right. Seconds later, Steve McManaman scored the winner for Liverpool.

I'm usually a fairly calm person, but I admit I lost it a bit that day, just like Willard had lost control of the game. He was no stranger to confrontation because if it wasn't hard enough to be a referee, he was also an Inland Revenue officer! He was so arrogant in the way he dismissed the players. That's not the way to do it, and the sending-offs were very harsh and difficult to take. I don't think he was against us because we were Barnsley; he just had a bad day like we all have.

At one stage, he apparently abandoned the game and left the pitch, but didn't consult me, Roy Evans, or any of the players. He just walked off down the tunnel. When he returned to the field of play, twelve or so Barnsley fans ran onto the pitch and tried to get at him. Jan Åge Fjørtoft rugby tackled one lad to the ground in what was the best tackle I've seen in my life, especially as I'd never seen Jan tackle anyone before then! Liverpool's Paul Ince was great too, helping to calm the fans down before things got too serious. Jan saved us from a massive fine and possible points deduction. There was an enquiry because fans had invaded the pitch, but fortunately, we just got a slap on the wrist.

I still don't know what happened that day. Willard lost the

plot in my view. I'm not writing this to have a go at him because he had a good career as a referee, but that game certainly wasn't his finest hour and a half.

I tried to go and see the ref after the match, but he didn't want to see me. Nowadays, you have half an hour after every game, but back then, you could only speak to them if the ref agreed to see you. I suppose it was a blessing really, as maybe my frustrations would have come out in private.

I didn't try and play it down during my post-match interview, but I had to choose my words carefully. I didn't want to get in trouble with the FA, so I made it clear that I was fuming without leaving the door open for anyone to fine me.

There are suggestions that referees should be interviewed after a game and asked to explain their decisions, but I don't agree with that as it'll open a can of worms. Their job is difficult enough as it is, and if you bring them in front of the cameras every time they make a mistake, I think there is a danger that we'll lose respect for referees completely. You've seen what it's like when reporters start to dig out managers when they are having a bad time, and I can't see how doing the same to refs will help them. As a manager, I would like an explanation privately, but I don't think it'll do anyone any good if you haul them in front of the cameras after every game.

On the subject of referees, I never really bought into the train of thought that the big clubs get the big decisions. When you're playing for a smaller team, there is the feeling that these small decisions, and sometimes big decisions, are going against you all the time, but I don't think they are. You need to have a siege mentality as a smaller club, and you perhaps get more bookings because you're going into tackles in a more aggressive manner because you're fighting for your lives.

If the referees genuinely favoured the big clubs, we'd have a massive problem in English football. I think we have an organisation of referees and officials where you cannot question their integrity. I can honestly say that I've never seen any bias. There are one or two things that may happen in a game that go against you, but that's not bias. Referees make mistakes, and so do players. So do managers, and so do chairmen. Refs are under enormous pressure; they get stick from all areas; fans, players, media, and chairmen. Like goalkeepers, they can have a good game and then make one bad decision, and that's all people will remember.

It's not an easy job, and I think that VAR has heaped even more pressure on them, even though it should have eased it because it isn't being used properly. I'm sure it will get better. At least, I hope it will. Refereeing is one of the hardest jobs on a football field.

The Liverpool match was a big punch in the face for us and we never really recovered. We lost three key players, not just for that game but also for the following few as they were suspended. We didn't have the squad to replace them.

We fancied our chances in our next game, against Blackburn, but we got beaten 2-1 with a late goal from Kevin Gallacher. Maybe the suspended trio could have made the difference – who knows?

The remaining games were all very close, but we kept losing by the odd goal. Sometimes that's harder than being battered 6-0.

On the 2nd of May 1998, we lost to Leicester City at Filbert Street, and relegation was confirmed. We looked a bit nervous and didn't play with the freedom we usually did. They scored a scrappy goal, and I knew then that it wasn't going to be our day.

I never wanted to admit that we would be relegated. Everyone had expected us to go down; most thought we would be adrift at the bottom, but to get to the penultimate day of the season shows that we went down fighting. We were all absolutely gutted, and the fans were in tears. They'd had the dream, and all of a sudden, that dream was over. It was hard to take.

It was a total contrast of emotions from twelve months previous: from the euphoria of promotion, to the devastation of relegation. My immediate thought was that I wanted to get us straight back up. That's what I told John Dennis directly after the game. I'd enjoyed my season in the Premier League, had learnt some lessons on what we lacked, and I knew what we had to do to put things right. We had a big pre-season in front of us to bring in some more quality and prepare the players for an instant promotion charge.

I didn't know it at the time, but I wouldn't be at Barnsley by the time the new season began.

CHAPTER 15
Return to Hillsborough

People had taken note of 'little Barnsley' and the way we played. Our attacking game had won over the public, and we were most peoples' second team during our stint in the top flight. Everyone wanted us to beat the big boys, and those clubs outside the Premier League looked at us as proof that dreams do come true. We had a lot of support in football, and one or two teams out there were taking note of my position because of what we'd achieved.

Our chairman, John Dennis, was very candid, and we had an agreement that he would tell me if anyone came in for me. That's not always the case, but I had such a good relationship with John and a tremendous amount of respect for him. Not that I was looking to leave, I just wanted to be kept informed.

Everton and West Brom had previously knocked on the door, and I told John to thank them very much but tell them that I was happy at Barnsley.

And then Sheffield Wednesday came calling.

In July 1998, John told me that Dave Richards, chairman of Wednesday, had made an enquiry about me. "I've told him to fuck off unless he's prepared to pay a lot of money for you," John explained. When the Owls returned and agreed to pay the compensation, John asked me what I thought.

Sheffield Wednesday were the only club I would have considered at the time, but I needed to go home and discuss it with my family. I returned the next day and told John that if I didn't take the job, I would regret it for the rest of my life. I remember Neil Warnock saying that he once turned down the chance to become the Chelsea manager, and he has regretted it ever since. I didn't want to have any regrets.

I wanted to stay at Barnsley, and if anyone else had come in for me, I would have turned them down. But the lure of returning to Hillsborough was too strong.

It was very difficult for me to leave Oakwell. The hardest thing I've ever done, even though I've always prided myself on my ability to make difficult decisions. I loved Barnsley and Wednesday, and I felt torn between two lovers. I didn't enjoy leaving, but I knew that it was the right thing for me to do.

John was fantastic about the situation, as I knew he would be, and said that he wouldn't stand in my way. Although, the one thing I have to say to put the record straight is that he had told the fans that I was staying. I never said that. I love John, but he got that a little bit wrong.

Barnsley got a lot of money for me, which softened the blow for them a little. They appointed John Hendrie as manager and moved on.

A new chapter in my career began.

The reaction of the Barnsley fans was mixed; half were calling me a traitor, and the rest were thankful for what I'd helped the club achieve. It wasn't nice to read or hear their comments, but that's football. It wasn't pleasant at the time, but I just had to accept the criticism and try and move on. I certainly didn't expect it to be all rosy when I walked away. No one was going to pat me on the back and say, "Off you go, enjoy yourself." Not when I was leaving to join their Yorkshire rivals.

I never thought about going back to Oakwell to sign any of my former players, although I would have liked one or two. Unless the club was struggling for money, I didn't think that was right, and it wasn't my style. It would have caused even more problems if I'd started nicking their players, so I dismissed that idea straight away. Nor did I think it was right to poach Eric Winstanley, so I appointed Frank Barlow as my right-hand man.

I wasn't Wednesday's first choice manager. In fact, I may have even been tenth in the pecking order. The media had reported that Walter Smith had verbally agreed to take the job, before turning it down at the last minute and joining Everton instead. I think the fans would have loved Walter after all the trophies he had won at Rangers. Whether I was second, third, or fortieth choice, I didn't mind. The Sheffield Wednesday supporters were great to me – still are – and welcomed me with open arms.

Wednesday had endured a tough season during the 1997/98 campaign, finishing in sixteenth position and only avoiding relegation by four points. As a result, my former boss, Ron Atkinson – in his second spell as manager – was sacked. Most bookies made us favourites for relegation, and that was why their first-choice targets had turned down the manager's role.

Before I accepted the job, I phoned Ron to ask his opinion. "Dan, you know the club inside out. The people upstairs know you, the fans know you, and they'll give you a bit of time, although they will also be very demanding," he said, before emphatically recommending I take the job. Receiving the backing of Big Ron was great.

He didn't tell me anything about the squad, and I didn't ask him. What I didn't want was to find out that he'd had an issue with someone, which would give me preconceived notions and could cause a problem when I didn't need one. I wanted my own opinions and I wanted to form them quickly with the help of my staff.

When I arrived at the club, there were a lot of opinions about certain players. I was bombarded with people telling me who the troublemakers were, and that wasn't helpful at all. Yes, it's important to listen to others, but I wanted to give everyone a clean slate and not receive so much negative feedback from day one.

I already knew a lot of the players, but it was important to sit down as a group to introduce myself and explain how I wanted us to play and what I expected from everyone. It takes time to get to know the lads, what makes them tick and what upsets them.

The first challenge for me was learning to deal with big-name players who expected to be treated differently. There are stars in every club – the creative ones, the goal scorers, the internationals – and they tend to have a different mindset to the others.

I soon discovered that there were a hell of a lot of egos in the dressing room, and some very strong personalities. Everyone thought that what they said was right, and that was the biggest problem we had. I had to try to get them on board straight away and for everyone to pull in the same direction. It was the biggest learning curve in my career, and looking back now, there are certain things that I would have done differently.

The biggest personalities were England international defender Des Walker and the two Italian boys, Benito Carbone and Paolo Di Canio.

I was supposed to meet Paolo on the first day of pre-season, but there was no sign of him, so I phoned him to introduce myself and find out where he was.

"Ah, hello mister. Mister Ron said I could have two extra weeks off because I had such a good season," Paolo told me. The Italians always called the manager 'mister', instead of 'gaffer' or 'boss'.

No one had told me that Paolo had been given an additional fortnight off, so I was in two minds about whether to call Ron and ask him. In the end, I decided not to because if he told me he hadn't given Paolo extra time off, we'd got a problem. I couldn't drag Paolo back when it was one man's word against another's, so I replied, "OK, Paolo. We'll speak again in a week or so, and then we'll meet when you come back."

At the start of the third week of pre-season, we were training at Bisham Abbey. By that time, the lads had been working hard and were getting their fitness up. We were doing some track work, starting at fifteen hundred metres and dropping in increments down to twenty-five metres, before going back up again. I can tell you from experience that it's not easy to do. It's hard work, and you definitely know when you've done it.

Anyway, Paolo arrived that day, and we shook hands and introduced ourselves. I told him to get his kit and go off with the fitness coach to work on some basics, before joining the rest of the lads a few days later. He turned around and said, "No. I'm not going with the fitness coach. I'm the fittest man here. I've been training all summer, so I'll join everyone else."

"No, Paolo. You're an important player for us, and I don't want you to pull a hamstring or anything like that on the track. It's for your own safety," I replied.

"No, mister. I want to do the track work with everyone else. I'm very fit," he insisted.

Right. Let's see how fucking fit you are then, I thought. So I put him with the group that contained the strongest runners and fittest lads we had. I explained what we were going to do and all the runs that we had planned.

Paolo won virtually every race he was in, and if he didn't win

145

it, he came second. I tip my hat to him. I certainly didn't expect that, but he was such a fit man with his own personal fitness coach over in Italy. He'd been working on his fitness all summer, so he knew that when he needed to perform, he could. I gained a lot of respect for him, and I quickly learnt that with players like Paolo, you have to give them a little bit of special treatment. He was a true professional and a role model for everyone else. He was exactly how I wanted my players to act away from the club.

Where Paolo was very strong-willed and full of opinions, his countryman, Benny, was the total opposite. They were chalk and cheese. Benny was more passive, certainly not as fit as Paolo, but possessed brilliant skills with both feet; he could place a ball on a six pence. From my point of view, Benny wasn't creative enough in the areas where he could do some damage, but he did things with the ball that took your breath away. He was exceptional at times, and a real fan favourite.

The problem we had was that we were Sheffield Wednesday, not Manchester United. We couldn't carry players on the defensive side and needed all ten players to defend when we were out of possession, so we had to give Benny and Paolo more set positions. They didn't like it, but we had to do it for the good of the team.

They were worried that it would take away their creativity, but we thought differently. We felt that by getting back into defensive areas to help the team out when out of possession, they would be in the right positions to spring an attack when we won the ball. Without Paolo and Benny getting back, the opposition would break through us like a knife through butter. They were our shield.

Sheffield Wednesday were owned by a hedge fund, Charterhouse, who were concerned about their return on investment, especially as the club had been struggling at the bottom end of the table for a few seasons. The bottom line was that I was told that I had no money to spend and that I had to bring the wage bill down. When I'd met the board before joining, I'd been told I would have £7,000,000 to spend. (The papers reported I had a war chest of £10,000,000 – I wish!) I was perhaps a little naïve, but the older I got, the more I learned to expect things like that from owners.

So I didn't get the financial backing I'd been expecting, but when I had a chance to fully assess the players at my disposal, I didn't think for one minute that we'd be in a relegation battle. My aim was to finish mid table or even higher. I was happy with the quality within the squad, but the culture of the club needed to change if we were to progress because there was a complete lack of unity.

There were a lot of factions within the dressing room, and I knew that it was going to be very difficult to fix. I didn't need players to go out for a meal or a drink with each other; I just needed them to have mutual respect for one another. Look at Andy Cole and Teddy Sheringham; it's been highly publicised that they don't like each other off the pitch, but when they played together, they put their differences aside and were fantastic.

One thing that was never a problem in the dressing room was the language barrier, as everyone spoke English. The only thing was I wished I spoke Italian, French, or Portuguese, as I might have known when I was getting some stick!

We had bags of quality going forward and were capable of winning games and scoring goals. When you have Di Canio and Carbone on your team sheet, opponents have to be wary, so I wasn't concerned with our attacking threat; it was our ability to defend that bothered me. When I looked back at the results from the previous season, the bottom line was that we'd conceded too many goals and lost too many games. That needed to be addressed straight away, but the personalities made it very difficult. That's when I realised why we had the problems; it wasn't a lack of ability, it was the players' egos that wouldn't allow them to stand down from their high horses.

Peter Shreeves, who had been at Wednesday for years in various roles, told me that Des Walker was a problem and didn't like to train. Under Big Ron's leadership, he'd been told to stay at home because he didn't want Des around the training ground. I knew Des very well and thought that was a bit harsh. I'd always gotten on very well with him, so I brought him back. But when it came to doing certain things with the back four, Des didn't want to do them. He'd been lightning fast when he was younger, and the fans used to sing, "You'll never beat Des Walker." Time had caught up with him, though, and as he lost his pace, he'd started to drop deeper, which gave us a wavy back line. When we wanted to play with a high line, the rest of the lads moved forward, and Des dropped off, which meant the system didn't work. Des Walker didn't agree with certain things that Emerson Thome was doing and vice versa. If your back four aren't united, you've got a huge problem.

First and foremost, when I looked at the players, I knew we had a good team, but they needed organising. They needed to be organised to play the style I wanted to play, and it all started at the back. I needed everyone to understand that clean sheets are everything, and I'm talking about the team here, not just the back four. I wanted the whole team to work together when we were out of possession, all hunting down the ball and winning it back. Then the results would come.

We needed a squad that believed in how we were going to play, so we could defend as a team and attack as a team. We needed to work as a cohesive unit. I expected my players to work their bollocks off, but not everyone agreed with that. Some only wanted to play when they had the ball at their feet and didn't want to do the other side of the game. So many individuals were just doing their own thing, and at times, it was sapping to try and get everyone on board. I respected everyone's opinions and viewpoints – maybe they were right in some cases – but I was the manager and Frank was the coach. I told the players that if they didn't want to do what we asked them to do, I'd have to go out and bring in someone else. Maybe that didn't endear me to one or two, but that was the simple truth.

You see it now with the best teams, like Manchester City and Liverpool. It doesn't matter how highly the attacking players are regarded, if they don't do the defensive work, they won't play.

It was very different to when I was playing because you can't get away with the old-school style of management. Can you imagine the uproar if I'd kicked someone's car like Mr Clough had kicked mine? That was all part of growing up in my day. It teaches you respect.

I was fortunate to have a good captain in Peter Atherton. He was a leader, fully committed to whatever he did, whether that was on the ball or heading and defending. Going forward, he wasn't of the same calibre as Paolo or Carbone, but he was a solid defender. He'd held the armband under Big Ron, and I could see that he had a lot of respect from the lads, so I stuck with him.

I needed more leaders like Peter, and I got another when I

signed midfielder Wim Jonk from PSV for £2,500,000. He was a class player, who'd been to two World Cups with Holland, won the UEFA Cup with both Ajax and Inter Milan, and had a wealth of experience. He was exactly what we needed, but unfortunately, we couldn't get him on the pitch often enough because he kept suffering with injuries, and we didn't half miss him.

In addition to his basic wage, Wim was reportedly paid £7,500 a game, even when he didn't play, which caused some discontent amongst the supporters. I don't know if that's true or not because I didn't get involved in the contract negotiations – that was done by the secretary or the chairman. I didn't know what any of the players were paid, and I preferred it that way.

My view was that if the club couldn't afford it, they wouldn't make an offer to the player. If we were handing out contracts like that, we only had ourselves to blame. You can't blame others for the consequences of your own poor decision-making. Be honest now, would you sign that contract? £7,500 every time you miss a game. I'd sign that.

How much clubs pay players is up to them, and the players aren't likely to say no to a pay rise or an inflated contract. Why should they? It's the individual's character that is the biggest factor, in my view. Again, look at Manchester City and Liverpool. You'd imagine their players are all very wealthy men, yet they still give it everything week in and week out.

The only other summer signing we made was Argentine defender Juan Cobian from Boca Juniors. We also brought in midfielder Danny Sonner from Ipswich for £75,000 a few months into the season. The lads said that Danny Sonner was an absolute snip at seventy-five grand, but not because of what he did on the pitch. It was because he was so funny in the dressing room, which was exactly what we needed at the time. He was absolutely magnificent, and everyone liked him.

The start of the season was quite mixed; in our first five games, we lost 1-0 three times and won 3-0 twice. We knew we had plenty of creativity and players who could score goals, although we had to adapt our style and play to our strikers' strengths. Di Canio and Carbone were fantastic geniuses who wanted the ball played to their feet. But there was no point playing balls into Andy Booth's feet and asking him to run at defenders. He needed a certain type of supply from out wide. Petr Rudi and Niclas Andersson could take players on and whip in crosses, which were ideal for Andy.

The first two clean sheets we kept were the most satisfying because that was the hardest part. We felt that if we got our noses in front, there was a good chance we were going to win the game, but if we went behind, there was a danger we'd concede again.

Paolo was on fire at the start of the season, but I decided to leave him out for an away fixture against Wimbledon. When you're playing against the Dons, you know that they are going to be very physical and try and bombard you by firing balls into the box. I wanted someone to come in and give them a little bit back, so I played Alan Quinn instead. As you imagine, Paolo wasn't happy about it.

The reputation of the Crazy Gang and their chairman, Sam Hamman, has been well documented. At the time, Wimbledon were ground-sharing with Crystal Palace, and the dug out at Selhurst Park was a few steps down from the pitch. During the game, I was standing on the touchline, shouting instructions to the lads, and as I walked down the steps backwards to sit in my seat, I ended up sitting on Sam's lap! He'd snuck down the side of the touchline while I was focused on the game and sat in my seat. "Fuck off, and get in your own dugout," I said to him, laughing. That was one of the daft things Wimbledon did to try and distract you from the match. He's made people eat sheep testicles, so I guess I was lucky.

We lacked the physicality to deal with the Dons, and we were 2-0 down after fifty minutes. I brought Di Canio on and he scored – and he let me know that he'd scored, by the way!

With three goals in six games, I restored Paolo to the starting lineup for our next game, a home match against Arsenal. The Gunners had won the Premier League and FA Cup double the season before, and were a very strong side. We won 1-0, but no one remembers the score. All anyone recalls is Di Canio's moment of madness.

CHAPTER 16
Paolo, what have you done?

It was always going to be a tough game for us, but in the first half we were playing very well against the champions. And then we lost Paolo Di Canio in incredible circumstances.

Paolo had been kicked from pillar to post all game and had received no protection at all from the referee, Paul Alcock. Every time he had the ball, he was fouled, and the ref did little to deter Arsenal. I was shouting from the touchline, and the crowd were becoming more and more agitated that we weren't being awarded free kicks, as were our players.

Just before half time, Nigel Winterburn came in and rattled Di Canio, knocking him down. Yet again, the ref gave nothing. Wim Jonk then fouled Patrick Vieira, who got straight back up and threw Wim down to the ground. Paolo's frustration boiled over. He ran over to Vieira and pushed him away. Then Martin Keown got involved, getting in Di Canio's face. There was a scuffle and Alcock showed Paolo the red card, which was like a red rag to a bull.

As most people know, Paolo pushed Alcock and the ref tumbled to the ground. The way he went down in instalments was just an embarrassment and still is to this day. Everyone still laughs at it, but it wasn't funny for Sheffield Wednesday at the time. The repercussions for the football club were enormous.

At half time, we had to put the incident out of our minds and focus on the game. What had gone on before had happened, and I didn't have time to start worrying about that. What we had to do was batten down the hatches and make sure we got a win, which we did. It was a great result for us.

I didn't speak to Arsenal's manager, Arsene Wenger, after the match. He stormed off the pitch very glum because he'd lost and didn't speak to anyone.

After the game, you can imagine what everyone wanted to talk about – it wasn't our 1-0 win, or Lee Briscoe's brilliant goal from twenty-yards. No one mentioned that, it was all about Paolo.

It was an unprecedented situation. If you put your hands on the referee, you're asking for trouble, and there is bound to be punishment. Having said that, I do feel that Alcock exacerbated the situation with his theatrical fall.

On the Monday morning, I phoned the referees' coordinator and asked for his number. "Do you mind if I speak to Paul?" I asked.

"We think you should," they replied, before giving me his telephone number.

So I rang Paul to apologise and ask for his help.

"Look, Dan," he said. "Maybe I overreacted. I'll speak to the FA and I will say that in my report. Don't worry."

And he did speak to the FA, but he went back on his word and told them that he'd been shoved aggressively. He didn't do what he'd told me he was going to do, which was really disappointing. Once the FA had the referee's full view, there was only going to be one outcome – and that was a lengthy ban and a big fine.

I'm not trying to defend Paolo here. What he did was wrong and completely unacceptable. But would the outcry have been the same if Alcock had stayed on his feet?

After receiving his red card, he walked down the tunnel, straight out of the ground, and caught the earliest flight he could find back to Italy, because he knew he had to get out of England and away from the media spotlight.

I tried to get hold of Paolo the day after the game and then every day for the next two weeks, but he wasn't answering his phone. We called him from loads of different numbers, but he probably recognised them, so didn't answer. Eventually, we phoned him from the club secretary's phone, and he answered. That was the only time that I spoke to him. I told him I wanted him to come back to Sheffield and that I still wanted him on the team.

Paolo told me that he wasn't in a fit state of mind to return to the club. He explained that he had medical certificates from Italian doctors that showed he was suffering from stress. He didn't apologise, but in his mind, he didn't have anything to apologise for. He was adamant that he'd been kicked all over the pitch with little protection, and that was what caused his reaction. In that respect, I can understand with viewpoint.

We had to pull together as a club and try to find the best solution for everyone involved, but it was surreal because everything was about Paolo. We'd been doing well, but no one mentioned that, which was demoralising for the rest of the lads. We were a football club, not a one-man team, and it affected morale. They all thought the same thing – *is there only one player at Sheffield Wednesday?*

After the brilliant result against Arsenal, we went on a dismal run, picking up just three points from six games. That was all down to the fact that we were missing one of our best players, and all the furore that surrounded it.

As I've mentioned, we were desperate for clean sheets. Kevin Pressman had been a fantastic keeper over the years; I'd even played with him, but we needed someone to challenge him. We didn't have anyone who could compete with Kevin and put a bit of pressure on him. That was why I brought in Pavel Srnicek in November 1998.

Pav had an impressive spell with Newcastle before going over to play in Italy. When I found out that he was available on a free, I couldn't sign him quick enough. He was a fit man with an impressive physique, and like Paolo, he looked after himself on and off the pitch. We needed someone with his stature, someone the defenders could trust, because we'd been conceding far too many goals. Whether that was down to Kevin or the defenders, I don't know, but we had to do something to shore up the defence.

The fact that I knew Kevin well had no impact on my decision. Players have got to know that there is competition for places. No one is guaranteed a first team spot. I explained all of that to Kevin, and while he didn't like it, of course, he accepted my decision and knew that he had to go out and fight to win the number one spot back.

Pav's home debut was against Manchester United. When you've got forty thousand fans in full voice, Hillsborough is incredible, and their support gave us all a massive lift. We were outstanding and beat them 3-1, with a brace from Niclas Alexandersson and one goal from Wim Jonk. We were one of only three teams to beat United that season as they marched on to win an unprecedented treble. That was as good a win as you're going to get.

Bear in mind that we hadn't won a game for two months going into that match, so to get a result like that against a quality side was fantastic and gave everyone belief. I'd changed a few players around, made some tweaks to the formation; to see the lads put on a performance like that showed that we were doing the right things. I couldn't have asked for anything more. After the fall out from the Di Canio incident, we'd become the bookies' favourites for relegation, but I never for one moment thought that would happen.

That win really kicked-started our season, and we followed it up with a draw at Stamford Bridge against Chelsea, which was never an easy place to go, and then beat Nottingham Forest and Charlton, which gave us a big lift and moved us up to thirteenth in the table.

During this time I was still trying to convince Paolo to return to Sheffield Wednesday. I was doing everything I could, but he just didn't want to come back. The longer it went on the less likely it was that he'd return. At the time, his value must have been at least £6,000,000. Dave Richards told me during a board meeting that he'd spoken to the chairmen of every other Premier League club, and they'd agreed that no one would touch Paolo.

But lo and behold, in January, West Ham came in and signed him for £1,750,000 – an absolute bargain. He had a fantastic career at Upton Park, which didn't surprise me because he was such a talented player. That really opened my eyes to what the Premier League is like. The clubs all had a gentleman's agreement not to sign him – nothing in writing – but when someone can see a bargain like that, they'll quite happily go back on their word.

That was very disappointing for me and the fans. I didn't want to get rid of him, and neither did the supporters. Paolo said he didn't want to come back, but I honestly believe we could, and should, have put up a better fight for him. He knew I valued him, but he didn't think he was wanted by others at the club. I think he felt he wasn't loved. Maybe now, after Paolo's modest stint as a manager, he may respect how tough the job actually is.

I think the board and owners saw it as an opportunity to get him off the wage bill and bring in a couple of quid. The fee we received was nowhere near what it should have been, and it certainly didn't help us out on the park. Paolo could give us a goal out of nothing. Where could I find a replacement for £1,750,000?

We had to try and plug the hole with a different type of player, and that's what I did, signing Richard Cresswell from York City for £950,000. Cressy was such a dynamic type of player who worked his balls off. He wasn't a replacement for Paolo as such. He wasn't as creative, but he could score goals, and the fans loved him because of his work ethic. It was a gamble to sign him from League One, but with the limited funds I had available to me, I had to shop around in the lower leagues. A lot of clubs were watching him at the time, and we felt he was a promising young player who might have a bit of value in the future.

We finished the season in twelfth place, which was satisfying considering all the turmoil we'd endured. Don't forget we were relegation favourites at the start of the year. The league table was always very tight, and you can look at mid-table spots as a positive or a negative. I chose to focus on the positives. We beat Manchester United, Arsenal, and Liverpool, which proved we had the quality to compete with the best teams, but a lack of consistency stopped us from pushing on and really challenging for a European qualification spot. That's the difference between the big teams and the rest – the big teams get the results when they need them. Whether they are playing Arsenal or Coventry, they go out and do a job every time. The top players are up for every game and have a winning mentality. That's what we needed more of.

Having Frank Barlow as my long-term assistant at various clubs helped as we developed a bit of a good-cop-bad-cop routine. Frank and I were very different in lots of respects. Sometimes my judgement may have been wrong, and that's where Frank came in, offering me suggestions, ideas, and a different perspective. As manager, I had to live and die by my decisions. Sometimes I'd get it right – other times I'd get it wrong. That's the beauty of football.

As the players went away for their summer holiday, Frank Barlow and I started to think about the season ahead. We felt we had the nucleus of a strong team, but we had to make some improvements, and we needed more depth. Each position had to have at least two challengers because we didn't want anyone to take anything for granted or become complacent.

I felt optimistic about the future. Little did I know that the 1999/00 season was to be the most turbulent year of my entire career.

CHAPTER 17
Downing Street want to speak to you, Danny

Our first bit of transfer business was signing Scotland internationals Phil O'Donnell and Simon Donnelly from Celtic on free transfers. Phil was a good midfielder who'd done very well at Celtic, but he suffered with a lot of injuries when he joined us and only played once for me. He was a lovely guy, a nice family man, who lived not far from my home in Chesterfield. It was a real blow when I heard he passed away in 2007, aged just thirty-five.

Simon was also unlucky with injuries, which meant we never really saw the best of him at Hillsborough, but at the time I was quite excited to have them both on board to strengthen the squad.

And then we went abroad and paid PSV £3,000,000 for Gilles De Bilde, a Belgian international striker. Sir Bobby Robson had tipped me off about him, and we felt very excited about his arrival.

Gilles had a reputation as a bit of a hot head; in 1992, he received a suspended prison sentence for headbutting two scout leaders, and four years later, he received a lengthy ban for punching an opposing player in the face, breaking his nose, during a match in Belgium. So it's fair to say that there was a certain stigma attached to Gilles! But he was a lovely boy, and we never had any disciplinary problems with him at all.

De Bilde loved his dogs and had some Dobermans back home in his native Belgium. Any dogs entering the UK from Europe have to go into quarantine, something Gilles publicly disagreed with. The *News of the World* ran an exposé shortly after he signed, reporting that he'd smuggled his dogs past customs illegally, although Gilles denied it.

On the pitch, he was a quick, skilful player, and very brave for a little fella. He scored goals for us, which was exactly what we needed, but he didn't really settle in the area, and he found it difficult to adjust to the English game. To be fair, we didn't create enough chances for him.

Our final signing was Gerald Sibon, another striker, who joined us from Ajax for £2,000,000. He was a giant of a player, standing at six foot six. I'd been over to Holland to take a look at him, and was impressed with his skills and quick feet. With his height, I expected him to be good in the air too, but we soon noticed that when the ball went high, he seemed to lose sight of it or he'd mis-control the ball, particularly during night games. In training he was fantastic, so we couldn't understand what the problem was. Eventually, I asked him if he'd ever had his eyes tested. He hadn't, and it turned out that he needed glasses. We got him some contact lenses, and he went on to have a good career at Wednesday.

If winning games wasn't hard enough for a manager, I was having to sort out dogs and glasses!

It's never as simple as signing a player, putting them into the side, and watching them hit the ground running. We always tried to do our due diligence, but there are always one or two surprises. Bear in mind that the foreign lads are coming into a different country – a different culture; it takes a bit of time to adapt. Nowadays clubs have player liaison officers – there might already be other players in the squad from the same country, so there is a lot of support for new signings. We had to do it all ourselves.

It's easier for English players to adapt to a new club, but we couldn't afford them because the market was crazy. Even if we could afford the transfer fee, the players' wage demands were too high, so we were forced to sign foreign boys.

I'm not saying that Gilles and Gerald wouldn't have been on the list of players we'd identified; they would have been, although they maybe wouldn't have been as high up the list if it weren't for the extortionate transfer fees the English players commanded. When we identified our targets, I took the list to the board, and they'd tell me whether they would make an offer. Most of the time at Wednesday, the answer I received was no.

There is always a risk when you sign someone without any Premier League experience. When a player had been performing in their home country, the expectation is that they will become an instant hit, but it's much harder than that. They have to find a place to live, keep their family happy, and fit into the English lifestyle. Football is an unforgiving business, where fans and the board expect players who have cost millions to come in and do the business on the pitch from day one.

We were backed by Charterhouse, an investment firm based in London, and they wanted to see an instant return on their investment, not wait six months. If a player wasn't performing, I was asked to explain myself, so there was a lot of pressure. It was a world away from Barnsley, where John Dennis ran the club in a different manner.

If I'm honest, we needed more players, but the financial constraints meant I couldn't sign anyone else. I went over to Monaco to spend a couple of days watching players. One particular player I saw was Thierry Henry, a young boy at the time, who stood out like a sore thumb. But he wasn't the one I had gone to watch because he was already spoken for. There were clubs queueing up for him. I spent two days watching my target and compiling a report. I really liked the player and felt he'd fit right in, but when I came back to England and spoke to the board about signing him, I was told there was no money. *What happened to this £10,000,000 war chest I was reported to have received?* By the way, the player I wanted went on to have a terrific career at the top level.

Maybe I could have been more forceful and demanded more money. I could have spat my dummy out and taken my frustrations public. I'm sure the fans would have been on my side, and they could have forced the club's hand. But on the other side, if I had done that, I would have been just as guilty as anyone else for putting the club in a position where they were spending money they couldn't afford. I loved Wednesday, still do, and although the lack of transfer funds and letting players go on the cheap was affecting us on the pitch, I had to consider the longer-term impact on the club.

I've never stamped my feet and made demands; that's just not my style. What I did was go in to see the chairman or finance director to explain the problem, give them the name of the player I needed it and tell them that we needed to go out and see if we could afford them. If I was turned down for anything, I fully accepted it. It's pointless kicking and screaming as it doesn't help anyone in the long term. My expectation was always to get the best out of the players I had within my squad, and if I could add to it, great. If not, I'd just get on with it.

When the season began at Hillsborough on the 7th of August 1999, we played OK, even though we narrowly lost 2-1 to Liverpool. We lost 4-0 to Manchester United in the next game, and that started a terrible run, where we didn't win any of our first nine matches. It was the worst start a coach could envisage.

We were still trying to get the team to gel together, and that takes time. Whether you are given that time is another matter. With the results that we had, I felt under pressure, of course I did. But I remained positive and focused on turning it around. What may or may not happen to me and my job was not part of the bigger picture; my priority was always the team. We were suffering from a lack of confidence, and the players didn't trust each other.

By far the worst moment of that dismal run came on the 19th of September at St James' Park. Newcastle had also endured a difficult start to the season that had resulted in Ruud Gullit resigning as manager. His replacement was Sir Bobby Robson, and we played them in his first home game as manager. The prodigal son returns. Alan Shearer was the best striker in the country, and we were a team who weren't defending particularly well. It was the worst situation that we could have asked for.

At halftime we were 4-0 down. By full time, it was 8-0, and Shearer had scored five. We had started the game really well, and could have been two up inside the first ten minutes. If one of those chances had gone in, it would have been a completely different story. But they didn't go in, and when you look in the history books, they tell you the result, not the performance. An 8-0 defeat is something that very few managers can survive.

After the game, our chairman, Dave Richards, spoke to the press and really dug out the two Italian lads, Paolo Di Canio and Benito Carbone, saying that they had got us into the position we found ourselves in because of their high wages and Paolo's high-profile incident the season before. Although it was difficult for me to say anything publicly because I was the manager, I sat on Paolo and Benny's side of the fence. The club had given them their contracts, so it wasn't anyone's fault but our own if we couldn't afford to pay them.

It's very difficult when your chairman criticises your players in public. It certainly doesn't make things any easier. My job was to try and pick them back up, which is hard when they are reading in the papers what the chairman has said about their teammates.

We returned to the North East the following week and suffered a 1-0 defeat at Sunderland, which was a bitter blow. I didn't need people to tell me that I was under pressure. I'd been around football long enough to know that the results weren't good enough. In football, patience is a virtue, and it's probably even worse now.

We finally got a win in our tenth game of the season, against Wimbledon, which was a great result. They were a team who were never easy to score against. They were very physical, direct, and capable of grinding out a result. We were the complete opposite of that, and one thing I could have done was improve the physicality of the team.

But we beat them 5-1! We weren't five better than them, though, just like Newcastle weren't eight better than us. You get those results sometimes – games where you take all your chances. It was a good win, but it didn't paper over the cracks. We knew we still had a long way to go.

By now, the owners were putting huge pressure on the board to cut costs and bring some revenue in. The only players we could sell were the better players, so the club – not me – decided to sell Benito Carbone to Aston Villa for £850,000, which was ridiculously low. It was a financial decision taken by the board to reduce the wage bill. It was not a footballing decision, and not my decision either. Every player has a value, and Benny's was much higher than that. Villa got an absolute bargain, just like West Ham had with Paolo a few months earlier.

As if that wasn't bad enough, we then sold Emerson Thome to Chelsea for £2,700,000, which was very cheap. They sold him to Sunderland less than twelve months later for £4,000,000, making a tidy profit.

There was no way I could replace players like Carbone or

Thome, but I didn't even have the chance to because the money we brought in wasn't reinvested into the team, it just went into the bank. I ended up picking players who may not have played if I'd been able to bring others in. Players aren't stupid, they know where they are in the pecking order, and they knew they were our last resort. That does nothing for confidence at all. When a player has been on the sidelines for a period of time, they are understandably disheartened, and when I brought them back into the team, they knew they were only playing until we could find someone else.

My job was becoming very, very difficult. I had results going against me, the chairman criticising the team, and our best players being sold without me being consulted. The squad were completely demoralised, and my job was to motivate them. However, they were being paid a very good wage to play football for Sheffield Wednesday. They shouldn't really need any more motivation than that. If they do, they are in the wrong business.

You need to have a high amount of self-belief to go out there and show people what you can do. This is a big problem in football, and I'm sure a lot of managers, if they're honest, will agree with me. You get fed up as a manager having to put your arm around players and plead with them to play football. They are under contract to play football matches, not to sit around, moan, and sulk. That was the problem I had, and I couldn't understand it. If someone was paying me £10 a week to play football, I'd go out and give everything I had. After that, if they gave me £20, I'd say thank you very much, I've earned that. During my playing days, I never wanted to be criticised for sitting on my arse, not playing, and getting money for doing nothing.

I wanted to see commitment from the lads. OK, some players had left, and results had gone against us, but so what? That's football. It was up to us as a group to turn that around and prove to people that we aren't a crap team. We aren't a team who deserved to lose 8-0. We aren't a team who are going to be relegated.

We had a glimmer of hope on Boxing Day when we beat Middlesbrough 1-0, and followed that up with some fantastic results against Bradford, Arsenal, and Spurs that gave us a fighting chance of getting out of trouble.

While we were on that run, a group of MPs came out with a load of shit and stirred things up. On the morning of our home game against Bradford City, I read the following quote from MP David Blunkett. "In my opinion, it would be best for the club if Danny Wilson was to leave."

Blunkett, along with fellow MPs – Clive Betts, Bill Michie, and Joe Ashton – had met with Charterhouse Bank, who owned a third of the club, and called for my immediate dismissal. So instead of preparing the team for a crucial Yorkshire derby (a game we won 2-0, by the way), I was giving interviews to the press who wanted to know what I thought of their comments.

"I just think it is pathetic timing. I would have thought people of their stature would have known better. If they want to keep blasting their mouths off, I can't do anything about that. I've got broad shoulders," was the response I gave to the media.

What really surprised me was that Joe Ashton, a former director of Sheffield Wednesday, was one of the MPs having a go at me, because I had previously supported him through a very difficult period in his life.

Joe was a very brash – very blunt – character. He'd say that he was a Yorkshireman, through and through, which entitled him to say anything he wanted. In November 1998, he'd been caught in a Thai massage parlour during a police raid, and the *News of the World* printed the story. As soon as I read the article, I phoned him and said, "Joe. I'm not interested in what's gone on. I'm sorry for the situation you're in and imagine it can't be easy, but if you need any support, I'm here for you."

And then a year later, he turned around and did that to me. He didn't even have the decency to phone me to tell me that he'd given an interview that would put more pressure on me. He didn't have the courtesy to warn me. That about sums up his character. And people wonder why politicians are vilified.

As I have mentioned, Joe had been a member of the board for almost a decade, so he was just as culpable as anyone else for the situation the club had found themselves in.

This was at a time when the government was trying to get people back into employment, and here were four MPs publicly attempting to get me the sack! Their attack against me didn't sit well with the general public or the government.

The League Managers' Association, John Barnwell in particular, were incredibly supportive, as were my fellow managers, many of whom backed me publicly. There was a swell of discontent amongst the general public, and I received hundreds of letters of support, not just from Wednesday supporters but from people from all over the country – even Sheffield United fans – which was amazing. The public turned on the four MPs, and I think they soon regretted getting involved in something they shouldn't have.

One Sunday morning, I was sitting at home, reading through the sports pages, when the telephone rang. Karen answered. A few moments later, she came running into the kitchen and said, "Danny, it's Downing Street for you."

I picked up the phone and it was Alastair Campbell, the Prime Minister's official spokesman. "Danny, I'd like to apologise to you for everything that has happened. I'm not apologising on behalf of the four MPs, but because of them. It will not happen again. You will not hear any more from those four in the newspapers or anywhere else. I can assure you of that," he said.

Wow, I thought. *Downing Street phoning to apologise to me, a little lad from Wigan.*

I had thought they were out of order, but when I received that call, I *knew* they were out of order. To this day, I do not forgive any of them. They stepped out of line and tried to use their political power to voice their personal opinions, which was very wrong.

While the MP row was going on, I won the Premier League Manager of the Month award for January 2000. That says it all really – those four calling for my head while I won an award!

The four then turned on Dave Richards, and he was eventually forced to step down from his role as chairman of Sheffield Wednesday. Dave was very good to me, and I had a strong relationship with him. He has since apologised to me and said that, in hindsight, he could have done more to support me, but in fairness, he himself was under pressure from our backers and his hands were tied.

Howard Culley became our new chairman. I didn't know much about him, other than the fact that he was a solicitor. I didn't ever get to know him either, as we had very little dialogue.

But I didn't worry about the boardroom comings and goings because I couldn't control that. What I could control was what happened on the football side.

In an ideal world, I'd love to say that I was able to switch off from it all when I went home, but I couldn't. I was living not far from Sheffield, and a lot of my neighbours and friends were Wednesday fans, so I couldn't really get away from it.

The job as a manager is twenty-four hours a day, seven days a week at the best of times, and you'd like to think you can have an hour with your family without talking about football, but it doesn't happen. That phone is always ringing with another problem; one player is injured, another isn't happy. There are the constant meetings with the chairman and the board; maybe the press needs a word with you too. You cannot escape it. As a player, you can walk away from it. You can go home after training, play with the kids, and switch off for a bit. But you can't do that as a manager. Football management consumes you. As my career developed, I got better at handling it.

It didn't just affect me either, it affected my family. There were loads of Wednesday fans at Laurie's school – he's an Owl too – so he was getting into situations at school where kids would argue with him about my team selections. Karen and the kids came to watch the games, and fans sitting around them would be saying some awful things about me, not knowing who they were sitting near. Karen was fantastic. She is such a brilliant, understanding lady, and her unwavering support was a massive help to me.

The abuse footballers and managers receive is scandalous. It is seemingly OK for managers to be hammered from pillar to post. The treatment Steve Bruce received from the media at the start of the 2021/22 season was awful. There are no limits to what the media can say, and they are often more than happy to light the blue torch paper. If you fall out with a journalist, that's it. If you win a game, there'll be a cool report. If you lose, it'll be damning.

The public takes notice of what the media and pundits say. There have been some shocking examples recently, with people criticising others from the comfort of their television studio. They seem to forget that players and managers are human beings with families who watch and read all these comments.

It's easy for them to make a throwaway remark and walk away, but it sticks with players, managers, and their families.

Tony Pulis has said that this abuse is going to wind fans up so much that someone will be attacked. I hope it never happens – I really do – but sometimes the frenzy that's whipped up will drive someone to do something daft, especially with the spate of pitch invasions at the end of the 2021/22 season.

Fortunately, I've never felt threatened myself. I've experienced disgruntled fans and been sworn at, but I've never had any physical confrontations. One or two fans have heckled me, and I've told them to fuck off, which is a natural reaction. But then I'm the one who's criticised! Why should footballers and managers take constant abuse that is often vile, personal, and sometimes takes place away from the stadiums, and not be able to respond? Yes, I understand that the paying fans have a right to air their grievances, but it often goes too far and oversteps the mark. You wouldn't be expected to receive that kind of abuse in any other walk of life. It wouldn't be acceptable, yet football tolerates it.

At the end of February, we played Newcastle at home. We were 1-0 down after eleven minutes, and with memories of the 8-0 defeat still fresh in their minds, the fans weren't happy, and started to have a go at the players and me. I was stood on the touchline, as I usually was during a game, while Frank was sat in the dugout. The next thing I knew, he was stood by my shoulder.

"What are you doing here?" I asked him.

"I just thought I'd stand by your side for a bit," he replied.

That was Frank all over. If I was getting pelters, he'd come and take them too. I've seen situations where the manager is taking stick and the coaches hide away, but Frank was never like that. When he had been a coach at Chesterfield years earlier, the board sacked the manager and the coaching staff but asked Frank to stay on. Such was his loyalty that he left the club too.

On the 11th of March 2000, we beat a strong West Ham United side featuring Frank Lampard, Rio Ferdinand, and a certain Paolo Di Canio, who was returning to Hillsborough for the first time since his departure just over a year earlier. He took a bit of stick from the Wednesday fans, but still managed to set up Lampard, who put the Hammers in front in the first half. We came back to win 3-1, and move to within seven points of safety. After the game, I shook Paolo's hand and wished him well for the future. There were certainly no hard feelings on my part.

Ten days later, I was sitting in my office at the training ground, when there was a knock on the door. Howard Culley walked in and said, "Danny. We've made a decision. We're going to release you from your contract; I've got a statement here that I'd like you to sign, and then we can part ways." He held two envelopes in his hand and passed one to me.

"Leave it with me," I said.

I read through the letter and was shocked to see that it said I'd resigned. I stormed into Howard's office and said, "You can shove this up your arse."

He looked at me, surprised, and asked me what I meant.

"It says here that I'm resigning, and you know that's not the case," I replied.

"Oh sorry, Danny, I think I might have given you the wrong one," he said before handing me another envelope. This one contained a statement that said I'd been sacked.

Howard was a solicitor, so I imagine the wording in both statements was spot on. He must have thought I was stupid and would sign anything. I didn't have an agent, but I'd seen enough contracts in my time, so when I read the word 'resignation,' it was like a red warning light flashing.

Why would they do that? Well, the simple reason was that if I resigned, they wouldn't have to pay me any compensation. That was very sneaky. I signed the second letter and handed it back to Howard, who apologised again.

"Have you released the news yet?" I asked.

"No, not yet."

"Can you do me a favour please? Can you give me an hour before you release it? That way, I can clear my desk and drive home to tell my family first."

"Of course, Danny," he agreed.

So I emptied the office of all my belongings, said goodbye to the few staff who were still at the training ground, and drove home. When I got to the corner of my street, forty-five minutes after my meeting with Howard, I saw a photographer who I knew very well. I asked what he was doing there, and he told me that his editor had been informed that I'd been sacked and had sent him round to my house to take a picture of me. Despite promising me they'd wait an hour before releasing the statement, the club did it straight away and didn't have the courtesy to tell me.

After all I'd been through over the past year, I just wanted to make a difficult situation as easy as possible for myself and my family, and they did this! It still hurts to this day. There was absolutely nothing for the club to gain by releasing the statement when they did compared to an hour later. I feel I walked away from the situation with my head held high and with my dignity intact. I've never told my side of the story until now.

I'm often asked if we'd have stayed up if I'd remained in post until the end of the season. My answer is always yes. I will always back myself and I still felt we had enough quality to survive. People may disagree with that, and there is no way we'll ever know for sure. But I am one hundred per cent certain that we wouldn't have gone down if the club – not me – hadn't decided to sell Paolo, Benny, and Emerson.

Looking back on my time at Sheffield Wednesday, I will never forget my three years as a player. We played some of the most exhilarating football I've ever seen under Big Ron and Trevor Francis. The success that we enjoyed will always be remembered fondly by the supporters. But what I can't forget, for the wrong reasons, are the four MPs and their actions towards me when I was manager that marked the beginning of the end. They could turn around with arrogance and say that they got what they wanted because I was sacked, but did they really get what they wanted? At the end of the season, Wednesday were relegated and have not returned to the Premier League since. The MPs were disowned by their own government. I'll never forget the pain the situation caused my family at the time.

I didn't go back to Hillsborough for a long time afterwards. The first time I returned was to watch my son play for the reserves under Chris Turner. Laurie was trying to make his way in the game and was a good player. I sat out of the way, as far away from the directors' box as I could. I didn't want to get involved with the press or directors; I just wanted to watch my son play football.

I GET KNOCKED DOWN

In 2017, Sheffield Wednesday held a one-hundred-and-fifty-year anniversary dinner and invited a host of former players and managers. I didn't receive an invite. I heard that it was an oversight, but I don't believe it. How can you overlook someone who played in three cup finals, was part of the side who finished third in the Premier League, and managed the club for almost two years? That didn't go down particularly well with me. I've received apologies since, but they aren't sincere.

In contrast to the club's behaviour, the supporters have been absolutely fantastic towards me. They remember me most fondly as a player, but I think they also understand that we were going through a really torrid time at board level when I was manager. They didn't get on my back, and even when I was sacked, I received letters of support from fans, thanking me for my efforts. I cannot thank them enough for their encouragement over the years and they will always hold a very special place in my heart.

It's sad to see the Owls where they are now. A club the size of Wednesday, with the fan base they have, should be in the Premier League, no doubt about it. They aren't, and I don't think you can blame the managers they've had. For me, the problems run a lot deeper than that.

Trying to win the ball back from, Republic of Ireland's, Steve Staunton in a World Cup Qualifier. It was a huge honour to represent Northern Ireland on twenty-four occasions.

hung up my boots after the 1994/95 season. It was too demanding to play and manage.

I got a completly different view of the game when watching from the dugout.

Eric Winstanley and I celebrating Barnsley's promotion to the Premier League in 1997.

We played some fantastic football during our promotion winning season – it really was like watching Brazil. The rain didn't stop the Barnsley fans joining us to celebrate.

disapointing end to a terrific year. I honestly ought we'd stay up, but it wasn't to be.

Frank Barlow became my assistant when I rejoined Sheffield Wednesday in 1999

peaking to Paul Alcock after the Di Canio push. I still think he went down too easily.

While four MPs were calling for my head, I won Manager of the Month in January 2000.

Dear Mr Wilson

I felt that I must write to you in light of recent events.

I am actually a Spurs fan but I feel disgusted at the way you have been treated lately by those 4 MP's calling for you to be sacked.

Firstly I am a football fan and just because I support one team and you manage another this does not mean I can't support you.

I wish you all the best for the future and I really hope you can keep Wednesday up, not only to shut up those idiots but to prove what I have known for a while that you are a good manager who deserves to be left alone to do his job.

You have my full support and I wish you all the best for the future.

Yours Sincerely

Ann R.

January 17, 2000

Dear Danny,

My eleven-year-old son, Matthew, and I are season ticket holders in the South Stand at Hillsborough. I felt I had to write to register our support for you following the utterances of the four Sheffield MP's last week. The performance against Bradford was the best reply the team could have given. I cannot believe the arrogance of these people who should be supporting the club not splitting it apart. The last six months have been hard for everybody connected with the club and I think you have acted with dignity and honour throughout this period and you do not deserve to be treated like this by these so called supporters.

Best of luck for the FA Cup replay and for the rest of the season. Keep up the good work.

Yours sincerely

DEAR SIR,

DON'T LET ALL THIS SHIT GET YOU DOWN.

KEEP YOUR CHIN UP.

AND FOR CHRIST'S SAKE DON'T QUIT!

Yours faithfully,

Mr Danny Wilson
Sheffield Wednesday F C
Hillsborough
Sheffield

Dear Mr Wilson

Like many other people, I read of the comments of the four local MPs with amazement. What right have they got to exploit their prominent position in order to voice what should be personal opinions? They would be better advised to devote their time to trying to improve their Government's performance. Several ministers' jobs would be in jeopardy if they were judged in the same way as football managers.
As it has turned out, the team seem to have rallied behind you, and Saturdays crowd certainly have. Good luck for the rest of the season - I hope you are able to avoid relegation, and stick it to the MPs in the best possible way - on the pitch.

Yours sincerely

Dear Danny

As a life long Blade, and proud of it, never in my wildest imagination have I envisaged a situation where I would write to the manager of the Owls for any reason but particularly in a supportive manner.

However all that has changed following the recent action of the 'gang of four'. Like M.P.'s I have always viewed football managers as individuals who speak with dual standards and clearly have only their own particular agenda for their own particular good.

I believe the actions of the infamous four have only reinforced my views whereas the way you have conducted yourself is a shining example to us all and in stark contrast to the standards set by some of your predecessors, eg, Mr R. Atkinson to name but one.

I have thought for some time about writing to you as I feel it is important that standards of sportsmanship and fair play are maintained and you clearly aspire, by your repeated actions and comments, to that view.

I wish you well for the future and sincerely hope the victory yesterday is the springboard for more that ultimately leads to the Owls avoiding

---

League Managers Association

44 Holly Walk, Leamington Spa
Warwickshire CV32 4YS
Telephone: (01926) 882313
Fax: (01926) 886629
E-Mail: LMA@League-Managers.demon.co.uk
Website: www.leaguemanagers.com

JB/LJH/khoey jb

17th January, 2000

Miss Kate Hoey MP
Minister for Sport
Department for Culture, Media and Sport
2-4 Cockspur Street
London SW1Y 5DH

Dear Minister,

We feel compelled to write and express our concern and massive disappointment at the scheming of the four Sheffield MP's who are attempting to secure the dismissal of Danny Wilson as manager of Sheffield Wednesday FC.

Whilst accepting that football supporters can voice their opinions publicly and that club managers have to accept public scrutiny we believe this outburst is at best ill-timed, ill-judged and totally unacceptable.

Our member Danny Wilson has dealt with this unfortunate incident in a very professional manner even though it has caused considerable embarrassment to both himself and his family.

At the very least we expect some public censure by the government of the actions of these few MP's.

We look forward to your response.

Yours sincerely,

John Barnwell
Chief Executive

I received hundreds of letters of support from all over the country during what was a very difficult time for me and my family. I will never forgive those four MPs.

Winning the Football League Trophy with Bristol City in 2003 is one of my proudest moments in football, but I'd have swapped it ten times over for promotion.

I think most people wanted MK Dons to be relegated during the 2004/05 season. It was very satisfying to prove them wrong. We stayed up by the skin of our teeth.

A leaky dressing room roof at Accrington Stanley turned our season around. Hartlepool won promotion straight back to League One in 2007.

We were relegation favourites at the start of the 2009/10 season but managed to reach the Play-Off final. Unfortunately, we narrowly lost to Millwall at Wembley.

While I was holding this press conference, a number of Blades fans were protesting outside the ground. I knew that the fans would accept me as long as we got the results on the pitch.

Leading Sheffield United out at Wembley in 2012 was a very proud moment. We couldn't have been any closer to promotion.

I retired from football management in 2017. I don't miss the pressure of the competition, but I do miss working with the lads on the training ground and seeing players develop.

My family are the most important part of my life.
From left to right: Laurie, Carrie, Karen, Amy (my daughter in law), and me.

CHAPTER 18
Don't lose to the Gas

Despite that horrible experience, I wasn't done with management. I wanted to get straight back into it and prove that Wednesday's decision to sack me was wrong. I wanted to manage a winning team and enjoy success again.

Rather than put me off, those last few months had the opposite effect. They galvanised me and made me stronger. I was perhaps a little naïve when I took the Sheffield Wednesday job, but I learnt so much during my eighteen months at Hillsborough. I now knew about football politics. I knew all about the pressures surrounding a football club. It's not just the managers who are under pressure either; the directors and chairman feel it too. The whole experience toughened me up. What the press were writing about me, what others were saying. You can't ignore it, but I learned to compartmentalise the criticism so it wouldn't impact me again in the future.

But before I got back in the saddle I wanted to take a little bit of a break away from football so I could spend some time with Karen and the children. Not a year off, just a month or so away from everything to get myself together. There were one or two clubs rumoured to be interested in me, but I didn't apply for any jobs. I've never had to apply for a job throughout my career.

The longer you're out of the game, the quicker you are forgotten. When you've been away for a while, people begin to form doubts and wonder why you haven't got another job. For that reason I always wanted to dive straight back into it, and in the summer of 2000, I received a phone call from Bristol City – a massive club – inviting me to go down to Ashton Gate for a chat. I didn't know it was going to be an interview!

As I arrived at Ashton Gate, I was shown into the boardroom and discovered that all the directors had been summoned. I hadn't done much homework on Bristol City at that time, as I thought it was just going to be an informal chat. So I didn't have a full dossier containing stats on the players and the previous season's results; we just had a conversation about the way I liked my teams to play football. I was offered the job, which was a big surprise to me. A very pleasant one.

Bristol City were in League One at the time, but when I looked at the set-up of the club, the size of the city, and the fan base, I saw a sleeping giant. Dropping down two divisions didn't bother me as I felt that the potential was there to get them up.

During my playing career, I'd travelled all around the country, so moving to Bristol wasn't an issue for me. The concern Karen and I had was around the children and what was best for them and their education. Laurie and Carrie were settled in a fantastic school, St Mary's in Chesterfield, so we kept our house in Derbyshire, near Karen's family, and bought an apartment in Bristol. I lived in the apartment during the week and came back home for a day or two when I could. Karen and the kids came down to Bristol some weekends. It worked out really well, and we had a lot of good times down there. Bristol is one of my favourite places to live; it's very cosmopolitan, an up-and-coming city. The fans were great to me, which is always a nice bonus, particularly when you're away from your family.

Friends of ours would come and visit at the weekend too, and we were frequent diners at San Carlos, the Italian restaurant. Sue and Dave Galley, who was the physio for England and Liverpool, and Julie and Chris Colton were always great company. Sadly, Julie was to pass away some years later, aged fifty-one, from a brain tumour. That was a big wrench for both of us, particularly Karen; they were like sisters.

For Chris, her husband, and son James, it was a massive blow.

It was a very, very tough time for us all when she passed, and Julie is still greatly missed.

*****

The club was in a mess, although not so much on the football field as we had some decent lads there. The problems – as they are at so many clubs – were in the boardroom. The chairman when I joined was Scott Davidson, who'd been a member of the boy bands Pet Shop Boys and Bros. The board meetings were full of arguments between the various factions. It was very unsettling from my point of view as I might get the go-ahead from one director only to be turned down by another. It was very strange.

There was a lot of turmoil at board level, and it didn't take long before Scott and some of his friends who were also directors, stood down. Scott was replaced by John Laycock. John and another director, Steve Lansdown, couldn't agree on the running of the youth team, so eventually in 2002, Steve became the chairman. Steve has done fantastically well with the club and has put a lot of his own money in to strengthen the team and improve the ground. But while I was manager, there was no money available, so we were scrimping and saving on transfers and making the best of the players we had.

I tried to implement the same philosophy at Bristol City that I'd used at Barnsley, a system that is pleasing on the eye to the supporters. You have to play attractive football, but you also need the three points on a Saturday. It's about winning football matches at the end of the day. The key was to get everyone pulling in the same direction, and I couldn't complain in that respect. The lads were fantastic from day one; we had some terrific players.

Brian Tinnion was an old soldier in midfielder, Steve Phillips was our goalkeeper, and the brilliant Scott Murray impressed me from the off. I didn't make too many signings, but one who stood out was Lee Peacock, who we got from Manchester City. He did really well for us, more than well actually. He was a revelation. We had the basis of a good squad, and there was a nice balance of senior players and youngsters.

But I wasn't going into a club that was full of confidence. I took over from Tony Fawthrop, an interim manager who'd only been in the role for a few months. Morale was low; I sensed that straight away. There had been so much disruption; they'd lost so many players and they needed some stability. They needed a permanent manager who was going to be there for a while. Someone who could impose something different and inject a bit of confidence.

I'd come from the Premier League, which pleased the fans, and they were behind me from the start. I didn't know too much about Bristol City when I joined, so those first few weeks were about me learning about the players: how they played, what their strengths and weaknesses were, and what made them tick. Some lads trained well all week and then froze on match days. Others were crap in the week, but come Saturday, they were flying. I needed to have a little bit of time with them to find out what sort of characters they were, and I needed a good half a dozen games to see how they played.

We beat Wrexham 2-0 in my first game in charge, but then failed to win any of the next six. Players had to gel, confidence had to improve, and that takes time. The biggest challenge was getting the lads to believe in what we were trying to achieve. I knew that if I could get them into a position where they felt they were going to be valued for their contribution, they'd go a long way for the club. Players will run through brick walls for you if you can get them on board.

Despite the difficult start, we then embarked on a fourteen-game unbeaten run, which was great and showed that the lads were buying into the way I wanted us to play.

In December 2000, we faced Bristol Rovers at home. I'd played in the Steel City derby, which was intense, but I didn't really know much about the rivalry between the two Bristol clubs. I soon discovered how vicious it was, but in a good way. Ian Holloway was the Rovers manager, and he was hyping it up in the media. I thought the build up to the game was brilliant, absolutely brilliant. The whole city was alive.

I knew from my experience of playing in derby games that you can't be placid; you have to have a little bit of oomph. It's important to have that passion, but you also need to retain the work you've done in training all week. You cannot let your emotions distract you from what you're supposed to be doing. As Frank Barlow used to say, "You have to have ice in your head and fire in your belly."

Olly was pumping the match up all week. I was too wise to get involved, always preferring to do my talking on the pitch. It turned out to be a cracking game that we won 3-2. From a personal point of view, that was a big match to win. If the fans had any doubts about me before that game, they certainly didn't afterwards. They had the bragging rights.

We drew the return fixture at the Memorial Stadium later in the season. The Rovers games were always an important day in the calendar for both sets of fans. Getting a good result in those matches gives you a bit of goodwill from the supporters – just don't lose to the Gas!

Another match that stood out that season was on New Year's Day 2001 – my forty-first birthday. We beat Cambridge 6-2, which was a great result and a terrific birthday present!

There were lots of goals in our side, and putting the ball into the back of the net was never a problem for us. Our main strikers, Tony Thorpe and Lee Peacock, scored thirty-eight goals between them, and Scott Murray chipped in with eleven from midfield, which shows how attacking we were as a team.

Scott was a little Scottish winger – what a character. He was funny, dry, and ran his heart out for the team. You ask Tony and Lee who made most of their goals, and they will say Scott. The supply from the middle of the park was exceptional. Scott and Brian Tinnion, between the pair of them, made or scored ninety percent of our goals. They built up a great telepathy in the middle of the park and made it easy for the strikers.

We were pretty solid at the back too, and we never got hammered. If we lost, it tended to be by the odd goal. We had a good core of players – a decent squad, but the line-up I put out was the best eleven, no doubt about that. We were fortunate that we had very few injuries, so I was able to pick a settled side. The lads were in form and wanted to play; the team were scoring goals and the fans were loving it. When you get that sort of feeling, the players don't want games to end and they always want to play, so it was quite easy from my point of view when it came to team selection. The way the lads were playing and training, they picked themselves. We had others in the squad who were capable of coming in and doing a job, but I generally stuck to the same eleven wherever possible.

On the 7th of April 2001, we beat Bury to extend our unbeaten run to six, but then we only won one of our last five games and that cost us a spot in the play-offs. We didn't produce enough points at the front and back ends of the season. Those games really hurt us, and we finished in ninth place, just seven points behind Wigan, who made the play-offs. You can look back and think, *If we'd won this game or that game,* but every team can do that. I still felt it was a good season and I didn't feel particularly disappointed. We'd made progress from the previous campaign. Not just in terms of the points returned, but also from what I saw on the pitch. Some of the lads were young, and we were improving all the time. They were brimming with confidence, ready for the next year.

The fans were very much on board, even at the end of the season when we lost a couple of games. They remained supportive of me and the team, and we had record season ticket sales for the following year, which was great, all while reducing the wage bill by a third.

But although things were clearly moving in the right direction, an unusual thing happened to me during that first season at Ashton Gate.

I returned to my office one day after training to find a sealed envelope sitting on my desk. There was no indication of who it was for, who it was from, or the reason for it being there. It had just been plonked on my desk with no explanation. I curiously opened the envelope and read the letter inside that explained that the club were giving me six months' notice due to financial reasons. It was signed by John Laycock, the chairman at the time.

I couldn't believe it. Nobody had spoken to me about the possibility of me leaving the club. No one had come knocking on my door. So I treated the letter with the disdain it deserved, put it in my pocket, and never said a word. To this day, no one has ever mentioned that letter.

There was further progress in the 2001/02 season. Bristol Rovers had been relegated the previous year, but we were drawn against them in the quarter-final of the Football League trophy – a big game for both clubs. We won 3-0 and knocked Rovers out of the cup. Our fans loved that result. Anytime you beat the Gas, you're held aloft, but a cup win was special. We felt we were the strongest team in the city, but derby games are never easy, and form goes out of the window. I tried to relax the players like I always did. I was never one to hype things up; that's not how

I am as a person. Sometimes, you can be like a duck on top of the water – even I had a few butterflies at times – but it was up to me to be a calming influence on the players. If the lads saw that I was nervous or excited, they'd take that out onto the pitch with them.

We played Cambridge United in the two-legged semi-final. We'd beaten them twice in the league, so we were brimming with confidence going into the first leg at the Abbey Stadium. We drew 0-0 and then lost 2-0 in the return leg at Ashton Gate. That defeat, in front of our own supporters, was hard to take. We were so close to a place in the final. We knew we were a better team than Cambridge, and that may have been our problem. We never really got going in either game, and maybe that was down to complacency. Fair play to Cambridge because they got their tactics spot on, but we let the fans down and I was bitterly disappointed not to give them a day out at the Millennium Stadium.

Our league form was pretty good throughout the season, but again we suffered at the end of the year again, winning just one of our final five matches, so we finished in seventh place, just five points and one position away from the play-offs. Yes, we missed out on promotion, but we had finished two places higher and with a better points tally than the season before, so it was progress. We knew we were getting stronger, and the lads were growing in confidence. The players knew their jobs; it was ingrained in them, and they didn't need as much instruction or coaching as they had before. They knew what was expected of them.

There was progress off the pitch too. The crowds were increasing and the club, who were in the red when I joined, had balanced the books and now very much in the black.

Everyone associated with Bristol City felt optimistic for the following season.

CHAPTER 19
Silverware at last

We had a mixed start to the 2002/03 season, winning five and losing five of the first ten games. It took us a little while to get going, but when we did it was fantastic, and we went three months unbeaten. Sometimes you can't put your finger on it, other than the fact that the lads knew their jobs. Yes, Frank Barlow, my assistant, and I would still give them little pointers, reminders, and gee ups when needed, but we didn't have to do much more than that. We got stronger as the season went on.

We enjoyed another run in the Football League Trophy, seeing off Queen's Park Rangers, Boston United, Wycombe Wanderers, and Bournemouth to set up a semi-final tie against Cambridge United, the team who had beaten us at the same stage the previous season. We couldn't have had a better draw as the lads were already fully motivated and were determined to make amends. The first leg, held at Ashton Gate, resulted in a 4-2 victory for us, but it could have been 8-2; we absolutely mullered them.

It was a good result, but there were still only two goals in it, so we had to remain switched on for the second leg a few days later. Louis Carey gave us an early lead and they were never going to recover. We battered them again and won 3-0. Deep down, we wanted to put that game to bed, and we did. I wouldn't call it revenge as such, but it was a very satisfying win.

Reaching my first final as a manager was a huge achievement. It had been almost twenty years since Bristol City's last cup – the Football League Trophy, back in 1986 – and it was a great opportunity for us to win some silverware. Wembley Stadium was being rebuilt, so the final was held at the magnificent

Millennium Stadium in Cardiff. Our fans were magnificent; forty thousand of them were in full voice as we walked out of the tunnel onto the pitch. It was incredible. Our support was enough of an incentive for the players. It was terrific – a great day out.

Carlisle were our opponents, and as they were in the division below us, we were the bookies' favourites. But finals are one-off games, and I couldn't help but remember the 1988 Full Members' Cup final when my Luton Town side lost to Reading. It reminded me that upsets can and do happen, and I didn't want to be on the receiving end of another one.

We played very well, controlling the game from kick-off, but just couldn't find the breakthrough. We kept going and got our rewards late on when Lee Peacock put us in front in the seventy-seventh minute. That first goal made the difference. Carlisle had virtually given up by then, and Liam Rosenior got our second just a minute from time.

That feeling when I lifted the trophy in front of our jubilant supporters is right up there with all my other achievements in the game. The players were on cloud nine and celebrated with the fans, rightly so. The victory was as much about them as it was about us.

To go through a process of elimination and get to a final was great; to win it was even better. But I'd have swapped it ten times over for promotion, no doubt about it. Our league campaign had been fought over seven or eight months, through all types of weather, dealing with injury and trying to maintain our form.

Unfortunately, we finished third in the league table, missing out on automatic promotion by just three points. We played Crewe – who pipped us to promotion – in April, and drew 1-1. Had we beaten them, we'd have gone up instead which just goes to show how close we were. It was a bitter blow. At the start of the season, we'd have taken the play-offs, but to come so close to going up automatically and to miss out was difficult. I had to pick the players up and get them ready for another round of games. We just had to get on with it. Yes, they could have been lying on a beach, drinking sangria, but instead we had to go through the next challenge, and that was hard. The players all felt so low because we'd fallen at the final hurdle.

We'd beaten Cardiff – our opponents in the play-off semi-final – twice in the league, but they had snuck into the final play-off spot on the last day of the season, so they had momentum with them. Psychologically, they had the advantage. We had to get the lads' minds in the right place because you can feel very lethargic if you're not right mentally. There wasn't anything physically we could work on – we couldn't get them fitter at that stage of the season – so we focused on improving their mindset.

I don't think Cardiff were better than us. Maybe I was biased, but we always felt we had the better of them. Robert Earnshaw was outstanding that season and a big, big threat. Without him and his thirty-one league goals, they wouldn't have made the play-offs. We set up to contain him, which we did, but that meant we lost a bit of our attacking threat. We were very unlucky over the two legs. It was nip and tuck all the way, but a 1-0 defeat at Ninian Park was enough to send Cardiff through to the final, which they went on to win.

We were incredibly disappointed to miss out on promotion, but I tried to look at the positives. There was definite progress once again. To finish third and win a cup has to be considered a good season.

The key for future success was going to be keeping our team together. We were getting better and better, closer and closer. We had to go for automatic promotion next season; we couldn't leave it to the lottery of the play-offs.

Scott Murray scored twenty-seven goals for us during the 2002/03 season. That's a good return for a striker; for a winger, that is an unbelievable amount. Not many can get that kind of goal return from a wide position. He was a phenomenal player. He'd run through brick walls for you. If I told him to try and get over a barbed wire fence, he'd give it a go. He'd come back bloody, but he'd have tried. He was that sort of player. He was a great kid, and I had an enormous amount of time for him. The dressing room loved him because of his dry sense of humour.

I wasn't aware that Scott wanted to leave us. He was never one who'd come in and say he was looking to go elsewhere. He never knocked on my door or caused us any problems. So when Reading came in for him, I didn't for one minute think he'd go to them, even though they were in the Championship at the time. I didn't think they were his type of team, but they came up with the money, the board accepted it, and Scotty left us. It was a massive blow, but you can't fault the boy for moving to a club in a higher division and trying to better himself. We got £650,000 for him, which I suppose was good for the club, but it wasn't anything that would be given back to me to reinvest in the squad.

The whole team felt the loss. Scott was the catalyst for a lot of our goals, and we all know that scoring is the hardest part of the game. For some reason, it didn't really work out for Scott at Reading, and he came back to us on loan in March 2004. The fans absolutely adored him and still do. He's back at Bristol City now as kit man and is a club legend. We missed him when he left.

It wasn't just the players receiving offers; I also had an opportunity to leave Bristol City. As a manager, I was always committed to the teams I was managing and never consciously chased any other jobs. In 2003, I was approached by the Northern Ireland Football Association to become national team manager. What an incredible opportunity that would have been, but I felt I still had unfinished business at Aston Gate. I don't think I was ready for international management at that stage of my career. I was still cutting my teeth at club level, and I wanted to coach every day of the week. I didn't want to go and watch games once a week and work with the players every two months. That wasn't for me.

At my age now, I'd be more suited to international management. It's less exhausting than club management, and you don't have to do the day-to-day work. Travel wise, you're out and about all the time watching players which isn't a bad thing for an older, more experienced person. International management would possibly suit someone like me, but I think that ship has sailed now.

Despite winning our first game of the season 5-0, we got off to a slow start again before eventually kicking on and finding some form.

On the 16th December, I returned to Barnsley in the FA Cup for my first game back at Oakwell since leaving them five years earlier. I got a mixed reception from the supporters – a few boos and a few claps. To be honest I didn't expect it to be mixed, I thought it would have been very anti-me because I'd gone to Sheffield Wednesday. We lost the game 2-1 but beat them in the two league fixtures.

I also returned to Hillsborough as Wednesday had been relegated the previous season. The fans were great and gave me a fantastic reception. They've always been good to me. After the game, I kept out of the way of the boardroom and the directors' lounge, and just had a drink with my old mate Chris Turner, who was the Wednesday manager at the time.

We finished third in the league again, missing out on automatic promotion by just one point. What a big disappointment. It really hit us hard because we'd put so much work in, but we just fell short. In that respect, maybe one or two doubts were starting to creep into people's minds. You couldn't fault us in terms of how we wanted to play because the football was very good. We just didn't have that little bit extra to push us over the line.

We beat Hartlepool United over two legs to set up a play-off final tie against Brighton at the Millennium Stadium. Scott Murray was suffering from an injury which kept him out of the starting lineup and restricted him to the bench, which was a blow. It was a really tight game and a big kick in the nuts as we conceded late on and lost 1-0. We did enough to win the game ourselves, but we were nowhere near as good on the day as we had been in the matches leading up to the final. That in itself suggested that we needed a little bit of a change amongst the squad, someone to come in and give us that extra yard that we needed.

The play-off final was on a Sunday, and the following day I had a meeting at Ashton Gate with Steve Lansdown, the chairman. Obviously, he was disappointed – we all were – but he was also optimistic. We discussed recruitment and freshening up the team. The meeting didn't last long, but it was very positive. I then had the difficult task of telling the players who were being released that we weren't going to be renewing their contracts. I always had those conversations face-to-face. It was something that had to be done, although it was one of the hardest parts of my job.

The kids were off school, so we flew off to La Manga in Spain for a holiday. We'd had to change dates because of the play-offs, and I was looking forward to getting away for a bit and enjoying some time with my family.

While I was away, I got a call from Brian Jones, the club's psychologist, who told me that the club were letting him and Frank Barlow go for financial reasons. I wasn't happy at all and didn't understand the reasoning. I knew the club had been in the black for the last three seasons. That really disappointed me because the success that we'd enjoyed over the past few years was partly down to Frank and Brian. I couldn't understand the decision, or the fact that I hadn't been consulted.

I phoned Steve Lansdown and asked him what was going on. I asked why he hadn't told me during our meeting. "We didn't know then," he replied.

I'm convinced they did it to force me to resign, because Steve then said, "We're going to part ways with you and bring in a new manager."

I couldn't believe I was being sacked over the phone! I felt it was a bit crass, cowardly even, particularly after the positive meeting we'd had just days earlier. They'd let me do the dirty work with the players who were being released. I felt that I at least deserved the courtesy of being sacked face-to-face. I left Bristol with a bitter taste, which was a shame after all the success we'd brought to the club. We'd made progress season after season. In the history of the club only three managers have a higher win rate than me.

It's a real shame how it ended. The fans were shocked too. We were one point away from automatic promotion and lost 1-0 in the play-off final – we couldn't have got much closer. The crowds were flocking to Ashton Gate; season ticket sales were increasing year on year, it was all positive. I don't think I deserved to be sacked, certainly not over the phone, and not while I was on holiday. Sadly it happens in football. I've heard of other managers who have been sacked via text message! Football doesn't have a conscience. One day you're there mixing with the players, planning for the future, the next you're gone, and you don't even have a chance to say goodbye.

A couple of days later, while I was still on holiday, my phone rang again. I answered it, and although no one said anything, I could hear someone in a car singing "The King is gone, long live the King." I looked at the caller ID and saw that it was Brian Tinnion's phone number. I'm not sure what happened – maybe he called me by accident while his phone was in his pocket – but that must have been embarrassing for him. That's when I should have read the situation. He ended up getting the manager's job, which was a complete surprise from my point of view because he was still a player, not a coach at that stage.

When I was sacked, I thought they must have had someone else lined up, and they did – Brian. Things like that don't happen overnight; I'm sure discussions must have taken place while I was still manager. Brian would have cost them less than me, but it was a strategy that didn't work out for them, as the following season, Bristol City finished seventh and missed out on the play-offs altogether.

I returned to Ashton Gate on the 27th of August 2005, as opposing manager. The fans were absolutely brilliant and gave me a standing ovation. To get that kind of reception showed that I must have done something right while I was there. Brian was still in charge at the time and it got his back up that the fans were cheering for me and not him, but you need to earn that respect – and a forty-seven per cent win rate helps too!

I'd always got on well with Brian, there was no reason not to. He was a fantastic player, one of the first names on my teamsheet. He was a major cog in the success that we had. But when I went down the touchline to the dugout, and he tried to shake my hand, I told him to sit down. He knew what he'd done. When I heard what I had when he phoned me, accidentally or not, that was it. When the game finished – a 2-2 draw – I just walked off.

Time is a healer, though, and now when I look back at my four seasons at Bristol City, I remember the great games, the goals, the incredible supporters, and the success that we enjoyed together.

CHAPTER 20
Against all odds

To say I was disappointed with how my time at Bristol City came to an end is an understatement. I felt we were on the right lines, progress was being made, and the club – on and off the pitch – was getting stronger after years of problems.

The situation didn't dampen my enthusiasm for the game though. In fact, it drove me on a bit more. From my point of view, I realised that people from outside Bristol thought I'd done a good job, so I knew I wouldn't be short of offers for a speedy return to management.

I was still going to watch lots of games, keeping my eye on various teams and players for when I did get back into management, but I was wary of which matches I attended, as I didn't want my presence to set the rumour mill into overdrive. I decided not to go to a game if either team's manager was under pressure at the time. I didn't want to add to their pressure by people seeing me in the stands, putting two and two together, and coming up with ten. I was always very cautious of that. But I did enjoy going to watch football games, just for the hell of it really.

After a nice break to recharge my batteries, I was in a positive frame of mind, ready for the next challenge. And when it came, it was a huge one.

In December 2004, I was approached by MK Dons. It was their first season as a football club following the change of name from Wimbledon. They were struggling in League One at the time, and I was intrigued, although I knew that going from managing a team chasing promotion to a side battling relegation would be a tough ask. Not only results-wise, but the whole club was getting bashed from all angles because of the controversial relocation of Wimbledon football club that had led to the creation of MK Dons. The chairman, Pete Winkelman, was taking so much criticism. A lot of people felt that MK Dons should have started from scratch at the bottom of the football pyramid, instead of replacing Wimbledon in League One.

I sat down with Pete for a chat, and I was blown away by his passion and enthusiasm for Milton Keynes, not just the football club, but for the whole town. He was absolutely brilliant. I couldn't believe his ambition for the club. He told me about his own background as a music producer, his vision for the town and the club. He sold it to me fantastically and after about an hour, I told him I wanted to be a part of it. It sounded so interesting and exciting.

But with my manager's hat on, it was always going to be a very tough gig. The playing side mainly consisted of young, untried boys, and that was always going to be very difficult in League One, which is a very physical league, full of experienced pros. It wasn't just the playing side that concerned me, though. There was so much animosity surrounding the club. A lot of neutrals were taking pleasure in seeing MK Dons struggle. There were some very well-known journalists who wanted to have a pop and wouldn't let it go. One in particular, Martin Samuel, had a real bee in his bonnet about what had happened. He was relentless in his criticism and it really got to Pete. We had all this to contend with, as well as building a new stadium, and I was charged with getting the results to keep us in the division, which was always going to be very difficult.

The way Pete, and everyone associated with the club, saw the situation was that MK Dons were a new club and it was a fresh start. Milton Keynes is located just forty-five miles from London, and lot of the town's residents were people who commuted to the capital, and typically supported London-based clubs. Pete was targeting them and their families with the aim of the local children becoming Dons supporters. He went into schools with MK Dons shirts, giving them out for free to try and get the youngsters interested. It was fantastic. Pete used to tell me, "There are two hundred and fifty thousand people living in Milton Keynes, twenty-one percent of whom are kids. We want them to grow up to become MK Dons fans." He was so enthusiastic in his approach. He championed the club and was always going out and about and into the community, telling people what we were trying to achieve. That was what started the ball rolling really – Pete's all-round belief that he could get the football club going.

At the time, we played our home games at the National Hockey Stadium, which, quite honestly, was crap. It had nothing going for it at all from a football sense. There was absolutely no atmosphere within the ground, no matter how many people were inside, because there were no walls, nothing to keep the sound in. The pitch was rock hard too. It had been an artificial surface before, and it felt like they'd just laid the grass on top of the artificial stuff because the ball bounced so much. None of our players enjoyed playing there.

Pete kept telling me about the plans for a new stadium: where it was going to be located and what it would look like. It sounded absolutely brilliant, but at that time I just thought it was a bit of a pipe dream. I couldn't see him building it within a couple of years; it felt like too big a job in such a short space of time. I didn't say that to him, though, because I didn't want to dampen his enthusiasm. But by hell he did it. He did unbelievably well to build a magnificent thirty-thousand all-seater stadium. No matter what people say about MK Dons, I take my hat off to Pete and I have an enormous amount of respect for what he achieved. And his family: his wife, Berni, and his two children. They were so up for the challenge that was in front of them, and they backed him to the hilt. More importantly, so did the people of Milton Keynes – the council and the public.

Pete told me that they needed someone with a bit of credibility at the helm. Someone experienced, like myself, who knew what it was like to manage a team at the top end of the table. I was fairly well known within the game, and that was one of the reasons I was offered the post. Pete was getting battered from pillar to post by the media, the general football public, and even by people within the game. No one thought he was a serious proposition.

I too saw MK Dons as a brand-new club, not an incarnation of Wimbledon. Apart from the word 'Dons' at the end, there was no resemblance to Wimbledon, although one or two players had moved from Wimbledon to MK Dons, like Dean Lewington, who's still there now. He's been very loyal to the club and has had a fantastic career. I wouldn't be surprised if he becomes manager there one day because he has all the credentials. His dad, Ray, is also a great coach.

Pete wanted us to become the type of club that nurtures young talent. He wasn't averse to producing young players, selling them on for a profit, and then bringing through the next generation. He achieved this in later years, with Dele Alli – his biggest success.

We had a lot of young lads who became good. Izale McLeod was a very talented kid, who scored quite a few goals for us, which eventually earned him a big move to Charlton.

David Martin, our goalkeeper, later played in the Premier League for West Ham United.

Jamie Mackie had two seasons in the top flight for Queen's Park Rangers, and Jason Puncheon was another who made it to the Premier League.

The talent was there, I never had any doubts about how good the players would eventually become, but we didn't have enough experience in the squad to help the younger lads mature. We needed a bit of toughness.

My objective was purely to stay in the division. No more than that. I didn't have any transfer funds to spend. All the money coming in was going back into the football club and towards the new stadium, and I accepted that. The bigger picture was to get the infrastructure right to move MK Dons forward, so I had to rely on loans and free transfers. Clive Platt, a big centre forward, came in from Peterborough. He had the experience we needed and linked up well with McLeod.

Paul Mitchell joined us from Wigan. A northern lad, and a real leader, which was what we were missing in the dressing room. He sadly broke his leg, so didn't play as often as I would have liked, but his presence off the pitch had a huge impact on the younger lads. He's now very highly rated in the recruitment world. He is the current sporting director at Monaco and has also worked with Spurs, Southampton, and RB Leipzig.

I played with a back four at MK Dons, rather than my the three that I'd used before. We tinkered with it a little bit at first, but you've got to have a formation and system to suit the players. Three at the back didn't suit us. We had a fantastic left back in Dean Lewington, and Gareth Edds had come in during the summer to play at right back, although he was so versatile he could play anywhere really.

Pete didn't want me to be just a manager. He wanted me to go out and promote the club around the town and the surrounding areas, in an ambassadorial role. I did that to a certain extent, but it wasn't my strength, I'm not one of those people who can go out there and shout from the rooftops. Within the football club itself I can chat away with anyone, no problem at all, but to go out and act as a salesman, if you like, that's not me. I did a bit, although not as much as I'm sure Pete wanted me to do. The most important thing in my eyes was survival rather than bringing in a few more fans to watch our games. My focus was on results, and they hadn't been great.

We'd only won three games before I joined and were on a nine-game run without a win. We had to turn it around. We had no choice, but it was going to be tough to change a losing mentality. Morale was at rock bottom. These young boys had never been in a situation like this before. A lot of them had been YTS or reserve team players at Wimbledon and then all of a sudden, they were part of a club nobody liked. When they picked up the papers, more often than not, they'd read something detrimental about the club. We were in a position to erase a lot of that negativity but you can only do that by getting results.

It took a while, but after losing to Brentford on 5th February 2005, we were unbeaten for the next eleven matches. That little run gave us a great chance, although we still needed to win our final two games to keep us in the league. Fortunately for us, Wrexham had been handed a ten-point deduction for entering administration that had sent them down, so that left one remaining relegation place. It was between us, Oldham, and Torquay.

On the penultimate day of the season we beat Peterborough 3-0. Torquay won and Oldham lost. Those results gave us huge belief because no matter what happened elsewhere, we knew that if we beat Tranmere in our final game of the season we'd stay up. Our fate was in our hands.

Tranmere Rovers had finished third in the league, so we knew they were a good team, but we were fairly relaxed going into the game. There were over seven thousand fans packed into the Hockey Stadium; it was virtually a full house. Pete was pleased as it showed that the demand from the public was there. We took an early lead through Gareth Edds, and then Tranmere equalised in the second half. A draw was no good to us, though, because Oldham were winning. A draw would send us down. Full credit to the boys because they kept going and didn't give up.

Eddsy was a fit boy, an Australian who could play at the same pace from the first minute to the last. With just six minutes on the clock, he burst forward and unleashed a shot that flew into the goal. The crowd went absolutely bananas, as you can imagine. Going 2-1 up so late in the game was enormous, and I had no doubt that we could see the game out. It was a very emotional moment when the ref blew the full-time whistle and we realised that we had stayed up.

A last-gasp winner on the final day of the season was immensely satisfying, especially as we knew that everyone outside the town was against us. People may talk about us only just staying up and question why we celebrated. It was a massive day for the club. We'd proved to people that we could compete. We hadn't gone into free fall. Success isn't just about winning trophies or league titles. Success stories happen up and down the country, and this was one of them. People still didn't agree with what had gone on; some still don't even after all these years, but we had worked damn hard to stay in League One and we deserved to enjoy the moment.

Pete was so happy that he presented me with the Player of the Season award, believe it or not! Before I joined, we'd lost eleven games, drawn four, and won just three. We went on to lose eight, draw ten, and win nine. It was a complete turnaround.

After a short break, I turned my attention to the following season, although I knew it would be another tough campaign, especially due to the challenges we faced when it came to recruiting players.

For a start, we had no money, so we couldn't pay big wages or transfer fees. But also, the negative media publicity surrounding MK Dons meant there was a stigma attached to the club. It's not easy trying to convince a player to join a side who are constantly being criticised by the media.

When the new stadium began to take shape, it was a great selling point to potential signings, but that all came a little bit late for me.

Our training facilities were OK, but no better than that. We trained on a council-owned field, and getting the grass cut was a bit of an ask at times. The stadium was Pete's priority, and rightly so, but from a manager's point of view, the training pitch was key. That's where you spend the week preparing the boys for the games. When you've got people walking their dogs over the pitch, or people riding bikes past you when you're trying to coach players, it becomes very difficult to concentrate.

I did manage to bring in a few players. Paul Mitchell came in on a permanent deal, and he was soon joined by Craig Morgan, a centre back who became a Welsh international. Stephen Quinn came in on loan from Sheffield United. He was a cracking lad and a great little player. His brother, Alan, had been at Sheffield Wednesday during my spell as a manager there.

We needed another striker as there was a lot of interest in Izale and we didn't know if we'd be able to keep him. Izale aside, we didn't have goals in that team, so we brought in Aaron Wilbraham, a target man who'd just been released by Hull City. Later in the season, I signed Scott Taylor, who was a recognised goal scorer in the lower leagues, and we paid money for him, the first time I'd spent anything at MK Dons. Unfortunately, he had a spate of injuries and we hardly got him on the pitch, which was so disappointing. We were expecting big things from him.

It was a difficult start to the season, and we never really got going. Our biggest problem was scoring goals. Izale bagged eighteen, Clive Platt got eight, and Gary Smith scored seven from midfield, but overall that wasn't enough. If you can't score goals, you're always going to be in trouble. Aaron was a good all-round player, but he only scored six goals, and Scott Taylor played just seventeen games because of the injuries as I've mentioned. I spent all our budget on one player, so I had to look at myself and question if I'd spent wisely. I think we did because when he did play, he was very good.

In January, we lost our goalkeeper when David Martin joined

Liverpool, and I made the decision to release Jason Puncheon. Jason had so many chances, but his discipline was a constant issue, and it got to the stage where I thought it was best for all parties if he moved on. There were times when he'd go missing, literally go missing. We had no idea where he was. There was never any doubt in my mind that he was going to be a good player in the future, but it wasn't going to happen for him at MK Dons. I don't think he was ready to play regular first team football at that stage of his career and he needed a fresh start. He needed to go away and resurrect his career, which he did.

Towards the end of the season, we won four games on the bounce, which gave us a chance of survival. Again, we went into the last two games of the season needing at least one win to stay up. I honestly thought we could do it again.

Ironically, we lost a crazy game to Tranmere in our penultimate match. With ninety minutes on the clock, the score was tied at 0-0. They scored, we equalised, and then they grabbed a very, very late winner in stoppage time. Talk about an emotional rollercoaster! As Mr Clough used to say, "It only takes a second to score a goal." You can't rest on your laurels and assume the game is over until the ref has blown the whistle, yet that's exactly what we did. We lost concentration, which was bitterly disappointing.

We then went into a shootout with Rotherham on the final day of the season. We needed to beat them to stay up and relegate them. But if we drew or lost, Rotherham would avoid the drop and send us down.

We drew 0-0 and were relegated. We were so close, just two points away from survival. Did we deserve to stay up? I don't know, but when you get fifty points, you think you've done enough. Fifty points would have been enough to stay in the Championship and League Two that season, so I felt we were a tad unlucky.

The reaction from the media was very harsh, with many people saying we deserved to be relegated, not for footballing reasons but because we'd replaced Wimbledon. That was incredibly unfair on the players because the decision to move from Wimbledon to Milton Keynes was made years earlier – it wasn't their fault. A lot of people took satisfaction from our relegation, and that hurt.

I had an inkling that I'd be leaving the club. Pete was doing so much to sell Milton Keynes as a town and a football club. He wanted everyone to buy into his vision; he wanted everyone to be a part of the area, and I wasn't. I stayed in a hotel for a large part of the week and went home to Derbyshire as often as I could. I was never going to move to Milton Keynes on a permanent basis and take my children out of school, especially not with the uncertainty that surrounds managers. I think that was one of the reasons, not just the relegation, that led to Pete's decision to sack me.

When you've just been relegated, you expect to be questioned, but we were always going to be relegation favourites with the squad we had. In League One, your weaknesses will be exposed, and our biggest weakness was a lack of goals.

Pete and I sat down and discussed the future. I respect him a great deal for speaking to me face-to-face. There wasn't going to be a phone call or text message with Pete; that wasn't his style. People think he's a nice guy – and he is – but he is also a very strong and determined man, and when you talk to him you can see that. He certainly isn't soft. He explained where he wanted to take the club and told me that I wasn't part of his plans. I was disappointed to be relieved of my duties, of course I was, but at least he had the decency to explain why he made that decision.

Nobody likes to be relegated, but it made me even more determined to get back into football management and enjoy success again.

CHAPTER 21
A leaky roof

During the times when I was employed as a manager, I was away from home most of the time, so between jobs I liked to spend as much time as I could with my family. We had a place in Spain for a number of years, so we'd try and get out there as often as we could and get away for a bit. We'd eat well, enjoy a few drinks, and play a bit of golf in the sun.

After a short holiday in the summer of 2006, I got straight back on the saddle with Hartlepool. They had also been relegated from League One, and I received a phone call from Chris Turner, who I'd played with at Sheffield Wednesday. Chris was working for Hartlepool as Sporting Director, and he asked me if I'd consider going in for a chat. Paul Stephenson was the caretaker-manager at the time, and he later became my coach. He was a very good coach, and I got to know him well.

So I went to have a chat and I was given the manager's role just weeks after leaving MK Dons. Hartlepool was about the same distance from my home as Milton Keynes, so the club put me up in an apartment on the harbour side of the town, which was ideal as it was less than five minutes from the ground.

Anybody who knows me will understand that money is not something that drives me. In fact, it's quite the opposite at times, as I've taken jobs on, got a load of grief, and hardly been paid anything. It's not money that motivates me; it's the love of the game that's kept me involved for so long.

As a manager, you are battered from pillar to post. Very rarely are you in the position of Jurgen Klopp or Pep Guardiola, where you're winning games every week and getting glorified in the press. That's a dream I'd love to have, but it just doesn't happen.

More often than not, you're vilified for one decision or another that you've made. Management for me was about the enjoyment of working with players, seeing them develop, grow, and go on to bigger and better things. I took a lot of pride and satisfaction from that.

Hartlepool had a good name in football, and I knew they were a well-run club. Increased Oil Recovery (IOR) owned the club. Their head office was based in Aberdeen, but the company's owners were Norwegian. I soon learned that they ran the club differently to others I'd been at, which caused problems for me later, but they were a stable company who would often bail the club out by injecting cash to keep Hartlepool afloat. But they didn't do it willy nilly. They put a structure in place, and it was solid. No matter what you wanted, your request had to go through IOR, and if they said no, that was it. Ken Hodcroft, our chairman, was the link between the football club and IOR.

As soon as I took the job, I knew it was going to be a challenge. Everyone expected Hartlepool, like they do most relegated teams, to bounce straight back up at the first attempt, but as we know, it doesn't always pan out that way. No matter who you are or what league you're in, there is always an ambition and an expectation from fans and the board; whether they are realistic or not is open to debate. So there is always pressure. Managers are never far away from pressure, and perhaps that's what I thrive on in a perverse way. Maybe I need pressure.

The jobs I took throughout my career were all clubs with challenges. I was generally going into a football club that was feeling quite sorry for itself and picking up the pieces – I was a firefighter really, often having little money to spend and inheriting a team low on morale. My job was to quickly assess the situation, identify the reasons for the problems, and then rectify them. Very rarely can a manager go in and turn things around without changing anything. You occasionally get one or two good results from 'new manager syndrome,' but in the main, you have to make changes. You have to be ruthless; there's no room for sentiment in football.

Every year, Hartlepool went to Holland for their pre-season camp, and I saw no reason to change that. We didn't fly there, though, because of the expense. The way the club was ran, we sought sponsors to pay for the ferry or pay for the kit. That was how they did it; if they could get funding rather than put their own hand in their pocket, they would, which was great.

We had two friendlies lined up: one against Top Oss and the other against Den Bosch. So, we're on the overnight ferry to Holland and – bearing in mind this is pre-season – I have never seen so many pissed men in all my life! The lads were absolutely plastered. We got out there and drew both games, so I gave the boys a day off and said they could have a couple of drinks. They got plastered again –it was ridiculous. One of the lads cut his foot on broken glass, which ruled him out for the start of the season.

It was a real eye opener, and I immediately noticed what was wrong, and why they'd been relegated – they were a good team, but the players had lost their focus. They'd forgotten what was required of them, especially during pre-season. They'd done this every year, and they must have thought I wouldn't mind.

They were wrong!

When we got back to England, I came down on them very hard. There were some harsh words said and some tough training sessions given. There is a balance to be found between having a good time to foster that vital team spirit and remembering that they are professional athletes. Don't get me wrong, they were fit boys, but it was pre-season. They'd just had their holidays, enjoyed their booze, and had four weeks off. Pre-season is a time for putting in the work – trying to find an edge that'll give you an advantage over the other teams. I didn't think that was a good starting point, to be honest. Going out for a pint or a glass of wine isn't a problem. You can do it every night of the week for all I'm concerned, but there is a line that needs to be drawn. There are times when you can drink as much as you want and times when you can't. Pre-season isn't the time for drinking.

The other challenge was financially. The club were losing money and they weren't flush with dough, so we had to cut our cloth accordingly, and that meant selling players. Adam Boyd, our centre forward, was the biggest loss when he was sold to Luton Town for half a million quid. Tom Butler went to Swansea City and Chris Llewellyn joined Wrexham.

Ritchie Humphries was already at Hartlepool when I joined. Ritchie was a player I'd managed at Sheffield Wednesday. He was a fan favourite, and I knew how good he could be, but he wasn't doing it on the pitch, so I sent him out on loan. The fans went bananas because he was their hero, but he wasn't performing to the standard I knew he was capable of. I knew Ritchie's character and had every intention of bringing him back to the club. The loan move was just a short-term solution to give him a change of scenery and a chance to recharge his batteries.

Our season got off to a dreadful start – it took us five games before we won our first game, and by mid-September, we were in twenty-first position in the table. It was a transitional period, where we had to change the players' mentality. Relegation was still fresh in everyone's minds and the majority of the lads were still feeling low.

No one thought we'd do anything at that stage because there was no consistency in our results. Most people were surprised with our turn of fortune, but not me, because I knew we had good players. A good mix of youth and experience, combined with pace. To not get results was criminal because the fans deserved more.

The turning point for us came in November 2006, during an away game at Accrington Stanley. It was a miserable winter's day and it was absolutely pissing it down with rain. We were losing 1-0 at halftime and I was not happy. When we got back to the dressing room, the players sat down, and I noticed that the rain was coming through the roof, dripping onto the treatment table. The place was a tip and I ripped into the players.

"This is what you want, is it? Coming to a shithole place like this, letting a team like that take the piss out of you. You're pissing your careers away. You've just had one relegation and the way you're playing you're going to get another one." But with a few more expletives thown in as you can imagine! I really went to town on the boys; it was the angriest I've ever been in football.

People who haven't worked with me have this perception that I'm a nice guy. Well, when you've been managing for nearly twenty-five years, you need to have a ruthless side. You can't be a nice guy in football. I'm a totally different person at home – very patient and it takes a lot to rile me. But if I am riled, I'm not a very likeable person. I can count on one hand the number of times I've really lost it.

It was possibly the biggest bollocking they've had in their careers, and it worked. The players responded, and we won 2-1, with a last-gasp winner from the rejuvenated Humphries.

The comeback victory against Accrington kicked off a twenty-three-match unbeaten run that propelled us up the table. We set a record for the number of wins in a single season which was fantastic and put us on track for promotion. So I thank Accrington for not mending the roof on the away team's dressing room!

The return of Ritchie Humphries was a huge factor in that amazing run. He was like a different player when he returned, almost like a new signing for us. Ritchie is a fantastic pro, very well respected in the game, and was chairman of the PFA during the latter stages of his career.

We also brought in Andy Monkhouse, a six-foot four-inch winger, believe it or not. He was devastating on his day. Great feet for a big lad and all that. He could create and score goals.

One of the biggest signings I made that season was bringing in Richie Barker from Mansfield Town for £80,000. What a signing he turned out to be for us. He hit the ground running and scored nine goals in eighteen league games.

During the season, Len Badger, the former Sheffield United player, and his wife, Mel, came to visit me in Hartlepool for a weekend. They stayed in a local hotel. This was around the time John Darwin, a Hartlepool man, had apparently gone missing in his canoe. They eventually found him in Panama, and he was sentenced to six years for insurance fraud. Anyway, Darwin was still missing when Badge came to stay, and he was convinced that Darwin was hiding in the walls of his hotel room because he could hear voices! Len was such a good character and a very funny bloke. I miss him so much. He died in April 2021, and he was a big, big pal.

In March 2007, we went to Darlington for a crucial local derby. It wasn't going to be easy, as they were also in the promotion hunt, but we took four thousand fans there and won 3-0, with two goals from Eifion Williams and one from Monkhouse. That was a big result. That was when we realised that we had a good chance of going up. We were in great form, and to go to our rivals, Darlington, and get an emphatic victory in front of ten thousand fans – unheard of for League Two – was terrific.

In our last three games, we drew 1-1 with Notts County, lost 2-0 away at Rochdale, and lost 2-1 at home to Bristol Rovers, and had to settle for second place. We lost focus a little, and that was the only disappointment for me, that we didn't go up as champions.

The Rovers game was tough. There was a party atmosphere during the match. The fans were happy and clapping the players – even when they gave it away! They were celebrating our promotion, and maybe that led to the players losing focus.

We were actually 1-0 up, but they scored the winner with four minutes to play through Rickie Lambert. He was a player I'd have loved to sign. He was a terrific goal scorer and, obviously, went on to play for England and Liverpool. He was always a threat throughout his career. Rickie actually started out as a midfielder and ended up as a striker because he was such a good finisher. I had enquired about him at the start of the 2006/07 season, but getting him to move up to the North East wasn't easy because we'd just been relegated.

At the start of the campaign, my objective was to win promotion and that's what we achieved, so it was a good year and expectations were high for my second season.

*****

From one of the best moments of my time at Hartlepool, to possibly the saddest moment of my career ,was the passing of our twenty-year old midfielder Michael Maidens in a car accident in October 2007. He was a talented winger and a complete gentleman. We were in Wales preparing for an away game against Swansea when we heard the tragic news. We were all completely shocked.

Roberto Martinez, the Swansea manager, and I asked the authorities if we could postpone the game out of respect for Michael, and thankfully everybody agreed.

As you can imagine, his mum and dad, Heather and Doug, were beside themselves. I think any parent would understand their grief at losing a child. They followed Michael to every game he played, and he was a massive loss, not only to his family but also to everyone at the club.

Hartlepool retired his number 25 shirt as a mark of respect.

Michael is still remembered fondly at Hartlepool, and he will be forever.

*****

As I've mentioned, the way IOR ran the club was completely different to anything I'd come across before. After every game, whether that was a Sunday or Monday, the chairman wanted me to write down my assessment of the match, so he could post it to the company in Aberdeen, to then be sent on to Norway. I did it at the start, but then got fed up and stopped writing the reports. The chairman was at every game, so he could quite easily have reported back, but that's not the way they wanted to do it.

Everything had to be put down in writing. If you wanted a pen, you had to complete a requisition form and send it to Aberdeen, who'd forward it to Norway for a decision. Then the form would go from Norway to Aberdeen and back to the club. Whatever you asked for had to go through that process, and, as you can imagine, it meant things took ages to get done. That was a big frustration from my point of view. In the end, I spoke to Chris about it.

"Chris, I want you to tell IOR that I don't want to be doing this. I want to spend more time on the training pitch with the players to try and win football games. I'm out every night watching matches, trying to scout players or assess the opposition. I don't have time to write a report on our game when they can get a video and watch it for themselves."

Chris took it to Ken, the chairman, and I think Ken got frustrated with me. He wasn't going to change his ways, and neither were IOR.

There were a lot of things that were frustrating me, to be honest. We'd won promotion with a team who had been relegated from League One twelve months earlier, and we did well, finishing fifteenth in League One during the 2007/08 season, a great achievement, I thought, as did a lot of people.

The problem was that I found myself spending more and more time filling in forms and writing reports, than focusing on the team. Eventually, I just decided not to do it anymore.

We had a meeting every Monday morning, with the minutes going from Ken to Aberdeen, etc. During one meeting, they were discussing another pointless process, and they asked what I had to say on the matter. "Fuck all," was my response. I was so frustrated. It wasn't my job to say whether company decisions were right or wrong; I was only interested in the football side. I felt that all these extra tasks were diluting the time I had available to spend with the players, which was my job. The players were the most important part of the football club, and I wanted to focus on them and not worry about what was said during a meeting about insignificant things. I couldn't get my head around it.

So I told Chris Turner I was leaving it all to him, but that wasn't good enough in Ken's eyes, and he eventually called me into a meeting and told me that it was time to part ways. We were thirteenth in the table at the time, having a decent season.

I don't think it was a shock if I'm honest. I could sense the end was approaching. There was more than one occasion when I had my desk virtually cleared, ready to go. The disappointing aspect for me was that I wasn't sacked for footballing reasons. I was dismissed because I didn't work in the way they wanted me to operate.

I went into the club to fight a fire, create a team, and then win football games. That's the essence of football management. I always had the belief that I could come in and save teams – get them into a solid position. I did that at Bristol City, I did it at MK Dons, and I did it again at Hartlepool. It was just a shame that I wasn't allowed to take it to the next stage. Most of the time, when the clubs I was managing sacked me, they ended up falling on their arse. It gave me no pleasure to see Hartlepool fall into the National League a few years later. The fans deserved better.

CHAPTER 22
An ice bath and a penalty shootout

The fact that I was dismissed by Hartlepool made me start to question my own ability. I thought I'd been doing a good job, but part of me began to doubt myself a little. Another part wanted to prove Hartlepool wrong. Fortunately for me, I wasn't out of work for very long.

On Boxing Day 2008, less than two weeks after leaving Hartlepool, I was appointed manager of Swindon Town. There were reportedly over fifty applications for the role, and as soon as I was sacked, I jumped to the top of that list. I don't know the reason why. Maybe it was because people had realised that I had actually been doing a good job and that my dismissal from Hartlepool was harsh.

Whatever the reason, I was delighted to be back in the game so quickly. I met with Andrew Fitton, the chairman, and we got on very well. We still do today. Swindon were sitting just one point above the relegation zone in League One, and Andrew explained that my target was survival.

I had no doubt that we could get out of trouble when I looked at the players we had.

Kevin Amankwaah was one of the best attacking right backs in the division. A really athletic player with lightning-fast pace, and standing at six foot three, he could play centre back as well.

In midfield we had JP McGovern, who was terrific at sliding balls to the strikers through defence or getting into wide areas and putting balls into the box.

Hal Robson Kanu, who later starred for Wales in the European Championship, was another very creative player we had in the ranks.

Lilian Nalis was an articulate guy whose professionalism rubbed off on the other players. I enjoyed managing him, but unfortunately, he got injured quite a lot and we missed his quality on the pitch.

Up front we had Simon Cox, who was on fire at the time, and ended up scoring thirty-two goals for us during the 2008/09 season. Alongside him was Lee Peacock, who I knew from my time at Bristol City. Lee was absolutely fantastic, but he kept having problems with his back. Billy Paynter was the third striker in our ranks, although he too was struggling with injury.

Andrew Fitton and I discussed the fact that we needed another striker, but the only ones who were available weren't cost-effective. I didn't want to bring someone in for the sake of it, so we agreed to wait until the end of the season and see what happened.

We won my first game in charge, lost a couple, and then went on a five-match unbeaten run. One of the games during that run was against Leicester City, who won the league that year. They were managed by my former teammate, Nigel Pearson. Nigel had been a great captain for Sheffield Wednesday while I was there, and we had some great times together. But when it came to the match between our sides, we were rivals. We got a 1-1 draw, which was a great result.

We only lost two of the final ten games, and finished in a credible fifteenth position. I was quite happy with that, and so was the chairman, who told me that my target for the 2009/10 season was to get into the play-offs. Our results at the back end of the campaign had given him, and me, the belief that we could do it.

However, it was quite a demanding challenge, especially when we lost Simon Cox, our top goal scorer, at the end of the season. West Brom made a £1,500,000 offer, which the club accepted. It was a good move for Coxy and also helped Swindon out financially, but it left me with a big gap in the team.

We still had Billy Paynter, of course, but we needed to bring in a new striker. The chairman gave me a little bit of money, not in the hundreds of thousands, but enough to rebuild. We also needed to strengthen other areas of the squad, so I couldn't blow my budget on one player. I had to spend it wisely.

I've always trusted my scouts to find players and make recommendations, but I always liked to have a look myself before I signed anyone to see if I thought they could fit into the team. There are lots of things to consider, not just their ability. I liked lads who worked hard, especially out of possession. For my system to work, I needed team players.

It was a busy summer for Swindon in terms of recruitment. Fifteen players left the club, and a high number came in, including goalkeeper David Lucas from Leeds; Scott Cuthbert, a defender from Celtic; and Alan Sheehan, a good left back who could also play as a left centre back.

In midfield, Danny Ward was a good attacking left-sided player who scored a lot of goals for us. Alan O'Brien was another winger we brought in.

Jon Douglas came in from Leeds. Dougy was a continuity player. He was so good at keeping possession.

We also brought in Franck Nouble from West Ham. Frank was a remarkable young talent but never really got it together, which is a shame as I think he could have played at a much higher level.

Simon Ferry came in from Scotland. Simon had terrific ability in midfield and two great feet. The lads we brought in were of a creative ilk.

Vincent Pericard, who'd played for Juventus and the French Under-21 side, was an old-fashioned target man. He wasn't a prolific scorer, but if you wanted someone to play around him, he was excellent. You could get the ball up to him in the air and he could play people in from around him. His body strength was fantastic; he was so strong. Vincent worked hard and was a terrific lad. He contributed a great deal to the team and was brilliant on the training pitch, but unfortunately, he suffered a lot of injuries that hampered his career.

I was happy with the new signings, but we still needed a proven goal scorer, and that's when we signed a lad from non-league Poole. A striker by the name of Charlie Austin.

Andrew Fitton knew a bit about Charlie. Not a lot, just that he was scoring goals at non-league level. Charlie had been invited to train with Bournemouth, but they were having so many problems financially at the time, and they couldn't afford to take him. I went down to Poole to watch him in a game and, although he didn't score on the day, his movement was great, and I could see why he was so prolific at that level. I watched some videos and was impressed. He just always seemed to get into good positions inside the six-yard box, and he finished everything. He was scoring goals for fun.

I saw enough and said, "Let's take him." We paid in total, I believe, about sixty grand for him, which was a very good deal. Charlie became a very good pro and has enjoyed a fantastic career.

The one thing about Charlie was that he had the physical strength to compete with anyone, so I wasn't worried about him stepping up to League One. At the time, he was working as a brick layer for his dad's cconstruction company. He was a tough boy who was used to getting up at five or six each morning to work on a building site, so hard work was never a problem for him. He took to professional football like a duck to water and was one of the best signings I ever made.

The biggest challenge at the start was keeping him out of the pubs. He liked a drink, did Charlie. He was used to going for a pint with the lads after a day's graft on the building site, and we had to help him develop a footballer's lifestyle. When he first joined us, we allowed him to continue working with his dad, but then he stopped to focus on becoming a professional footballer. He took on board everything we said, and he's scored goals at all levels, including the Premier League.

With the new squad assembled, we went to Austria for our pre-season camp. Kenny Moyes, David's brother, had a company that specialised in pre-season training tours across Europe. I'd used him a couple of times before, and he always put on a good tour. We wanted to go somewhere with very few distractions so we could focus on getting to know each other and getting the lads' fitness levels up. Austria was ideal in that respect.

We stayed deep in the mountains. The weather was fantastic, but there was snow on the top of the mountain, so the water flowing down the side of the mountain into the river was absolutely freezing. At the time, people were raving about the health benefits of ice baths, and we had our own natural one, so after training we'd sit in the river for half an hour. Even I joined them in the water – I had to, didn't I? I'd like to say I led by example, but I think I probably crept in when they were already completely submerged in the water. It was great, though. The best feeling in the world. If you're feeling any pulls or niggles, they've completely disappeared by the time you get out of the ice-cold water.

I think we were one of the favourites to be relegated that season. People outside the football club saw a team who had only just finished in mid-table and then lost their top scorer. But deep down, I was quietly confident that we could make the play-offs, although I certainly didn't shout it from the rooftops. There was an inner belief that we could achieve something that season.

I was really pleased with the boys who had come in, and the pre-season trip to Austria was a huge success, so we were full of confidence ahead of the first game of the season, which was away to Gillingham and . . . we lost 5-0!

It was a shock, a huge shock. After all the hard work that had gone on during the summer, to then get walloped, I thought, *Oh no!*

But I'd been involved in football management for long enough to know that promotions and relegations are not won or lost on the opening day of the campaign. There were another forty-five games to play, and we wanted to gradually build momentum. So although I was disappointed, I wasn't overly concerned. We always believed that we'd get better and better as the season went on. Mind you, it couldn't get any worse than a 5-0 loss, could it?

It takes time for a new team to gel, and that's where the hours you spend on the training pitch come in.

As an attacking midfielder myself, I'd look at that position first to see if they were providing the right kind of service to the strikers. What I liked to do was spend time with the midfielders, strikers, and wide men and help them get to know how they each like to play. If you've got a striker who likes to come deep and have the ball played to his feet, it's pointless sticking the ball into space because they won't get on the end of it. You've got to understand the players you have around you and where they want the ball.

We had little Anthony McNamee on the wing, and he could

go past anybody. But he'd want to try and beat them again, and by that time, the strikers who had made their runs had to come back, so the option was no longer available. We had to encourage Anthony to get the ball in earlier and he started to do that. The challenge as a manager is to identify these problems and try and resolve them as quickly as possible. You have to give it time, continue to work hard on the training ground and keep the repetition until they get it.

We tried to get people into key areas where they could supply the strikers and create chances, and you could see how that worked as the season progressed by the high number of goals we scored.

The attacking side of the game was my forte, but I brought in specialists for the defensive side of the game. Peter Shirtliff– who I'd played with at Sheffield Wednesday and had signed for Barnsley – came in to be my defensive coach. He was so calm and assured, and coached the same way that he'd played. He looked after the defenders. We liked to get the full backs forward, and Peter's job was to ensure the back line were well organised.

George Woods was our goalkeeping coach. He'd enjoyed a fantastic playing career with Arsenal, Everton, Crystal Palace, and Scotland, and he passed on his experience to our keepers, David Lucas and Phil Smith.

After the Gillingham game, we went on a great run and didn't lose again for fourteen matches. Our first league win came against Southampton, the promotion favourites. That was a fantastic result as the Saints had players like Rickie Lambert, Morgan Schniederlin, and Adam Lallana. We also earned a draw against Premier League side Wolves in the League Cup, which was another huge confidence boost, although they eventually beat us on penalties.

Although we didn't win a lot of the games during that run, the most important thing for us was that we didn't lose. We were improving all the time. The young lads started to believe in what we were doing, and it's very satisfying when you can see the team moving up the league table.

Our run came to an end with a 3-0 defeat at home to Hartlepool. We then lost 1-0 to Norwich in the next match, before embarking on another fantastic run that saw us lose just once in eighteen games, including a 3-0 win over Leeds United, who were promoted at the end of the season. We'd proved that we could compete with anyone.

One of the biggest reasons for our impressive form was the number of goals we scored. When we introduced Billy Paynter to. Charlie Austin, they developed a great understanding. They were like Bonnie and Clyde, the pair of them! They formed a fantastic partnership that got better and better as the season went on. They ended up scoring nearly fifty goals between them, which is a manager's dream.

In March 2010, I was playing Kevin Amankwaah as a central defender, and I needed a right back. I knew Kenny Dalglish pretty well, so I phoned him and said, "Kenny, I need a right back. Have you got anyone at Liverpool?"

"There's a young lad called Stephen Darby you can take on loan," Kenny replied.

"What's he like?" I asked.

"He's a great kid, a great pro. I'll go so far as to say that you would let him marry your daughter, he's that good a kid," Kenny said.

That was a massive statement to make of someone's character, so I brought Stephen down to Swindon, and he was absolutely brilliant; a terrific signing.

We had a great chance of achieving automatic promotion, but we won only one of our final six games, which meant we finished fifth in the league, just four points away from Leeds, who were runners up.

There was definite progress from the previous season, and we played some very good football. I was delighted that we managed to qualify for the play-offs, even though there was a tinge of disappointment that we hadn't gone up automatically. We only lost eight games all season, the lowest in the division, so we were certainly a team who were hard to beat. Our problem was that we drew too many games, and that is what cost us.

We were drawn against Charlton in the play-off semi-final. We won the first leg 2-1 in front of our supporters at the County Ground, and three days later we travelled to London for the return leg.

We couldn't have gotten off to a worse start – we lost David

Lucas, our regular goalkeeper, to injury just five minutes into the game, and we were 2-0 down at half-time.

To make matters worse, in the sixty-seventh minute, our captain, Gordon Greer, was sent off, but we kept going. We kept working hard. And we got our reward just twenty minutes from time when Danny Ward scored after a great run from JP McGovern. That put us level on aggregate, and we were unlucky not to score a winner in extra-time.

The tie finished 2-1 to Charlton on the night, 3-3 on aggregate, so the match went to a penalty shootout. I've managed teams that have won on penalties and I'd managed sides who have lost. Either way, as a manager, you are completely helpless. You cannot do anything. Before the game and during training, the lads practised penalties, so I knew who the takers would be, but then it's all down to how the boys handled the nerves on the day. They've got to have the composure to put the ball where they've put it all week during training. Sometimes, players forget that. They've practised going the same way all week, but then, all of a sudden, they are in front of a different goalkeeper in a pressured environment and they change their minds. That's lethal. It's so important to maintain a clear focus on what you're trying to do. We just told the boys to try and clear everything out of their heads and to execute the penalty like they'd been doing all week. But you don't know if that's going to happen until they actually step up.

A penalty shootout isn't just about the players taking the spot kicks; the goalkeepers are key too. We'd lost David Lucas early in the game, which was hard enough, but going into a penalty shootout without our first-choice goalkeeper was a huge challenge. Phil Smith hadn't played a great deal of games for us, but he was very athletic, agile, and a great shot-stopper, so we knew we still had a good chance. Smithy had been outstanding in the game, and he had nothing to lose. He felt no pressure whatsoever and went into the shootout feeling very relaxed.

We already knew the players who would take the penalties; we just had to sort out the order and check where people felt comfortable. The first and fifth penalties are generally the deciders, so it was important to get the order right.

JP McGovern went first for us and scored. Charlie Austin,

Kevin Amankwaah, and Danny Ward, all scored theirs before young Stephen Darby stepped up to take the deciding spot kick in a very hostile atmosphere. The words that Kenny had said about him were ringing in my ears as he placed the ball on the spot. He knew what was needed, and he smashed the ball into the net with a terrific penalty.

We were on our way to Wembley! What an incredible feeling.

I couldn't go to the extremes of Big Ron and bring in a comedian to relax the lads, but we gave them all a couple of days off. When we did train, we didn't go flat out, we just kept it fun. When it came to the crunch, we did a bit of work about the opposition, the same stuff we did before every match. We tried to keep the whole build up the same as any other game, without the added pressure.

We always felt it was going to be a close game. Millwall, our opponents, were a good team and had a bit more experience than us. We tried to play a possession-based game and it was important that we didn't give the ball away unnecessarily because they were a very direct side. Steve Morrison was leading the line for Millwall, so any ball that went into our box, you could pretty much guarantee that he'd be on the end of it, so we had to try and neutralise that threat. The best way of doing that was to try and stop them having the ball, and that's what we worked on.

The atmosphere around the town of Swindon was brilliant. Considering that eighteen months earlier we'd been on the brink of relegation, to see the smile of the supporters' faces was great. They were determined to enjoy their day out at Wembley, and we were desperate to win the game for the fans. They were in great spirits and just reaching the final was an achievement because no one expected us to get there.

Unfortunately, we lost a very tight game 1-0. There was nothing between us and Millwall, and we could have scored with a chance that Charlie had, but the ball hit a bobble. The pitch was in a terrible condition and was being relaid between games because it was so crap.

Losing at Wembley in a game of that magnitude was a bitter blow, and I really felt for the fans who'd been great all season.

The players were devastated, and I tried to lift their spirits.

"Listen, lads. You've got here against all odds. You've worked well as a team, and every single one of you has been absolutely brilliant. We've scored goals, played some fantastic football, and we've got to build on that. It's disappointing now, but we need to come back stronger and go one step further next year," I said to them in the dressing room. But it's difficult to speak to the players after a game like that, at the end of a gruelling year, because they can't see beyond that result.

Andrew Fitton, the chairman, was true to his word. At the start of the season, he'd set me the target of reaching the play-offs. To reach the play-off final was more than he expected, and he congratulated me, and the lads, and told us that it had been a good season. I really appreciated his honesty and still have a lot of time for Andrew.

The players came in for a few days the following week for one or two things. The hardest thing I had to deal with was the retain list. That was so difficult because you're releasing young lads and spoiling someone's dream. I always have those conversations face-to-face, although I've heard some managers do it by text, believe it or not! I try and explain why I've made the decision, but generally most lads just hear the word 'released' and not a lot else. I knew how it felt. I had been released by Sunderland as a young lad, so I know it's not a nice experience. The other lads who have some experience will often find a new club, but for the younger ones, especially those who haven't played for the first team yet, they think it's the end. That's not always the case, but it's very difficult to convince a young lad that their dream isn't necessarily over.

After that, we'd do a few tests with the players and create fitness programmes for them to follow during the summer months. Yes, we wanted them to have a rest, but we expected them keep to things ticking over. After a short holiday ourselves, my coaches and I returned to focus on the next season.

CHAPTER 23
Where are the goals?

The fact that we had reached the play-off final showed we were up there with the top teams in the division. If we could keep hold of our best players, and maybe add one or two new lads, there was no reason why we couldn't mount a successful promotion charge in the 2010/11 campaign.

Unfortunately, success is not always beneficial to the football club because you get suitors for your players if they've had a good season. Billy Paynter had just had an exceptional year, scoring twenty-nine goals in all competitions, including four against Leeds United, who won promotion. If we'd gone up, we'd have been able to keep him, but Leeds came in and Billy left. It was disappointing to lose our top scorer for the second consecutive season, but I couldn't blame him. He wanted to better himself, and it's a short career.

We also lost our captain, Gordan Greer. Gordon was instrumental to the way we liked to play. He was brilliant on the ball and great at stepping out from the back. The top defenders do it all the time nowadays – we did it back then. He loved to play out from the back, and that was why we were able to break teams down like we did, because while they were chasing the ball, we could pick them off. We'd brought him in on a free transfer from Doncaster Rovers the year before, and he was sold to Brighton for £250,000, so we made a profit.

One of the biggest challenges for a manager is that you spend time coaching, developing, and giving players opportunities, and if they do well, you often lose them. If they don't do well, you lose games. It's a no-win situation. If the players take on board everything we said and worked hard for the team, they're going to attract interest. And when you're at a club like Swindon, the offers can't be turned down because the football club needs to be run in a sustainable way. It becomes a bit of a niggle because the fans want you to keep your best players – I did too, of course – but we just couldn't afford to. If we turned down an offer and the player ran down their contract, picked up an injury, or lost form, we've suddenly lost out on a decent chunk of money. For Swindon Town, the board just couldn't afford to say no.

It costs a lot of money to run a football club. The benefactors need deep pockets, and the way Andrew wanted to run Swindon was to be sustainable on its own. So we had a few sales, reduced the wage bill, and things were looking much better in financial terms than they had been when I started. That in itself is a type of win because I had the other side of the club to deal with too – it's not all about what happens on the pitch. But it did leave me very short on the football side and I was forever trying to find the next rough diamond to polish or to bring in players on a free.

We signed David Prutton, a very experienced midfielder. We still had Jon Douglas, who'd played with him at Leeds, so we knew they'd link up well. David was a great signing for us. He was one of those players who could change a game. He could run all day. But I wanted him to do a bit more at times, stamp his authority on the game. He had some very good performances for us, but I expected him to score a few more goals than he did.

I brought in two strikers to try and fill the void created by Billy Paynter's departure. We needed to find a prolific goal scorer, but when you've not got much money to spend, you have to take a chance, and that's what we did.

David Ball came in on loan from Manchester City, but he only managed three goals for us.

Thomas Dossevi, a French striker, came in on a free transfer, but he too only managed three goals. I looked at Thomas and felt that he had all the attributes to hit the ground running. He played for most of the season, and his all-round play was very good. He worked hard, but he didn't get the goal return we hoped for.

It was always going to happen, I suppose, but with the loss of some very good players – including a striker who'd scored almost thirty goals – we struggled to score goals. Expectations had been raised, but we had a weaker team at the start of the 2010/11 season than the side we'd put out in the play-off final, just a few months earlier. Everyone was asking the same thing – where are the goals going to come from?

It was a very tough start to the season, and we just couldn't seem to find enough form to put a decent run together.

In October 2010, we signed Matt Ritchie. He was a great player with a fantastic attitude. He was a little fella, even smaller than me! But he was a very tenacious kid with a terrific left foot. Although primarily a wide man, he got himself into decent positions and managed to score eight goals for us. He's since gone on to bigger and better things.

The only player who was scoring goals for us on a regular basis was Charlie Austin, who'd got seventeen during the first half of the season. He was attracting a lot of attention and, unfortunately for us, he joined Burnley in January 2011. We got decent money for him, but I didn't have the opportunity to spend that money on anyone else. So, in the space of half a season, we'd lost our two main strikers and our captain, and it was no surprise that we found ourselves at the wrong end of the table, battling against relegation.

After losing to Southampton on the 26th of February 2011 I was sacked, although the official announcement said that I'd resigned. Andrew Fitton felt that after two successful seasons, the word 'sacked' sounded a bit harsh to the fans, so they said that we'd "come to an agreement."

I didn't resign, though. I've never resigned from a job, and I've never given up on anything. That's not my style. At the time, I was still convinced that I could turn it around, although I knew the board weren't happy with the results.

We'd beaten the Saints twice the season before, so to lose to them at the County Ground was perhaps the final straw. Managers always think they need more time; we always believe that the next game will be the one where we turn it around. I guess someone has got to make a decision, and that's what Andrew did. It didn't quite work out for them in the long term, though.

We'd only just dropped into the relegation zone when I was dismissed, and the club eventually finished bottom of the league.

I am one hundred per cent sure that I'd have kept them up. I can say that honestly, because that's what I'm good at. Under that kind of pressure, I come into my own. When all those around me are panicking, I cope quite well. Just like when you are top of the league with twenty games to go, you don't celebrate like you've already won the league, you shouldn't give in when you fall into the relegation zone. I accept that the results weren't as good as they should have been, and I can understand why the club decided to relieve me of my duties. But there were still a lot of games left to play, and I know we'd have ground out a couple more results that would have kept us up. I'd done exactly that during my first season with Swindon, and I'd also done that at MK Dons. I was hoping Andrew would look back at that and give me a bit longer. But he didn't.

When you first join a club, that's when your bargaining power is at its greatest. I always made sure there was a clause inserted into my contract that ensured I was looked after if the club decided to sack me. I learnt that very early on in my career.

As soon as you're told you're being sacked, that's it. It's the final part of the process, and nothing you can say will change anyone's mind. Others have often been involved in the conversation; sometimes they have a replacement already lined up. Maybe the decision was made weeks earlier. So when you're told you're going, you just have to accept it and move on.

Little did I know that my next job was going to be the most unexpected move of my career.

CHAPTER 24
Agent Wilson

After leaving Swindon, I went over to our place in Spain with Karen for a break. La Manga was quite a popular holiday destination with other managers and former players, so I usually bumped into someone I knew while I was out there.

During my trip to Spain in April 2011, I bumped into Kevin McCabe, the chairman of Sheffield United. I'd known Kevin for a number of years as he had a place near ours. We weren't big friends as such, more acquaintances, but I'd enjoyed the odd beer with him early doors before I went out for a meal with Karen. We had a drink and a chat on this occasion too.

When I got back to England, I received a phone call inviting me to go down to London for a chat with Kevin about the vacant manager's job at Brammall Lane. I went down there, we had a good conversation, and he offered me the job. It was a pleasant surprise considering my background with Sheffield Wednesday. I knew that there would likely be a bit of uproar from the Blades fans, but to be fair to Kevin, it didn't bother him at all. He didn't mind taking a bit of stick if he felt that he was doing the right thing. Fair play to him. He put his neck on the block by offering me the job. I said yes straight away. There was no way I could turn down a club the size of Sheffield United.

The Blades had just been relegated from the Championship, but they were a huge club, with a big ground and good players. They ticked all the boxes for me. I never had any doubts about taking the job. With the team they had and the support they enjoyed, I knew that if we all pulled together, we'd have a decent season. I really believed that.

But I also understood that it wasn't going to be smooth

sailing. There was always going to be a situation where the Blades fans saw me as a Wednesday man. When we held the press conference to announce my appointment, I could hear the fans outside the ground. There were maybe a hundred people shouting and singing about me, making it very clear that they didn't want me to be manager of their club. I can fully understand why they felt that way, and I also realised that there might have been a lot more people across the city who didn't want me either. I knew I had a lot of things to overcome, but I also knew that if we could get the results on the pitch, I could turn the fans around. The sooner the season started, the better, as far as I was concerned.

The fans who were protesting about me because of my Wednesday connections were all gathered around the statue of Derek Dooley – a legend of a man who had played for and managed the Owls before becoming chairman and chief executive of the Blades. How ironic!

At the end of the press conference, we moved the journalists out and invited some of the protesters to come in and explain why they felt so strongly against me. A lot of them wouldn't come in for one reason or another, but around twenty did. Some of the misinformation about me really made me smile. What a load of bollocks some of it was too! One fan told me that I had a Sheffield Wednesday tattoo on my leg, so I dropped my trousers and asked him to show me where this tattoo was!

Another told me I'd been a Wednesday fan all my life. "I'm from Wigan," I replied. "I'm a Wigan rugby league supporter, and in football, if I support anyone it's Liverpool."

They had so much incorrect information, but they believed it. I tried to put them right on the facts, but the only way I could really get them on my side was by getting results.

One thing that really helped me was the support I received from three friends of mine – Len Badger, Tony Currie, and Ted Hemsley. Those three lads in particular were like my wingmen. They were all Sheffield United legends, and although they had nothing to do with the running of the first team, they were meeting with fans and season ticket holders and were always really positive about me. That eased a lot of pressure.

Frank Barlow – another ex-Blade – came in as my assistant,

and I appointed Chris Morgan, our captain, to the role of player/coach. I kept people around me who knew the club, and that really helped.

We made a concerted effort to go to pubs and clubs that were frequented by staunch United fans. I went there and held meetings with the supporters. It wasn't easy, and at times it was quite intimidating, but I thought it was the best thing to do – for me to go out there and ask them to give me a chance and judge me on the results that we got, not my history.

Surprisingly, I didn't get any stick from Wednesday fans. They actually nicknamed me 'Agent Wilson', joking that they'd put me in the role to do a job on the Blades!

The pre-season friendlies went well, and the first game of any meaning was away at Oldham Athletic. We won 2-0 with goals from ex-Wednesday player Richard Cresswell and Harry Maguire, with his first professional goal.

Harry had made his debut the season before, although he only played a handful of games. I picked him in the line-up for my first match, and he played virtually every game while I was manager. He made an instant impact and never looked back. He was a midfielder originally, but his previous manager, Micky Adams, had tried him at centre back, and I agreed that was his best position. He wasn't sharp enough to get around in the middle of the park, but I felt he was well equipped to play in defence, certainly with the system I wanted to use. He read the game so well, could pass the ball with both feet, and was able to step out into midfield and contribute to our attacking play. There weren't many people doing that at the time, and he was one of the standout players for his age. Harry was a member of the Sheffield United youth team who lost to Manchester United in the FA Youth Cup final in 2011, so a lot of people knew about him.

I knew Harry was going to be a very good player – he was always going to get better – but I had no idea that he would eventually become the most expensive defender in the world. He certainly had the ability to step up, but he exceeded all our expectations. He's done that because of the type of person he is. He has a great temperament and has reached the top because of his ability and strong work ethic. Although he is often questioned, he's got the right mentality and the character to prove people wrong.

That first win was good, but the fans still weren't convinced by me. The supporters were always behind the team and the players; I was just a side distraction really. As soon as the games got underway, the fans were all cheering on the team, and that was all I was bothered about. It was about those eleven boys on the pitch, not me. We went on a good little run and didn't lose a league game until the middle of September, when Huddersfield beat us at Brammall Lane.

In October 2011, I managed my first Sheffield derby. I'd played in a few, of course, including the 1993 FA Cup semi-final at Wembley, so I was used to the intense pressure, but ahead of this game, I was very nervy. It was the most nervous I have ever felt before a game as a manager or a player.

The atmosphere on the day was magnificent – absolutely electric. It was funny because during the game I had both sets of fans cheering for me. There was one song that the Blades fans began to sing as the season went on:

> "He used to be shite,
> but now he's alright."

That was the moment I realised that I was possibly winning some of them over. Not all of them, but a lot of them, which was great. I'd have preferred them to drop the first line, though! The Wednesday fans were singing my name too, which was nice, so there was a mixture of chants, some supportive and others taking the piss. But the only thing that mattered to me was what happened on the pitch.

The game was pretty nervy and finished as a 2-2 draw. We were 2-0 up, and they scored two goals in the last eight minutes. Gary Madine grabbed the equaliser, but it shouldn't have counted because there was a foul on our goalkeeper, Steve Simonsen. We weren't too happy about that, obviously.

In November 2011, we signed James Beattie, bringing him back to the club on a free transfer. Unfortunately, he didn't get the same number of goals as he did during his first spell at Brammall Lane, but you couldn't fault the other side of his game. He was a good link-up player who worked hard for the team, but he just didn't get the breaks in front of goal. Maybe he'd lost that yard of pace, but that was to be expected as he was in his thirties. Beats was a very bubbly lad, brilliant in the dressing room, with a terrific dry sense of humour. We needed someone like him in the club.

Later that month, we heard the tragic news that Sheffield United's former manager, Gary Speed, had passed away. The whole of the footballing world was shocked and in mourning. Everybody was stunned by it, and many still are to this day. It was very, very sad. Gary was such a young lad and a very talented manger. Most people at the football club knew him very well, and Brian Jones, a psychologist I've worked with for many years, offered support to anyone who needed it. He was on hand to try and help everyone through a very difficult time.

We improved as a team as the season progressed, and there was a spell between November and February where we won eight home games in a row, which was incredible. That run put a lot of confidence back into the team. At that stage, I didn't hear a lot about my background; the fans were too busy enjoying the games and results to think about me, which is exactly how it should be. We were playing some really good stuff as we pushed our way up the league table.

I won the Manager of the Month award for December as we picked up maximum points. People say that the award can be a poisoned chalice, but I think it's a bit of a fallacy that results don't go well after winning the award, so it didn't bother me. Mind you, we did lose the next match! It's a great honour to receive recognition, but the award belonged to all of us – players, staff, and even the fans who pulled us through games at times.

On the 14th of April 2012, we came from behind to beat Leyton Orient 3-1. That victory kept us in second place, four points clear of Sheffield Wednesday, with just three games remaining. Very few people were betting against us winning automatic promotion.

But then we lost our top scorer in totally unique circumstances.

CHAPTER 25
So, so close

Ched Evans was on fire during the 2011/12 season, scoring over thirty goals for Sheffield United. On the pitch, everything was going well for him, but off it, he was fighting some very serious personal issues.

In the summer of 2011, Ched was arrested and charged with rape. The club had kept it fairly low-key, so I didn't really know too much about the situation when I arrived at Brammall Lane.

There was a board meeting early on in my tenure to discuss how the club should handle the situation. Myself and the board members were sat in the boardroom, and Kevin McCabe joined us through video link. There was a strong push to get rid of Ched. I could understand that thinking because the club didn't want the stigma that was attached to the very strong accusations, but my argument was that he hadn't been proven guilty of anything yet, and we should allow him to carry on with his life and his football until the courts decided. The board agreed. It was a strong decision from us all because of the potential backlash from the public. But if you believe in something, you've got to see it through. I strongly believe that you are innocent until proven guilty.

Ched had an ankle injury at the time, so he missed my first few games as Blades manager, which gave me a chance to find out what was going on. I sat down with him most days to speak to him about what had happened and how his legal defence was going. I'm no expert, and only the people who were involved in the situation will know exactly what happened.

Our victory over Leyton Orient in April 2012 was our sixth in a row. Up until then, Ched had scored thirty-five times in all competitions, including sixteen goals in his last fourteen games. He'd also just been named in the League One PFA Team of the Year.

Ched's court case took place after the Leyton Orient match, so he didn't travel with the rest of the lads to Milton Keynes on Friday 20th April 2012 ahead of our game against MK Dons the following day. We were sitting on the coach heading down south, and I was on the phone to Brian Jones, who was following proceedings in the courtroom. All of a sudden, I heard screaming, shouting, and crying. "He's just been found guilty," Brian told me. I couldn't believe it.

I knew the other lads didn't have the live feed that I had, but within a minute they all knew. When we arrived at the hotel, I'd never seen or heard such a quiet bunch of players. The mood was sombre. How could I get the lads up for a match after that?

We played the game and were absolutely useless. We lost 1-0. We didn't even turn up, but I could understand why. Everyone was totally stunned. We all thought it was a foregone conclusion that Ched would be found not guilty because we all believed he was innocent.

Ched's conviction completely derailed our season. Losing your top goal scorer is hard enough, but the psychological impact his conviction had on the rest of the lads meant that we lost the whole team. The focus moved away from results to a certain degree, towards the press and media side of things. Everything became about Ched. We lost our focus and drew our final two league games, which meant we missed out on promotion by just three points. To make matters worse, it was our big rivals, Sheffield Wednesday, who pipped us to automatic promotion. With the run we'd been on, we'd have fancied our chances of winning at least one of those last three games. No doubt in my mind. Ched would probably have bagged goals in all three.

I was trying to think ahead, and finding a replacement for Ched was paramount. We'd set a striker up to come in on loan, knowing we had a void in that position. The total cost of the loan until the end of the season was around £16,000, but the board refused it. I couldn't believe it.

To accumulate ninety points and not go up is very unlucky, but we had qualified for the play-offs and my job was to try and pick the lads up for the two-legged semi-final against Stevenage. They were going to be two very tough games. Stevenage were very organised. Not a club you think of as a top team – they didn't have the fan base or the facilities to touch United – but they were very good on the pitch. They were a strong side, full of experience, and we knew that if we took them too lightly, we'd have a problem. We expected to have the majority of the game and we knew we'd win the stats – shots on target, higher percentage of possession, etc. But we'd have to be able to break them down, something that not many teams had been able to do, which is why Stevenage had finished so high in the league table. We had to be prepared to stem the counter attack, but finding a way to break them down was going to be the hardest part. We felt confident that if we could get our noses in front, we'd be alright. Thankfully, we won 1-0 on aggregate, which took us through to the play-off final at Wembley for a Yorkshire derby against Huddersfield Town.

When you look at the history of Sheffield United, you can see that they've played at the top level for many years and have been involved in some huge games, so the United fans expected us to either win promotion or get to Wembley. No disrespect to the other teams, but the size of our club compared to others in the division meant that our expectations were set much higher.

Everyone says that winning the play-off final at Wembley is the best way to get promoted, and I think most people thought we were about to find out how true that was.

The atmosphere on the day was brilliant. Our fans had flocked down to the capital, and so had Huddersfield's, to be fair to them.

Unfortunately, we had one or two key players missing. Kevin McDonald, who we'd signed from Burnley, was injured. Kevin was a very influential player for us, someone who made us tick, so we knew we'd miss him.

Chris Porter was our only available striker. So going into the game, we didn't have the best preparation, especially with everything that had happened off the pitch which didn't help us. But it helped Huddersfield no end. When they saw the team sheet, they must have thought they had a great chance. It must have given them a big lift when they saw who was missing.

The match itself was so tight that it could have gone either way. There was absolutely nothing in it and the game went to a penalty shootout.

I'd won a play-off semi-final through a shootout when I was at Swindon, and the one thing I'd learnt from that was that despite the hours of practise you put in, you cannot recreate the psychological aspect of taking a penalty in a big game. On the training ground, there is no pressure. The lads are taking the piss, putting it into the top corner for fun. But when you're standing in the centre circle at Wembley Stadium in front of over fifty thousand people, knowing that whether or not the club win promotion is solely down to you – that's a whole new ball game.

Some of our best penalty takers missed that day; lads I'd have put money on to score. Andy Taylor, our full back, missed one and he was absolutely different class at taking penalties usually. Neill Collins, a centre back who people thought was a little clumsy at times with the ball at his feet, stuck one in the top corner. A perfect penalty. *How does this work?* I thought to myself.

Huddersfield missed a few as well, and it came down to the goalkeepers. I still, to this day, do not think it is right to have goalies taking penalties in such a high-stakes situation where your club is depending on you. I don't think goalkeepers should be put in that position. People may say that you have eleven players – well, you don't. You have ten players and a goalkeeper. The keepers are mentally switched on the whole time as they are involved in every other penalty. They are under enough stress as it is and don't need the added pressure of taking one themselves. When the players have all taken one, it should go back to the person who took the first one and start again. I'd like to see the FA change the rule, but I don't think they will because it adds to the climax and the excitement.

Steve Simonsen hadn't practised taking penalties in training because I don't think anyone ever thinks it's going to go down to the goalkeepers. Steve stepped up and decided to put his foot through it, and the ball sailed over the bar. We were absolutely gutted for him, but he shouldn't have been put in that position. Alex Smithies scored his spot kick and Huddersfield were promoted.

To get ninety points and lose the play-off final in a penalty shootout that went down to the goalkeepers was devastating – we couldn't have been any closer to promotion. It was such a difficult year, full of turmoil. It's a season of sadness when I look back, knowing that we were inches away from automatic promotion – touching distance of winning promotion through the play-offs. We'd had a great year in terms of performances and results, and I don't think anyone was critical of us. I just felt numb. We all did.

CHAPTER 26
A series of strange decisions

The board restructured the club's finances at the end of the 2011/12 season. Missing out on promotion had cost us financially, and we had also lost millions from the Ched situation. I think someone would have paid £10,000,000 for him. But as soon as he had been found guilty, the club released him from his contract.

Our financial situation meant we lost a lot of lads I'd like to have kept hold of. Jordan Slew, a young lad who I was expecting to become a first team regular because he had so much potential, was one. Matty Lowton went to Aston Villa, and Steve Simonsen joined Preston. Beats left, Andy Taylor was another who moved on, as was Stephen Quinn. Chris Morgan retired too. A lot of the lads who had done so well for us had gone. We had to build again.

With money tight, I had to find free transfers or loan signings. It wasn't going to be easy, but I just had to get on with it.

I paid Crewe £60,000 for striker Shaun Miller, and Nick Blackman came in for a hundred grand, while Matt Hill, Danny Coyne, and Dave Kitson all came in on free transfers.

Dave Kitson was a decent player. He could be a bit lazy at times, but he was a good target man who could hold the ball up well. He was exactly what we needed at the time on the pitch.

But off the pitch, I wasn't too sure about him. When lads come into a new team, they tend to try and integrate themselves with the rest of the group, but he seemed to distance himself and didn't want to get too involved with the others, for whatever reason. He came across as quite aloof, but maybe that was just his character. I was warned to watch out for him. He was very friendly with the chairman's son, the same person who was pushing to get me sacked, as I was told later by an ex board member. I was never sure what Dave's intentions were. Maybe I am totally wrong about him, but I got the feeling he didn't like me. That didn't bother me, though, all I cared about was what he did on the pitch.

Despite the huge turn-around of players, we were flying at the start of the 2012/13 season. We didn't lose a league game until November 2013, although we probably drew a few too many. It was a great start, but not too surprising from my point of view, as we still had the nucleus of a good team. Kevin McDonald, Micky Doyle, and Harry Maguire just kept getting better and better.

In January, I was able to add to the squad and I brought in the experienced defender Danny Higginbotham on a free transfer. He was great for the young lads we had coming through.

Nick Blackman was our top goal scorer. We'd got him in the summer from Blackburn for next to nothing, and then he was sold to Reading for a big fee in January 2013. That was a big blow and really hurt us at that time of the season. It wasn't my choice to sell him; that was the board's decision. I wanted to keep him because we needed his goals, but my argument fell on deaf ears. Kevin McCabe felt the club needed the money. Obviously, he was putting a lot of his own cash into the club, so I couldn't really argue whether or not we needed the money, but it was disappointing from a footballing perspective.

The twenty-five thousand loyal blades coming through the turnstiles each week were really angry with Nick's departure. They couldn't understand why we were selling one of our best players, and I got the blame for that. The fans didn't realise that some of the decisions were made above my head and against my wishes. That's why transparency from the board is paramount. If you keep people in the dark, they will speculate, and issues get blown all out of proportion. But if you tell them the truth and explain why decisions have been made, although they won't always like it, most fans will accept the decision.

We went through a bit of a sticky patch in January where we didn't win for five games, but we recovered well and remained unbeaten during February, and only lost once in March. April began with draws against Carlisle and Walsall before we lost 2-0 to Crawley Town on the 9th of April 2013. We were still on the hunt for promotion, albeit a play-off spot rather than automatic.

And then I was sacked!

I had no inkling at all, it was a total surprise. We were heading for the play-offs, which was a good achievement considering the number of players we'd lost. Kevin McCabe told me that he felt we needed a change because we'd never won in the play-offs, and there was a mindset that we wouldn't win this year either. I thought that was an absolute load of bollocks. The experience we had gained from the previous season would have helped us go one step further – I'm convinced of it.

I'm not one hundred per cent sure that he told me the real reason for my dismissal, but that was what he said. I was absolutely gutted. Of all the times I've been let go by a football club, I felt this sacking was the harshest. If they'd replaced me with someone experienced, someone who had a reputation for taking teams up through the play-offs, it might have made sense. But they promoted Chris Morgan, who had never managed a team before and was still cutting his teeth as a coach. To appoint a brand-new manager at that stage in the season was a very strange decision. Maybe they thought Chris would give the lads a lift and add some freshness, but that didn't make sense either, because he was already at the club. He was one of my coaches, and he believed in what we were doing, so he was hardly likely to change anything.

From Chris' point of view, he was either going to be a complete hero and take Sheffield United up, or lose in the play-offs and never get another job. Unfortunately for Chris, he only won one of the final five league games, and the Blades lost to Yeovil in the play-off semi-final. No disrespect to Yeovil, but they were a team we should have beaten over two legs. They weren't anything we should have been worried about, so for me to watch it on television at home was mightily frustrating.

Not long after the play-off defeat, Chris was sacked, and his managerial career was over. Chris was a good coach, great with the players, and a good man manager. I thought he'd go on to make a good manager, but for him to be thrust into the role at that stage ruined his career. He's not involved in coaching or management now, which is a real loss to the game. We're still friends, and I have enormous respect for him.

I still believe that keeping me on until the end of the season would have made more sense. I felt the disappointment from the previous year would have been the tonic we needed to win promotion. Even now, Blades fans tell me that they can't understand why I was sacked. I still to this day do not understand the real reasons for my dismissal. Only Kevin can answer that question.

Kevin wrote me a letter after all the chaos had died down. I think he was trying to defuse what he thought was maybe a rift between ourselves. I respect the fact that he sent me the letter, but there will never be a rift between Kevin and me in my mind. We didn't always share the same opinions, but that's what football is all about. I just wish, personally, that Kevin was still at the helm of Sheffield United, as he and his family are Blades through and through.

I still don't think it was the right decision to sack me, and it didn't work out too well for the club. It took Sheffield United another four seasons to get promoted.

CHAPTER 27
It's football not Moneyball

I was out of work for eight months, which was the longest I'd ever been out of football. I had a few offers; one from Portsmouth and a couple from some London clubs, but they were too far away really, and I just didn't fancy the travelling. Although I wasn't ready to retire, I wanted a job that was close to my home so I could spend more time with my family.

In December 2013, I was approached by Barnsley. It made sense geographically, but it was a very different club to the one I had left fifteen years earlier. John Dennis had run it as a family club, whereas the current owners were running it as a business.

I didn't have any hesitation, even though people say that you should never go back. I understand why people say that because things won't be the same. We were never going to be in a situation where I could replicate the success we'd enjoyed before, I knew that, but I still felt I could achieve something.

Basically, Barnsley were in big trouble. They were bottom of the Championship when I joined. I soon realised that the problems weren't confined to the football pitch; there was no spark inside the club at all. It was like I had boarded a sinking ship. There was a horrible atmosphere around the club, and it wasn't a nice environment to go to work in every single day. Things needed a big shake up.

I still felt we had a chance of staying up, even though I knew it was going to be very, very tough. It looked like an impossible job, but I never gave up. Every day was a battle just to get the players to turn up for training. The lads wandered in looking miserable. You could tell that they were thinking, *Fucking hell. Here we go again.*

One of the biggest problems was that they had a lot of lads

who the previous manager had signed from clubs like Bury and Rochdale. The fans didn't take to them and neither did people within the club. The owner was telling me who needed to go. The board felt certain players were sucking the life out of the club and wanted them out, but maybe the board had created that situation themselves.

I wasn't bothered about personalities. My job was to keep them up, pure and simple, so I picked the players I felt had the best possible chance of getting a result for us. There were one or two whipping boys on the team who, as soon as they touched the ball, the fans would have a go at. It wasn't easy for those lads, and it wasn't easy for me to function against all that adversity. It was one of the hardest jobs that I've encountered, as everyone had resigned themselves to relegation. I think most people were just waiting for the season to end so we could start again.

I got a pretty good reception from the fans, and I think my appointment was made to lift them. But it wasn't about getting the supporters on side, it was the players we needed on board. That's where the problems lay. And the players were on the floor. There was no respite for them – the board didn't want them, the fans didn't want them, their agents were trying to find them new clubs. It made my job almost impossible. Trying to motivate a player for a match is hard when they turn around and say, "You don't fucking want me here and I'll be leaving at the end of the season anyway, so what's the point?" I had to convince them to play for us to help them secure the best possible move at the end of the season.

In some areas we had the quality, but ability alone isn't enough if you don't have the right mentality or any confidence. If you've got players within the club who don't feel wanted or valued, it has an effect on the rest of the dressing room. It only takes one or two negative players to bring everybody else down, even without them meaning to. Their negative demeanour and body language rubs off on everyone else. It brought me down at times too.

I didn't expect to have a bundle of cash to spend at Barnsley; I never had that anywhere in my career, but if I wanted to bring in one or two players to try and stay up, I thought there would be more money available than there was. But because of what had happened with their previous signings, they didn't want journeymen players who had been there, seen it, done it, and were coming to us for a payoff. They wanted to see some value in the team, which is fully understandable. That's the way a lot of clubs are operating nowadays, trying to bring young lads through so they can sell them on for a profit. But with the situation we were in, we couldn't afford to wait. That wasn't an option because we needed players to come in and make an instant impact to help the cause. My remit was to stay up. Could we have done it without bringing in senior pros? I don't think we could. We didn't have time to wait for the young lads to come in and find their feet. We needed results from day one, and to do that, we needed experienced players to come in and perform.

We won six games in the second half of the season compared to three in the first half, so there was progress, but it wasn't enough. That first part of the season was where the damage was done. The Championship is a very unforgiving league with some very good sides. We couldn't really bring anyone in, and that was the hardest part. We finished twenty-third and were relegated to League One. Even though it was inevitable, I was still disappointed.

The club needed a major overhaul, and it would take time to get it right. We had to rebuild a whole new squad. To do that, you've got to have the confidence from the people above you, and I didn't feel I had that at Barnsley. I don't think they really wanted me back; my appointment was made to appease the fans. If a board are bringing someone in, they have to give them their full support. I didn't have that. I didn't feel comfortable at any stage, I felt like I was just treading water and filling a gap until someone else came in. I never felt wanted and I always sensed that it was going to end in tears.

The expectation from the board and the supporters was that we could bounce back. That was my aim too, but I knew I couldn't do it with the team I had. It had to be completely disbanded, even though there were one or two I'd liked to have kept. One in particular was Tom Kennedy. He played virtually every game for me in the 2013/14 season, and he was a very good left back. Not the best defender, but very good going forward. The problem was that the fans didn't like him. Every time he touched the ball, they were on his back, so there was no way I could have kept him, even though I wanted to. He needed a fresh start.

The way I had recruited at previous clubs was by utilising my scouts, watching players, and bringing in lads I felt could fit into the system I wanted to play. But at Barnsley, the bulk of the recruitment was based on stats. That was the biggest frustration for me.

The Moneyball system is prevalent in American sports, mainly baseball. The system uses a stats-based approach to recruitment rather than the collective wisdom of scouts and coaches, who use their knowledge of the game to decide who to sign. After the 2011 film *Moneyball* starring Brad Pitt, some football club owners took note and decided to change their recruitment policy to focus on statistics instead of letting the manager's eye decide whether or not the players is right for the team. Barnsley were one of those clubs.

I've nothing against the use of statistics in football, but they don't always tell the full story. Don't get me wrong, it worked from time to time. Sam Winnall came in from Scunthorpe because of his stats, and he did very well for us, eventually earning a move to Sheffield Wednesday.

But most of the time, the recruitment policy was ridiculous. One day, I arrived for training and there was a player I'd never seen before, all kitted out and warming up. I turned to Chris Hutchings, my assistant, and said, "Who's that big lad over there?"

"I don't know, Dan. I thought you'd brought him in," Chris replied.

So I went over and introduced myself and asked who he was. His name was Mike Phoenix, and he'd been signed earlier that week. He was one of non-league's big scorers with great stats, so the board signed him. No one had even told me though, and that's what really annoyed me. They didn't have the courtesy to even consult me before making a signing. In other words, I couldn't identify a player, they could. That was their approach to all their managers. None of the managers really had a say on which players came in, which I think is barmy. If the club can sell one or two on for a profit, they think it's worth it, but what you get with that approach is inconsistency in results and a high turnover of managers.

It wasn't Mike Phoenix's fault. He was a great lad and I liked him as a person, but he was never good enough to play at League One level. I was under pressure from the board who kept asking me why he wasn't in the team, and I told them that he wasn't good enough. It wasn't fair on the kid to pick him when he wasn't at the standard we required. For them to give Mike hope and aspirations of becoming a pro footballer was very wrong.

I think a lot of players go under the radar now. Scouts with years of experience who have made a career from spotting talent on a playing field are not employed now, and a lot of players miss the boat because of it. The big clubs have so many youth teams that they are able to bring in anyone with an ounce of potential, and sometimes these boys get lost in the academy system. Not all players are outstanding from a young age; there are always some late developers, and scouts are the people who often find these little gems. David Platt, Jamie Vardy, Peter Beardsley, Ian Wright, even Charlie Austin are examples of players who came into the professional game late and enjoyed very good careers.

Stats may tell you how many kilometres a player has covered during a game or how many headers they've won, but they don't tell you what someone's heart is like. Stats won't tell you about a player's character. You can only see that when you watch them with an experienced eye. You can't put that on a piece of paper. I always liked to go out and watch any potential signings to see if they would fit into the team and the style of play. I asked around about the player to see how they get on with others and if they are likely to be disruptive in the dressing room. There are a lot of benefits to stats, but there is no substitute for an experienced human eye belonging to someone who understands the game. Someone who can see if all the ingredients that make a player are right. You can have perfect stats, but when the going gets tough, who knows how they will react? They could be playing for the best team in their league, but that could mean that they've never really been tested. Stats won't tell you how they will react to the step up in quality or how they deal with adversity.

I managed to bring in one or two players I knew about. Conor Hourihane came in from Plymouth for a quarter of a million and eventually played in the Premier League for Aston Villa. The owner and I signed him up in an airport hotel. He was a very good signing for us, I have to say.

We signed Andy Cole's son, Devante, on loan from Manchester City. Devante was so highly thought of at the time, he could have achieved anything in the game. When he joined us, he was inexperienced and a very raw player, but he was a good finisher, and his pace was electric. There were still things for him to work on. He could be erratic at times, and he didn't know the game in terms of where to make his runs or how to time them, and his link play needed to be worked on, but he had the raw ingredients to be a star.

He's not fulfilled his potential yet, but I still think he could come good because he's young enough. We were very excited when he joined Barnsley because of his potential. Andy used to come and watch his games. We hoped he could be half as good as his dad, and he wasn't bad, in fairness – he might even have had more pace than Andy – but he just couldn't quite cement his place in the side.

I just found the whole experience at Barnsley so frustrating because I was trying to win football games with my hands tied. I'm not really sure why they even appointed me because I think they wanted a yes man. Someone who was going to be grateful for the job and would go with the board's wishes. I was always my own man. I made decisions that I felt were the right thing to do for the football club, even if they weren't always popular.

I remember having a meeting with the owner and chief executive, and as they were talking, I was just looking at them because I didn't believe anything they were saying. I knew I was on borrowed time, and I'd gone past the stage of arguing with them. I'd stopped giving my opinion because it didn't make any difference, so I just let them talk while I looked at them with disdain. They didn't want a manager; they wanted a puppet. I knew the end was coming; it was only a matter of time.

Results were mixed throughout the season and on the 10th of February 2015, we lost 2-1 to Fleetwood Town. We were seventeenth in the league table, seven points away from the relegation zone but also only seven points away from the play-off places, so we had an outside chance of promotion.

The following day, after the funeral of my best friend's wife, I was called into a meeting. I knew what was coming, so when they said, "You're sacked," it didn't surprise me. I just wasn't the right man for Barnsley at that time with those owners, and I'm sure they will say the same thing; a real shame because if they'd backed me, if they'd allowed me to get on with the job, I feel we could have achieved a lot of success.

CHAPTER 28
One final job

I still had that fire in my belly for maybe one more job. In October 2015, I was invited to attend a meeting with Doncaster's board of directors. I suppose it was an interview, but it didn't feel that way. I went to the owner's house, just outside Doncaster, and was made to feel very welcome. The club secretary, chief executive, and the entire board were there. The meeting went well, and as I was leaving, I saw another manager going in. It must have been a day of interviews.

Later that day, I received a phone call from the CEO to say they liked everything they'd heard. I had the experience they wanted and they offered me the job. I accepted the position, and they organised an interview with Sky Sports News at ten o'clock the following morning to unveil me as their new manager. They said they would call me later that evening to confirm the interview time.

The night went on, but my phone didn't ring. When I awoke the following morning, I received a phone call from someone telling me that they'd heard that Darren Ferguson had been named as Doncaster's new manager! I couldn't believe it. To this day, they haven't had the courtesy to call me and explain. Instead, they sent me a letter that said they'd decided to go in a different direction. I have no idea what happened. It came as a huge surprise to me when I'd been virtually given the job. Maybe they thought Darren, as a younger manager, was the better long-term prospect. I've no axe to grind with Darren at all, I just thought it was a bit remiss of Doncaster not to call me to explain. They'd have known I was waiting to be unveiled, and their behaviour was very rude.

It didn't help at that stage of my career. The whole situation knocked my belief and my love for the game for a while. All I wanted was for people to be up front and honest with me. I felt I deserved a bit of an explanation. But I'd been around football long enough to know that these things do happen, so I put it to one side and two months later I began a new job – as manager of Chesterfield.

I had a lot of happy memories from my playing days with the Spireites; I won my first trophy with Chesterfield, and it was also the place I'd met Karen all those years earlier. I'd been asked to manage the club in the early 2000s when the owner at the time, Darren Brown, turned up on my doorstep one day. I don't know how he'd found out where I lived, as I kept my address private, but he knocked on the door, introduced himself, and asked if I'd like to be the manager.

"No thanks," I replied. I didn't like his approach at all, and something felt very off about him and the situation. I dodged a bullet as he was later jailed for fraudulent activity that almost led to the extinction of Chesterfield Football Club.

Anyway, in December 2015 I received a phone call from my old mate Chris Turner, who was chief executive at Chesterfield. They had just sacked Dean Saunders and were in a bit of trouble. Chris asked me if I could come on board to help them stay up.

It was a tough decision because I lived in the area and didn't want to manage a club too close to the family home because it can make things difficult for everyone. I went away to have a think and then arranged to meet Chris, and the owner Dave Allen, who had been chairman of Sheffield Wednesday after I left. Dave owns a casino business – I presume that's how he made his money – so we met at one of his casinos in Owlerton, just down the road from Hillsborough. We had a chat, and he asked me if I wanted the job. "Just give us a hand until the end of the season, Dan. All we want is to stay in the division," he said.

"OK," I said, accepting the job.

We won my third match in charge 7-1, which was a great start. I had no money – as usual – but I managed to bring in Gary Liddle, Connor Dimaio, and Jordan Slew on free transfers, and a couple of other lads on loan. Results improved and we managed to stay up, finishing in eighteenth place. Incidentally, Doncaster Rovers were relegated.

Towards the end of the 2015/16 season, the board started to say that they'd have to move players on and reduce the wage bill because the owner was having to put so much of his own money in to keep the club afloat. They were cutting back on everything they could.

Chris asked me if I'd stay on for another year.

"I'll stay, Chris," I replied. "But if we're selling our best players and you're expecting me to replace them with loans and free transfers, don't come moaning to me when the results don't go our way."

Nine players left in the summer of 2016, and I managed to bring in six free transfers, one of whom was Ched Evans, who'd been released from prison after being found not guilty at a re-trial. I'd like to think that in any walk of life, if you have a conviction overturned, you should be allowed to live your life and have the chance to earn a living.

I discussed it with Dave Allen, and he agreed to back me, so we brought Ched back to the club. He turned out to be a good investment as he re-joined Sheffield United a year later.

In November 2016 we'd just come out of a board meeting, and were about to go into an AGM, when Dave Allen said that he was resigning as chairman, and then he walked out. No one knew that was going to happen, so it was a big shock. I thought he was quite rude at times, very disrespectful to the other directors, and he often spoke to them with disdain. Maybe because he had put so much money into the club, he thought that gave him the right to be rude. Dave remained the owner, but the club was in turmoil.

We had a lot of injuries and results weren't great, but I always felt we'd stay up again. In January 2017, we went to Bradford City, who had a strong team at the time and reached the play-off final that year. There were seventeen thousand fans inside Valley Parade, and they beat us 2-0. That defeat put us in the relegation zone, but we were level on points with the team in twentieth, and I knew we'd do enough to stay in the division.

After the game, I did the usual pitch-side interviews, and when I was finished, I saw Chris walking down the touchline with the club secretary. "Dan, we've just had a phone call from Dave Allen, and he wants to sack you," the secretary said.

"The fucking cheeky twat," I replied. "I said to you at the start not to come to me and say results aren't good enough if you're selling our best players and not giving me any money to spend." I was fuming.

I walked away from Chesterfield, and that experience put me off football so much that I very much doubt I will go back. Dave Allen was a Yorkshireman, and I learned from the MP episode at Sheffield Wednesday, that some people use that as an excuse to say what they like. I don't think he particularly wanted to be at Chesterfield. I don't think he had a love for the club at that time. He'd done well with Chesterfield before and backed every manager, but he didn't back me. He says he did, but he didn't – other than backing me to get rid of players!

Every day during my twelve months at Chesterfield, I'd have Chris at my door saying, "You've got to get rid of this player. You've got to cut the wage bill."

Fucking hell, I thought. *I've got to win a football game; that's what I've got to do.*

Chesterfield finished bottom of the league at the end of the 2016/17 season, and were relegated to the National League the following year, which was a real shame. I hope they can get back into the football league soon.

CHAPTER 29
The final whistle

There were a lot of things that I didn't enjoy during my last two jobs at Barnsley and Chesterfield. So when people ask me to go back into management – and I've had offers from teams at home and abroad – I politely decline. Never say never, but I think I'm done with football now.

I've still got the passion for the game, but I go to matches now as a fan. I just enjoy watching football with a completely open mind, rather than with a manager's mindset. Occasionally, if I see a standout player, I'll talk to other coaches and ask if they've seen him, but it's nice to just sit and watch a game without any pressure.

I don't miss the pressure, and I don't miss the competitiveness either. You've got to have a passion to want to be involved in the game, and mine has waned a bit. I do miss the banter and the fun with the players. Being around the lads always made me feel young.

The game has changed completely since I started playing, back in the seventies. I'm impressed with the way that Manchester City and Liverpool play. Pep Guardiola came in and set a standard that everyone wants to adhere to, and every fan wants their team to play the same way. But only a few teams are good enough to do it. What amazes me is that when you go down the football pyramid, so many teams try to play in the same style when they don't have the ability. I've watched so many games where sides are caught out trying to play out from the back. The coaches are encouraging them to play football in certain areas, and that, for me, is bad coaching and bad management because they're not getting the best out of the players they've got. Sometimes you have to be brutally honest and understand when your team aren't good enough to play a certain way, so you don't embarrass them. Of course, you have to try to improve and develop the players, but not everyone has the ability to play the same way as Man City, and a good manager will always find a style of play that suits the players at their disposal. Look at Sean Dyche. I think he did a fantastic job at Burnley, playing to his players' strengths. When Burnley made the ludicrous decision to sack him, they got relegated!

I always tried to do the best for my teams and players by playing a style that suited their strengths, and I spent a lot of time coaching and developing them. I take a lot of pride and satisfaction when I see Harry Maguire starring for England in the World Cup, and Charlie Austin banging in a Premier League hat-trick.

I watch a lot of games. If I don't go to watch a live match, I'll find one on television. On a Sunday morning, I read the newspapers and always have a look at how my former clubs have got on. The trouble is, I've played for or managed so many teams that it often takes me until lunchtime!

If I had to pick one phrase to sum up my career, I'd say 'eat your heart out Cristiano!' When I look back, I'd like to think that I was reliable and that I was trusted as a player and manager. I like to think that I was honest in everything that I did. I didn't get every decision right, but every decision I made was done with the best of intentions and was what I believed to be the best thing for the team. I never went out to upset anyone or hurt anyone. I was very competitive, but I always tried to be fair.

I was possibly a player fans might enjoy having on their team, but I always preferred to heap praise on others and didn't expect too much myself. I was the same as a manager really, it was always about my players, never me.

I remember the words of my first PE Teacher, Dave Brown, "You've got to make something with all these attributes you have. I don't want to see your talent go to waste." When I reflect back on my career, I think I made the best of what I had.

I did alright for a little lad from Wigan.

Acknowledgements

Thank you to my beloved wife Karen for her unbelievable love and tolerance over all these years.

My son and best mate Laurie, and my gorgeous daughter Carrie for their amazing dedication and love they give to all our family without condition.

To Amy, Laurie's beautiful wife, who has given our families two of the most wonderful gifts in Arlon and Aoife.

My sister Mary, her son David, daughters Ann Marie and Nicola, without forgetting her wonderful son Christopher who passed away far, far too soon.

Margaret my eldest sister who has sadly departed, Frank her brilliant husband and daughters Michelle and Helen.

A massive thank you to Annie and Jimmy, my massively missed mum and dad. Without their support and guidance I would never have fulfilled many of my dreams.

A big thank you to my friend and sponsor, David Hopkins. Many people will know David from his very successful Markovitz company, or as chairman of Buxton Town Football Club, but the humble gent is a very generous man with various charities around the Derbyshire area - none more so than Ashgate Hospice, where I am honoured to be a Patron along with my good mate, Tony Nunn.

Ashgate has benefited from David and his family's hard work fundraising over many years to help them continue to support our loved ones as much as possible. Cheers Dave!

To all of you who have kindly contributed, good or bad to the pages printed. Many thanks.

From my playing days and throughout my managerial career it would be remiss of me not to say a big thank you to all my teammates, mentioned or not, the clubs, staff and officials and also the most important people, the fans who have been unbelievably generous towards me over many years, giving me some of the greatest times. I will be forever in your debt.

Finally to Mathew. How can I thank you for your time and hard work invested and the encouragement given to me to even think about writing a book. But now it's done I hope the football family will appreciate how much joy the beautiful game can give someone.

Memories - you can't buy them!

Danny
2022

Danny Wilson has collaborated with Mathew Mann to write his autobiography. Mathew has ghost written several books including What If? An Alternative History of Leicester City, Minding My Own Football Business by Barrie Pierpoint, You Must Be Joachim by Julian Joachim, and The Reality of the Dream by Malcolm Christie.

Mathew would like to thank:

Danny for taking me into your confidence and for giving me the opportunity to help tell your story. It's been an absolute pleasure and I hope the finished product does justice to your incredible career.

The team at Morgan Lawrence: Barrie Pierpoint (Director), Harry Worgan, Peter Taylor, Amy Memory, and Lee Clark.

My wife, Holly, for your continued support and encouragement.

And, finally, to my children, Dylan and Eve, who are my inspiration.

Playing statistics

	Appearances	Goals
Wigan Athletic 1976 - 1977	8	1
Bury 1977 - 1980	108	12
Chesterfield 1980 - 1983	131	16
Nottingham Forest 1983	11	1
Scunthorpe 1983	6	3
Brighton and Hove Albion 1983 - 1987	155	39
Luton Town 1987 - 1990	142	30
Sheffield Wednesday 1990 - 1993	137	14
Barnsley 1993 - 1995	89	2
Northern Ireland 1986 - 1992	24	1
Total	**811**	**119**

Managerial statistics

	Games	Won	Drawn	Lost	Win %
Barnsley 1993 - 1998	201	74	55	72	36.82
Sheffield Wednesday 1998 - 2000	80	23	17	40	28.75
Bristol City 2000 - 2004	226	107	55	64	47.35
MK Dons 2004 - 2006	82	25	25	32	30.49
Hartlepool United 2006 - 2008	133	58	29	46	43.61
Swindon Town 2008 - 2011	121	44	40	37	36.36
Sheffield United 2011 - 2013	106	55	31	20	51.89
Barnsley 2013 - 2015	63	19	13	31	30.16
Chesterfield 2015 - 2017	56	18	10	28	32.14
Total	1066	422	276	368	39.55

Honours as a player

Anglo-Scottish Cup	Winners	1981
Full Members' Cup	Runners Up	1988
League Cup	Winners	1988 & 1991
League Cup	Runners Up	1989 & 1993
FA Cup	Runners Up	1993

Honours as a manager

Division One	Runners Up	1997
LMA Manager of the Year	Winner	1997
Football League Trophy	Winners	2003
League One play-offs	Runners Up	2004 & 2012
League Two	Runners Up	2007

A MESSAGE FROM OUR SPONSOR
David Hopkins

I am delighted that my family company, M Markovitz Ltd, is the proud sponsor of Danny's book, recounting his amazing journey in football, as both a player and manager.

Despite his incredible track-record and significant professional accomplishments, Danny made an unassuming first impression when I met him at Buxton Football Club, a then-Northern Premier League team, which his son, Laurie, played for at the time.

There was no expectation of VIP treatment. I invited him into the Board Room and, as the season progressed, gradually got to know him better. It became increasingly obvious to me that, despite his role as manager of Barnsley FC, and the enormous successes he continued to enjoy in the game, this was an incredibly humble man, who was there very much in the capacity as 'dad' and who, despite the constant pressure he must have been under as a high-profile Manager, still found time, along with his lovely wife, Karen, to quietly turn up for games, sit at the back of the stand and support his son.

When Laurie moved on from Buxton, my path didn't cross Danny's again until he was arranging a fundraising dinner for Ashgate Hospice, a charity we are both very passionate about. We are both part of a small group of patrons for the charity, and it was only in the course of our work for them that I realised Danny, once again in his own quiet, unassuming way, was doing far more than his bit for this incredibly worthwhile local cause.

As Buxton FC has gone on its own journey in recent years, I have lent on Danny for support and advice many times, not least when I caught him boarding a train in London just after my First Team Manager had resigned unexpectedly. Danny, being Danny, didn't stop at offering advice; he donned his tracksuit, turned up to take first team training and oversee our next fixture against local rivals, Mickleover Sports FC, buying the club time to make our next managerial appointment (which he also assisted me in making!). The lads couldn't believe it. The gaffer had left, we were on a run of losses, but when they turned up for training, an ex-Premier League manager walked in to help. I think they thought I must have won the lottery.

I tried to pay him for his services, to which he simply responded with a laugh! And that is very much the nature of the man.

When I was approached by Danny's publishers to ask if I would be interested in sponsoring the book, it was an honour to say yes, supporting a friend who himself has only ever said yes to me.

As Chairman of Buxton FC and a lifelong Manchester United fan, I have met many people who have a deep and unerring love for our national game, but if there is a nicer man in football, I have yet to meet him. I hope you enjoy his story as much as I did.

David Hopkins
CEO M Markovitz Ltd & Buxton FC Chairman

Danny, in their words...

A selection of Danny's former teammates, players, colleagues, and friends have told their stories about Danny.

John Dennis
Barnsley Chairman

The Barnsley board and I were looking for a player-manager to come in and freshen things up, after the Machin era. Mel had done a great job, but it ran out of steam. We'd identified Viv Anderson, and when I met him at what is now the Cedar Court hotel, Ainley Top, just outside Huddersfield, I suggested he might want to have a little word with Danny Wilson to see if he would be interested in coming too. I'd been made aware that Danny's contract at Sheffield Wednesday had expired.

So, a few days later, I met Danny and Viv at a pub that I think was called The Highwaymen – it certainly felt like it after dealing with those two!

I'd already agreed terms with Viv, and assumed that the player-assistant would come for a little less money. My assumption was completely wrong. Danny made it clear that if he came to Barnsley, he had to have the same deal as Viv. It was one of those conversations where I knew that if I didn't go with it, it wasn't going to happen, so I agreed.

And that's the story of how Danny Wilson came to Barnsley.

Danny will be the first to admit that he found it quite difficult to adjust to his new player/coach role. He wasn't playing well, and the fans didn't particularly take to him at the start. But as he reacquainted himself with football at that level, he turned it around, and was voted our Player of the Season at the end of that year.

As far as my working relationship with Danny was concerned, he was an easy man to like. He was a very strong character and was definitely a man of his own mind. He was not easy to deal with in contract discussions, and I liked that about him. Someone who was strong, competent, and confident in his own ability.

When Viv left to join Bryan Robson at Middleborough, the board and I didn't contemplate too many alternatives. We felt that in Danny we already had someone on the payroll who could step in, so I met with Danny and asked him if he fancied the manager's job. "Yes," he replied. "Will there be any more money in it for me?" he asked.

"No," I replied.

"Will there be any money for me to spend on transfers?"

"No," I replied.

But he took the job anyway. That was Danny. He was a strong character, very self-assured without being arrogant. He was ready for the challenge; thought he could make a difference – and that's exactly what he did.

During his first season as manager, we narrowly missed out on the play offs, and in January of the following season Danny approached me and said, "Chairman, we need to change things up. Move some players on and bring in some fresh faces." We'd already signed Arjan De Zeeuw to replace Gerry Taggart. Peter Shirtliff had also come in as a senior player. The board and I agreed that Danny could spend whatever money he generated, and the new TV deal meant we had a bit more money available in the wage budget.

That summer, we sold Andy Payton to Huddersfield, Brendan O'Connell went to Charlton, and one or two others also went out the door.

We brought in Paul Wilkinson and Neil Thompson on free transfers, and Matty Appleton came in for two hundred grand. Clint Marcelle, a little winger, came in from Portugal, and we also signed Jovo Bosancic. Although they were all relatively cheap in terms of transfer fees, we did push the boat out in respect of salaries and bonuses.

Just as crucial as any of our new signings, was keeping our captain Neil Redfearn.

We got our business done early so Danny had a full pre-season to work with the team. And that was it. The following season we were playing Premier League football. What Danny and Eric Winstanley, his number two, and the squad did that year, was nothing short of remarkable. Because of Danny's achievements he will always be revered in Barnsley, and rightly so.

We got the promotion but failed to stay up by the skin of our teeth. Following relegation, Danny left to go to Sheffield Wednesday which was a big blow to the football club, and a big blow for me personally. I'm convinced that if it was any other club who had approached him, Danny would have remained at Barnsley. But there were no hard feelings. Danny and I stayed in touch, and we've still got a good relationship and a good friendship to this day.

And that is John Dennis' take on Danny Wilson.

Terry Mancini
Luton Town coach

In 1989, I went to Luton to help out an old friend of mine, Ray Harford. They'd won the League Cup in 1988 and, the following year, he took them to the League Cup final again. But as soon as Luton reached the final, they went from a comfortable mid-table position to the bottom three because no one wanted to get injured. They weren't putting their feet in and playing how they should have been playing. There was a strong possibility that they could win the cup and get relegated.

I've got to say that he had some hair 'em, scare 'em players, a few you wouldn't want to pick a fight with, that's for sure. Good players, but they were their own bosses. He was a very, very good coach, was Ray, but when the strong men stood up, he possibly wasn't what he should have been. So he phoned me.

"There's too many villains in the dressing room, Terry, and that's not me. You're the only person I can think of who can come in and help us out. With your personality and the way you want to do things, we'll have a chance of staying up," Ray explained.

"I'll come in," I replied. "But you've got to let me do it the way I want to do it."

"Of course, Terry. The League Cup final is on Sunday, so you can start then."

"Sorry, Ray. I've already got plans for the weekend, so I'll start next week," I said. I was actually going on a golfing holiday.

A week later, I met Ray in a café just off the M1 near Luton. Ray took me through the team; Mick Harford, Steve Williams, Steve Foster, Ricky Hill, Les Sealey – terrific players, and very strong characters. I'd never come across Danny before, but I soon realised he was very important to the team.

Over the three or four weeks I was involved with Luton, I got to know all the lads, and Danny was ace – still is. I laughed and joked, wound them up, and we nicked a few points here and there. When we faced Norwich, on the last game of the season, we knew that if we won the game we'd stay up.

Luton got a penalty in the first half, and Danny was the penalty taker. We desperately needed the goal. We desperately needed the win.

He didn't score.

The boys came in at half time with score tied at 0-0, and we wound them up. *Come on lads, you can do it.*

In the second half, we got another penalty. And all of those strong characters turned away and looked somewhere else. None of those big, tough guys, those superstar names, wanted it. But Danny did. He picked the ball up and placed it on the spot. Even though he'd missed the earlier penalty, he shouldered the responsibility, which is what he'd done all his life.

He smashed the ball into the net. We won 1-0 and stayed up. Danny went up ten-fold in my estimation that day.

I never worked with him again, but we've remained good friends. I run golf events now and I've taken him all over the world. He's a lovely man, very good with people. I've got a lot of time for Danny and his wife, Karen.

He's one of only a few managers to have managed over a thousand games. Danny glides in and out of clubs, and he's done a great job everywhere he's been.

For me, Danny will always be someone I'd want in my team, anytime, anywhere. Top Man.

Gareth Edds
MK Dons defender

I loved my time playing for Danny. I have the upmost respect for him as a manager, but also as a person. He was a very honest and caring manager. He cared about results, of course, but he also cared about the players as human beings. When he joined MK Dons, I was going through a bit of a rough time as my daughter was quite ill, but Danny was always very understanding in that respect.

One of the biggest impacts he made was the camaraderie that he built within the group. I remember he used to do a warm up where he'd stand at the front of us all and do a movement. All twenty-five players had to try and do the same movement in sync, which was always good fun.

Danny and his assistant, Ian Bowyer, were very good in terms of man management. Two people you could be completely open and honest with, and they gave us the confidence to go on and win games.

Although we spent most of the season near the bottom of the league, as we approached the end of the campaign, we started to get some good results and there was a bit of confidence brewing. We went onto the final game of the season, against Tranmere, needing a win to stay up. Thanks to Danny we had full belief in ourselves, and although we left it late, we managed to get the victory we needed.

I have a lot of fond memories of my time at MK Dons and I learnt so much from Danny. I have an academy in Australia now, where I pass on some of the things that he taught me.

Steve Phillips
Bristol City goalkeeper

The impact that Danny had on my footballing career was massive. He was the manager who gave me my opportunity.

At the start of the 2000/01 season, Alan Miller had joined us on loan from Blackburn and he was expected to be Bristol City's first choice keeper. But he was recalled the day before a League Cup game against Brentford. I remember sitting on the treatment table when Danny asked me if I was fit to play. "Definitely," I said, even though the physios were shaking their heads. I had dislocated my finger during training, a nasty injury where the bone had come through the skin, but I strapped it up and went out and played. It was my first game for Danny, and I played really well. I think he was going to release me at the end of that season, but after that performance, I was pretty much an ever present under him.

They were great years, the best years of my career. We won the Football League Trophy and were an inch away from winning promotion. I honestly think the club got rid of him a year too early, and I'm convinced we'd have gone up if Danny had stayed for one more season.

Danny and Frank Barlow were brilliant together. Danny was a great man manager and the players liked playing for him. He treated you properly, and never hung you out to dry in public like some managers. He was very relaxed, but if you were shit, he'd rip you a new arsehole! You knew where the line was.

I'd put Danny, along with Paul Trollope, at the top of the list of managers that I played under during my twenty-four-year career. When Danny left Bristol City in 2004, I was always hoping I'd get a move to one of the clubs he was managing. I almost joined him at MK Dons, but it didn't happen, which was a real shame. That shows you how much respect I have for him.

Ched Evans
Sheffield United striker

Danny, for me, will always have my total respect as a manager, and more importantly a man. As a manager, he was always approachable and willing to listen to players. He let the dressing room run itself, but the lads also knew he had a switch, so we never crossed the line. I think that is the most important part of being a manger – letting lads express themselves but not going over the line. In my seventeen years in football, he's the only manger I've played under who had that quality. He's simply the best manger I've ever had.

Chris Turner
Sheffield Wednesday goalkeeper

My first memory of Danny was when Big Ron brought him to Sheffield Wednesday. He'd been at Luton, and they'd sent us down the season before. He was a very skilful and talented midfield player, who became part of a very successful period in Wednesday's history. He trained hard and was a worker on the pitch too.

Danny was a very likeable person who would help anyone. He was very much one of the boys, always joining in with the jokes and the banter.

He was a very good, vastly experienced, manager. When I was at Hartlepool, we'd just been relegated to League Two and needed a manager to help us bounce back straight away. Danny was the perfect appointment, and won promotion at the first time of asking.

During our time together at Hartlepool, Danny and I were in a meeting with the chairman who was calling out two players; one who was in the team, the other who wasn't. The chairman was very aggressive and scathing about the lad who was playing, and supportive of the one who wasn't. I was sat next to Danny, and as the meeting progressed, it got worse and worse. I thought, *Danny's going to explode in a minute. He won't be liking this.*

The meeting ended and Danny hadn't said a word. As we were walking down the corridor I turned to Danny and said, "Fucking hell, Dan. You did well not to explode there."

He looked at me and said, "Play the game, Chris. Play the game."

It was absolutely brilliant, and that sums Danny up – he is a cool-headed sort of guy, nothing ever ruffles his feathers and he managed how he wanted to.

Frank Barlow
Danny's long-time assistant

I first met Danny when Arthur Cox signed him for Chesterfield in 1980. He cost us a lot of money for a twenty-year-old, but he was a very good player. He gave a hundred per cent in every game, was totally committed, and you knew exactly what you were going to get with him. When Arthur left and I became manager, Danny was one of the first names on the team sheet. When you're picking the team, there are some players you hope will turn up and others you know will turn up. I always knew that Danny would turn up.

Danny was a top-class player who lifted those around him. He was so quick. He was very aggressive too. Whenever there was any kind of physical skirmish, you'd see a little head pop up in the middle and it'd be Danny. So don't let him tell you he was an angel, because he wasn't!

I became Danny's assistant at Sheffield Wednesday, and we worked together at various other clubs. We achieved some success and I hope we were a decent management team. Danny is someone I trust one hundred per cent. He's a very honest, straight forward man, and I found it a pleasure to work with him, although we didn't always agree.

I couldn't believe it when Danny took the Sheffield United job. I'd been to Old Trafford to watch Sheffield United play Manchester United in the FA Youth Cup final, and I asked Billy Dearden if he knew who was going to get the Sheffield United job. When he told me he'd heard it was Danny, I was shocked. The first thing I thought about was the supporters. He wasn't going to be a popular choice and he'd be under a lot of pressure to win them over. But that was Danny. It showed his grit and determination. He always made his own decisions. He knew the fans didn't want him, he knew that he'd take some stick, but he also knew he would do a good job. And he did, although we were very unlucky. It's that determination that has enabled him to manage over a thousand games, which is an amazing achievement. There aren't many who have reached a thousand.

It's not easy to be a manager. It is a very, very demanding job – on yourself, on your family, on everyone around you. You know you're going to get the sack and you know you're going to receive criticism – most of which comes after a match which is quite a bit easier! *Why did you take him off? Why did you pick him?* Even if you're top of the league, you still get criticised.

Danny's been able to cope with all that by retaining his light hearted nature. I'd say he was mischievous but that's probably the wrong word to describe a man in his sixties! Danny is always full of practical jokes. When we were at Sheffield United, I received, in the post, a photograph of me as a teenager playing for United.

There was a letter enclosed with the photo that said, "Dear Frank. Could you please sign this photograph for my mother? She followed you as an eighteen-year-old and we'd like to give her the signed photo as a present for her ninetieth birthday."

It was from Danny! You always had to be on your toes around him.

I'm a big supporter of Danny. I don't really want to tell him how much I think about him, but I think he knows. He's just a great bloke.

Juan Cobian
Sheffield Wednesday defender

Danny brought me to Sheffield Wednesday in August 1998, and I became the first Argentinian to play in the Premier League. For South Americans it's always a dream to play in the English Premier League – it's probably the number one league in the world – and I'll always be grateful to Danny for giving me that opportunity.

He was a good manager, a very easy-going person who made it clear what he expected from us. We had a good group of players, but it was sometimes difficult for him because there were some strong characters in the dressing room, and he had to deal with the whole Di Canio situation. We finished twelfth that league and almost qualified for Europe, which was a successful season.

Danny had only retired a few years earlier and was still in good shape, so he used to join in the Friday eight-a-side games. He was still competitive, and I'll always remember one time Emerson Thome and I played head tennis against Danny and Peter Atherton. It was such a close game, and we must have played for over an hour and a half. At one point, Emerson and I were in the lead, but Danny and Peter came back to beat us. It was so funny because Emerson went into a bad mood and was very angry. We were begging Danny for another game, and he said, "Sorry, lad. We only play this once every four years like the World Cup." We never got the rematch.

I only wish I'd spent longer with Danny because he was an influential person in my career. But I was young and wanted to be the first-choice player straight away, so I left Wednesday after only one season, and joined Charlton.

I only have fond memories of my time at Hillsborough working with Danny and his assistant Frank Barlow.